THE PLAY
AND ITS
CRITIC
Essays for
Eric Bentley

THE PLAY AND ITS CRITIC

Essays for Eric Bentley

EDITED BY

MICHAEL BERTIN

UNIVERSITY
PRESS OF
AMERICA

LANHAM • NEW YORK • LONDON

University Press of America,® Inc.

4720 Boston Way
Lanham, MD 20706

3 Henrietta Street
London WC2E 8LU England

Library of Congress Cataloging-in-Publication Data

The Play and its critic.

Bibliography: p.
1. Drama—History and criticism. 2. Bentley, Eric,
1916-   . I. Bentley, Eric, 1916-   . II. Bertin,
Michael, 1947-   .
PN1621.P56   1986   809.2   86-18936
ISBN 0-8191-5640-X (alk. paper)

Typesetting by Eagle One Graphics, Inc.
Lanham, MD

Cover design by Anne Masters

TO
ERIC BENTLEY
FOR HIS SEVENTIETH BIRTHDAY
IN FRIENDSHIP

Publication of this book is made possible in part by a grant from the National Endowment for the Arts, Washington, D.C., a federal agency.

ACKNOWLEDGMENTS

I warmly thank all contributors to this celebratory volume. None of the essays has appeared in a book before; 19 are published for the first time in any form. Ruby Cohn, Rolf Fjelde, and John Fuegi volunteered sections from forthcoming books; while Irene Haupt offered her photograph of Bentley for the cover.

At the same time, I apologize to the many potential contributors I could not include. Eric Bentley is widely known and admired, and making this selection was difficult.

My friend and teacher, Bernard Beckerman, met his untimely death this past year. I thank his wife Gloria for enabling me to see his nearly-completed essay into finished form, and I am glad that a space in the book is reserved for Bernie's memory and living influence.

Meeting Norma Wardle in Bolton, England last year was a delight. She introduced me to C.S. Lewis's appreciation of Bentley; Father Walter Hooper, the executor of the Lewis estate, kindly interceded on my behalf with Curtis Brown Ltd. of London for permission to reproduce the item, and I should like to acknowledge the "Copyright © by C.S. Lewis Pte. Ltd." (All of the authors represented here hold the copyright of their own contributions.)

Sheila Dell, Mary Gonzales, Helen Hudson, Cheryl Keesee, and James E. Lyons of University Press of America; and Saundra Adkins, Carole G. Donohue, and Betty Hall of Eagle One Graphics produced the volume with me.

Those offering inspiration or performing essential tasks include Joanne Bentley, Bert Cardullo, Martha W. Coigney, Daniel Gerould, Maxim Mazumdar, Roy Park, Vincent Porter and John Shirley.

I am indebted to Jacques Barzun, Albert Bermel, and Lloyd Richards. They are among the most generous people I know, and their encouragement and advice were crucial.

I thank Maggie for all her tangible help, in editing, etc. But I mostly love her for the lesson of Shakespeare's sonnet, CXVI. Our children, Madeleine and Richard, are on their marks, ready for their play. A fair run to them both!

M.B.

Spring 1986

CONTENTS

III
ON ACTING

IV
THEMES

PREFACE

The Play and its Critic opens with a section of tributes to Eric
Bentley, but other tributes are interspersed throughout the
book, where I felt they would be most effective and
appropriate. The initial juxtaposition is between C.S. Lewis
and James McFarlane. Lewis was Bentley's tutor at Oxford
in the late thirties, and his appreciation of his student charge
is prescient; while McFarlane's citation of Bentley as the
recipient of an honorary degree shows the promise fulfilled.
The items span forty years and are nearly coterminous with
Bentley's career.

With the section on dramatists certain pairings leaped to
mind. I knew, for instance, that I wanted an essay on Shaw
from Jacques Barzun, one on Strindberg from Evert
Sprinchorn, and one on Brecht from Martin Esslin. Without
imposing subjects, I tried to steer authors to the subjects I
thought would make a book. Some selected the dramatist I
had in mind, others agreed to my suggestion, while a few
picked topics too good to ignore. Bernard Beckerman's essay
on Peter Shaffer, and Arthur Ganz's on Sam Shepard, bring
the section to the present day.

Gordon Rogoff and Albert Bermel make a third section
devoted to acting, and they underscore, among other topics,
aspects of Bentley's talent which are often neglected; while
the closing section, by Daniel Gerould and Herbert Blau,
concerns itself with thematic questions.

My ambition as an editor is to respect the style of each contributor. Rather than a solemn uniformity, I have worked for what I hope is an engaging variety of approach and manner; the whole being bound together by the occasion: the celebration of a man who in more ways than one created the occasion.

M.B.

INTRODUCTION

Real culture lives by sympathies and admirations, not by dislikes and disdains; under all misleading wrappings it pounces unerringly upon the human core.

William James

When Eric Bentley published *Bernard Shaw* in 1947, he set the stage for a Shavian scene. The scene is from the stage of life, and is set in the quiet of Shaw's study. I have often wondered how Shaw responded, really responded, to that alarmingly personal book in which Bentley seemed to discover the very secrets of Shaw's soul. And who was Shaw at the time? If he was not the sad old man many took him for, he was certainly a man much misunderstood and neglected in fame: A genius who had presumed to tell the world how it could be saved, and a wily personality concealing his innermost being behind the mask of the public clown, "G.B.S." Bentley saw past all that to write the book that all true Shavians treasure to this day; the one that brings them close to their man. As we return to our "scene," to look over Shaw's shoulder and to share in the concentration of his reading, what do we imagine his response to be? Many books on Shaw exist, and many others will emerge, but Bentley's is the one that reclaimed Shaw the artist from the recalcitrant facts. Shaw, in turn, with his profound understanding and lovely tact, passed over the book's private dimension, to praise it as "the best critical description of my public activities I have yet come across." Other critics could have given the world such a clarifying act, but is it too much to say that Bentley gave Shaw something more? Our scene is an encounter between great men, and not the least important part of their greatness is the ability to apply, in Lionel Trilling's phrase, "the perception that comes from love."

The time has come to ask the Shavian question of Eric Bentley himself. What is the significance of his career? To what purpose has he lived? What is the value of his words? Three questions that are three-in-one to a writer. He asked it of Shaw, and he announced Shaw in his answer. He invited every major figure in the modern theatre to live up to its ambition and worth. Now he is 70 and we ask it of him.

Born in England on 14 September 1916, Bentley left his Bolton home during the war to seek his name as a man of the theatre in America. And what a career he made! The record will show eventually, I think, that no single critical influence this century did more to release the energy of the important theatre into our world than Eric Bentley's. He argued into awareness an entire period of modern drama, and he gave to the American stage and university the potentials of language and history. The possessor of a near-Shavian richness of talents himself, he lives a variety of careers—as teacher, critic, scholar, historian, translator, anthologist, director, performer and playwright—each of which would make a reputation. But how trivial to list them thus and miss the big fact. In a profession that is often myopic, and in a society that is assuredly selfish, Bentley is perceived as a generous visionary. Many look to him for personal guidance, spiritual comfort, and sheer intelligence. His writing is felt as final and free. Interesting points to keep in mind when we weigh the criticism of the few who label him "severely intellectual."

Bentley is distinguished by a sense of mission, and it is helpful at the outset to recapitulate briefly the markers of his quest. In *The Playwright as Thinker* of 1946, Bentley finds the artistry, dynamic, and subversive power of the philosophically, politically, and socially radical modernist playwrights irresistible. Ibsen, Strindberg, Chekhov, Shaw, Wilde, Wedekind, Pirandello and Brecht express the ethical and moral force of a criticism of life, and Bentley takes up the challenge of connecting that force with the problems of modern, specifically, postwar American destiny.

His very treatment meets the challenge through a series of interpretations of drama which uncover meaning and reveal the stage as an art that "participates in the activity of the real."[1] For such participation to occur, for life and drama to join beneficially, a house cleaning of obstacles is called for, whereupon Bentley initiates a fourfold polemic aimed at journalistic, academic, commercial and aesthetic irresponsibility. He defends the present against the pedant, the past against the press, art against the grocery store, and the stage against the "dishonest beautification" that Paul Tillich defines as a staple of conformist culture.[2] Throughout, he affirms the need to preserve essential bonds: between the present and the past, the inner and the outer man, and the ideal and the real. The criticism of life as it should not be lived that he detects in the drama implies the moral beauty and humane joy he advocates.

His argument is overstated in part, and some of his ideas for reform of the stage may strike us as quaint today; as quaint, say, as Oscar Wilde's prescription for health in *The Soul of Man Under Socialism*. But Bentley and Wilde are unanswerable, because such solutions are nonexistent in a real world—or so our cynical half says—instead, they provide a utopian vision that improves morale today and thus provokes change tomorrow.

Bentley now turns his back on the Broadway stage, and journeys to Europe, *In Search of Theater* (1953). For packed information the book is unmatched. Given Bentley's talent for condensing a subject, each essay is a tome by any other name. London, Paris, Rome, Berlin, the backroads of Sicily in search of Pirandello, spot-checks back to the Great White Way—he sees it all and records it well. The influx of facts, the fixity of analyses, the additions to awareness are magisterial. He is learning to observe the actor, quintessentialize an artist's contribution, and compare a universe of conventions, qualities and styles. The list of firsts is impressive: the first essay to consider Yeats as a theatrical force, the first on De Filippo in English, the first to link Brecht and Artaud in significant parallel; in brief, the first summing up of theatre as a power in our world, in our century. But mostly it is a book to read for the display of Bentley's ability to love, unmawkishly and with precision, the men and women of moment in his life: Chaplin and Shaw, Stark Young and Martha Graham.

Home again, he dissects the Broadway stage as drama critic of *The New Republic,* and publishes his journalism in *The Dramatic Event* (1954) and *What is Theatre?* (1956). His concerns now issue from the vantage of an aisle seat; his style is charged with the ring of the moment. The image of Bentley laboring in this field is both funny and strange. He resigns after four years. Consider that these are among the thinnest of *Broadway* seasons; a span of boredom made just tolerable by *My Fair Lady, Tiger at the Gates,* and *Waiting for Godot.* Still, in the tradition of Shaw, he writes a record and creates a literature from an appraisal of an often idiotic subject.

Broadway, to say the least, is unprepared. Bentley weighs into the self-righteous and hypocritical liberal coterie of the McCarthy years, exploding false reputations as he buttresses talent. He proclaims the accomplishment of Brecht against the miscarriages of Miller and Williams; he argues for candor and for accepting our share of guilt against a melodramatic school of American playwriting that assumes innocence; and he continues, all the while, to champion the dormant power of the subversive masters.

His mission attains its summit with *The Life of the Drama* in 1964. A book of dramatic theory, it doesn't advance a theory of drama at all. Instead of asking "what should the drama mean?" Bentley asks "what has the drama meant?" He rejects as presumptuous the search for *the* theory of drama; instead, he seeks to discover a tradition of response. To define Shakespeare's "meaning" once and for all, as so many still presume to do, makes a silly assumption about culture: namely, that there is no tradition in which people have absorbed Shakespeare. In this light, the book's thesis is the need to respect the subjective response to art in its historical development; and this in contrast with the evasion of self and possible self-contempt implied in "objective" scholarship. A student of Nietzsche, Bentley knows "There are no facts, there are only interpretations," and the "fact" he searches for is the history of the imagination.

David Stafford-Clark writing on Freud says that "It is one of the signs of genius that its possessor asks questions which have simply never occurred to other people in the face of the same situation."[3] Maintaining that "the easiest questions are the hardest," Bentley enlivens a world we have neglected. A simple scan of his table of contents reveals his uncanny ability to find the "simplicities" that supposedly stare us in the face. For example: an actor thrills us. Bentley asks: what is a thrill? Or how to define the character of Hamlet? Begin by examining your own response to any human being outside of yourself. In what way do people exist for you? Hamlet starts there. The ABCs of psychology are marshalled to uncommon effect; the insight released from a consideration of the "obvious" is breathtaking. This is Brecht's "crude thinking" at its best. And the book has a material base. Bentley works from the ground up, "where the flowers of dramatic art have their roots in crude action." He avoids the obscurity of the metaphysical critic who equates obscurity with profundity, and writes a lesson on how to inform the common reader.

His capsule statement for the evasions he is combatting is, "Some resent life; others, art." He urges the raw emotional impact of drama against the genteel, and the need for design in art against the naturalist. He demolishes the snobbish prejudice against plot, type characters, melodrama and farce; and he outlines a goal of mature health that transcends their more infantile aspects.

The great closing statement for facing despair shows him confronting his fate. If he is incapable of accepting "the hope of a heaven," he nevertheless embraces his chosen art as the grace and "hope without which we cannot live from day to day." Pirandello is his inspiration here, and *The Life of the Drama* is dedicated ultimately to the Italian's acceptance of subjective human mystery.

Bentley's summation occurs in *The Life of the Drama*. It is lucky for us that the Vietnam War did not intrude upon the book's conception or composition. The war provoked in him an outrage that, of course, many shared. *The Theatre of*

Commitment (1967) and the *Theatre of War* (1972) show the strain. The first weighs as its theme the artist's right to privacy against the right of an urgent claim that intrudes upon that center; while the second, through its very diversity of topics (social, sexual, political and theatrical) reflects a society torn by conflict. Even the title, *Theatre of War,* with a play on words (*raw* indeed!), indicates the immediacy he is after and the price he pays.

Bentley has never been one for a foolish consistency. As an accomplished dialectician, who takes contradiction in stride, he knows how to change his mind when the world changes him. But with the shameful war raging, and perhaps with the certain security that several big books are behind him, he attacks with less than his customary civility and fastidiousness. The theatrical essays are as fine as ever, but those condemning United States policy are uncharacteristically shrill at times. Given the fire in the streets of America and in the jungles of Vietnam, we are not inclined to hold this against him. Indeed, *The Theatre of Commitment* and the *Theatre of War* are testaments of another sort: to a humanity made manifest in its brave subjective truth.

A consideration of Bentley's contribution would be incomplete without a mention of the anthologies he has edited and, with his knowledge of Latin, French, Italian, German and Russian, the plays he has translated; the latter helping to create Brecht's reputation in America. I won't fill my page with a list of titles, but taken together they show that Bentley has injected over 100 plays into the cultural stream; a mass of neglected work in the best available translations that Albert Bermel has characterized as the single greatest expansion of the English drama since the Elizabethans.[4] Recent anthologies of plays proudly announce the mammoth institutional apparatus that now discovers and disseminates new drama in America.[5] Bentley, we must point out, was doing it alone back then, on the top level of quality.

The polemic assembled from the various introductions and notes to the volumes is startling in its cultural effectiveness. Bentley argues for the classical impact of contemporary drama and for the contemporary impact of classical drama, always affirming the oneness of past and present, while simultaneously showing how permanence in art "is paradoxically achieved by a deep penetration of the present." This is quite possibly the strongest case ever made in dramatic criticism for viewing tradition as a living force. Zola said: "The drama dies unless it is rejuvenated by new life. We must put new blood into this corpse."

With all of this—and we haven't even touched upon his internationally produced play, *Are You Now Or Have You Ever Been (1972),* or his other dramas, which are beginning to find their audience—there is a danger of overpraising his accomplishment. Granted, he has written the best criticism on the best dramatists of the modern theatre, and there is even talk today of his "legendary" stature in the profession. But Bentley isn't ready for his pedestal yet; he is a living force or he is nothing.

As befits a human being, his range of consideration and depth of appreciation are incomplete. There are realms he mistakes or enters with difficulty. Chekhov, for instance, is a hard writer for him. Less obviously dialectically based than either Ibsen, Shaw, or Brecht; Chekhov's angry-tolerant and passionately-reticent nature is distant from Bentley's brand of argument. His writing on the dramatist is fresh and warm—we think of the good essay on *Uncle Vanya*—but I suspect it had to be coaxed into existence, and he hasn't written much else on Chekhov. The same applies to Beckett, who is approached obliquely and appreciated in stages, not immediately apprehended like his favorite dialectical playwrights. His writing on Strindberg is seminal, but seems just off, overlooking, as it does for the most part, the man's crowning achievement, the Chamber Plays.

The wrestling match with O'Neill is complicated by the phony accusation that Bentley is a critic dogmatically opposed to the American drama, and thus is informed by our sense that Bentley senses he is being watched. O'Neill, as *the* American dramatist, becomes a test of sorts, and Bentley indeed is amazing to watch in his stubborn inability to let go of the playwright. To his credit, he will not let go until he feels confident he has placed (pinned down?) O'Neill to his satisfaction. But his appraisal of *The Iceman Cometh,* brilliant as it is, still seems convoluted.

The defining instance occurs with a writer less known for his drama, Artaud. Though Bentley perfectly treats the negative aspect of the writer, he misses, I think, the positive aspect of the visionary; and history has proven him wrong; Artaud is used by directors to good effect. His shock is also a healthy charge in a world lost to bureaucracy.

Apart from instances where the work in question is frankly inferior, Bentley is criticizing or failing to engage drama he feels lacks a firm social base. He needs a writer to argue with, and a drama to explicate that lends itself to historical analysis. For these reasons, as he readily admits, he may have undervalued artists of a surreal tendency, those less connected with the here and now.[6]

So much for "limitations." What does Bentley do in his writing? He is the first critic of the modern theatre, certainly in America, to insist upon seeing both the playwright and his interpreter as figures held in time. Much follows from that: the conviction that the greatest drama is the drama most representative of its age, since it uncovers and formulates the essential problems of a society; the right to interpret the greatest drama polemically—hence with our fated imperfection and not with our ego-given presumption of discovering the universal significance of a work—and finally, the need to connect the greatest drama with our day by not shunning that responsibility. By accepting the men of the past, we accept ourselves; by accepting ourselves, we accept the men of the past. The beauty of this argument is self-evident.

Over his forty year career, Bentley offers a series of what he calls "periodic soundings" of the drama; his consideration of a play is actively influenced by what is happening in the world. His essays have greater value than those seeking the timeless in art, or than those pretending to definitive statement, precisely because they offer a record of change that becomes timeless and definitive in another way: they write the story of our time as they relate its reflection on stage.

But with Bentley there is another side to the question. He warns us against immersing the artist so deeply in his time that he loses his individuality. Here he is arguing against the statistic-hunting type of historian who loses the spirit in the flux of facts. Bentley urges that we always search for the idea behind the historically determined ideas. He is concerned to free Ibsen from Ibsenism, Shaw from Shavianism, Brecht from Brechtianism—indeed, all the artists from all the "isms"—and he will do this, as we know, despite each playwright's insistence on taking himself as an ideologue.

Bentley is forever searching for the source of energy that lives from age to age, be it a dramatic archetype, a heroic addition, or a recurring social dilemma which transcends its point of origin. What is most impressive about him in this line is his unequaled capacity to respect and appraise the intellectual content of drama without losing sight of it as art. This accounts for his ability to interpret the ideas *in* a play as the idea *of* a play, viewing Pirandellianism as Pirandello's subject or Ibsenism as Ibsen's, with the emotional beauty of the work binding all in a sum greater than its parts. It cannot be said too often that Bentley is first and last a man promoting men as artists in their art. He may emphasize the aggression in Brecht's drama in a passive age, or he may emphasize its pacifism in a war-torn time; in the end, he emphasizes the integrity of Brecht.

The support of his generous acceptance and the motor of his dramatic sense are conceptions of man he derives, surprisingly enough (but on second thought, it's not so surprising) from Shakespeare. Upon reflection, it seems fitting that our dramatic critic should take his image of man from Shakespeare, whose "spiritual strength is unique, for he is the teacher behind the teachers."[7]

While it is tempting to divide a man among his passions, as we have just done, we should avoid doing so to the point where no man remains a whole. Yes, Bentley's career has progressed through stages of strongly held admirations and allegiances, most recently, Kleist. But the crux of the matter is that the author of *A Century of Hero-Worship* (1944) has never settled for a single hero. We all know of men, some as strong as Bentley, who have lost themselves in the causes associated with a name. But Bentley has always protected himself from such error, correcting, to take one example, Ibsen with Brecht and Brecht with Ibsen.

So he is more than the sum of his passions, and his vision overflows the objects under his consideration. Committed, like Shaw, to a destiny larger than his own, he represents that rare and silently vanishing nature: the great moralist. If

Shaw stands behind him, Montaigne and Voltaire inspire them both. A philosophical socialist and humanist, Bentley's project is to occupy the candid center on behalf of human nature and the sociable society. Nostalgic as this may sound, he vitalizes the sentiment in a living struggle to achieve it. Retaining a dogged faith that overcomes his own pessimism, he refuses to surrender to our dispirited times. If his hard-earned optimism strikes some as naive, the fact remains that his open honesty catches us and a cynical society in an evasive lie.

A man so positioned needs a sense of humor, a knowing smile, and reserves of character. Think of the temptations thrown in his way to veer off course. He will be offered the cloistered security of the ivory tower; he will be enticed and torn by the conflicting claims of the individual and the collective (inviting him, at their most strident, to deny the world or his identity), and he will encounter the lure of easy money, fast times, and every conceivable fashion and fad. But though tempted, Bentley has resisted. He resigned, admittedly to his eventual regret, the senior chair in dramatic literature in America in protest over Columbia University's handling of the student dissidents during the Vietnam War; he fought off Brecht's urging to go all the way with Stalinism, and McCarthy's "urging" to go all the way with anticommunism; he refuses to indulge in the pseudo-Beckettian's pose of "nothing to be done," and he is above our theatre's too often compromised fame. Inevitably he is labelled an agitator by the pedants, a formalist by the Communists, a dogmatist by the conformists, an easy-optimist by the heavy-pessimists, and a snob by the self-seeking.

Influenced by several of our century's ideologies, most notably by Marxism, he has refused, again like Shaw, a doctrinal allegiance to them all in hope of finding the best in each. His continued political stance is for socialism extended through democratic means and, though a man immersed in his time and subject to its distractions, his vision has remained remarkably pure.

The reader's ultimate encounter is with his style. Open and transparent, it tells of an education conducted in public as Bentley experiences the world and seems to grow through the turns of his prose. Since every sentence is understandable at sight, there is no impediment to thought, and you are led to think; the exact reverse effect one gets from reading the jargon-mongers.

His sentences are long, but quick in the phrase. They are driven by a pragmatic search for truth, a spiralling dialectical range, a reach for the common reader, an attention to the text, and a passion for ethical utility. Add to this an uncommon common sense, a wit that is sharp without being mean, and the brilliance to order it all, and you have the quality of his voice.

That voice is felt as a civil conversation in which neither party interrupts the other. It speaks to the eye, neither looking up nor down at you. Through his writing on the modern theatre, Bentley registers the shock of twentieth-century life, and when he emerges, undaunted and sound in his unsentimental praxis, he encourages and, yes, helps us to live.

His skill as a dialectician is more than an attribute; it is the man, and as such contains a destiny. Deeply aware of the difficulty of attaining truth, this paradoxical thinker is wary of the flat assertion as reductive. With the gift of the best minds, he is more than able, in Jacques Barzun's formulation, "to hold two opposed and mutually tempering ideas simultaneously"[8]; while the assembly of his sentences, essays, books and plays is best read as a chorus of answering calls.

Early in his career, his road must have been a lonely one. In a postwar American theatre largely devoid of argument, his talent for assertion and counterassertion created a discussion in a wilderness. Debating the "pros" and "cons" of Ibsen and the rest, he advanced a vision of theatre and of life. His influence inspired fellows for the great conversation.

Poised between thesis and antithesis, containing within himself much of the yes and no of our culture, he lived his richly ambivalent and contradictory destiny, expressing his faith in a search for a synthesis. The boy and girl the world destroys in his most recent and beautiful play, *German Requiem (1985)*, say it best:

Otto: Separate, each thinks his own one thought. What if each could bring himself to . . . think the other's thought?

Agnes: Two thoughts are better than one! And lead to a third thought that might save the day![9]

The wish is heartbreaking, even out of context, but the hope is real. Searching, arguing, writing, when Eric Bentley contends with the angel of history, he fights for the child of the future.

Michael Bertin

Notes

1. For this serviceable phrase, I thank Henri Arvon, *Marxist Esthetics,* trans. Helen R. Lane, Intro. Fredric Jameson, Ithaca and London, 1970 (Eng. ed. 1973) p. 114.

2. Paul Tillich, *The Courage To Be*, New Haven and London, 1952, p. 147.

3. David Stafford-Clark, *What Freud Really Said*, New York, 1966, p. 25.

4. Albert Bermel, "Adventures in Translation," *The Kenyon Review* (Winter, 1962).

5. See for instance the preface by James Leverett to *New Plays USA 2*, ed. M. Elizabeth Osborn and Gillian Richards, New York, 1984.

6. In an interview conducted by Richard Kostelanetz, the editor of *American Writing Today*, 2, a USIA publication, Washington, 1982, p. 44.

7. Eric Bentley, *The Life of the Drama*, New York, 1967, p. 91.

8. Jacques Barzun, *A Stroll With William James*, New York, 1983, p. 95.

9. Eric Bentley, *Monstrous Martyrdoms*, Buffalo, 1985, p. 202. (See my descriptive note on Bentley's drama in *Contemporary Dramatists*, Third Edition, New York, 1982, p. 85.)

I
TRIBUTES

ERIC BENTLEY: AN APPRECIATION

BY C.S. LEWIS

MAGDALEN COLLEGE,
OXFORD.

Mr. E. Russell Bentley of University College has been my pupil while reading for the Final Honour School of English Language and Literature. I regard him as one of the two best pupils I have had in a tutorial experience of thirteen years. His knowledge is very great, for a young man, and is at present very evenly distributed over the whole field from Beowulf to Auden, and he has a real interest, not very common among our students, in the general theory and presuppositions of criticism. As my pupil he has needed very little teaching in the ordinary sense, for he has always been able to find out for himself anything he wanted to know. This has enabled us to devote our tutorial hours mainly to discussion; in which I found him, though a good tempered, a formidable dialectician. I have no doubt at all that if he is given the opportunity he will one day make contributions of the highest distinction to our subject.　　　　　C. S. Lewis

P. T. O.　　　　　March 12ᵗʰ 1938

4

I had forgotten to add that I know nothing
of his character but what is good and that,
socially, he is very agreeable. I have been
present both when he was the chief talker
and when he was the most silent member of
the party: in both rôles he seemed to fit in
equally well.

C. S. L.

Mr. E. R. Bentley, of University College, Oxford, was my pupil while reading for the Final Honour School of English Language and Liter- -ature, in which he achieved First Class Hon- -ours. Since then I have, on the occasion of several absences from work occasioned by illness, entrusted my own pupils to him for tuition. The results were most satisfactory and I found that discussion of tutorial prob- -lems with him was often illuminating. I have no hesitation in saying that Mr. Bentley is one of the two best pupils who have passed through my hands in a teaching experience of sixteen years. He is a real scholar and a man of highly original and penetrating mind, for whom I would venture to predict (if anything were now predictable) a truly distinguished future; and if I were given carte blanche to form a Faculty of English in any university I should certainly include him in my staff. He combines in a high degree the power of being thorough and profound in his own work with that of descending easily and genially to the level of minds greatly inferior to his own. He is also a man of principle and is usually liked in general society.

C. S. Lewis

Fellow & Tutor of Magdalen College,

Oxford.

April 1940

ERIC BENTLEY: A CITATION

BY JAMES McFARLANE

Buy any of the many Eric Bentley books currently in the bookshops, and before you even reach the title page you are confronted with evidence attesting to the astonishing versatility, the prodigious productivity of the author. "Also by Eric Bentley" it will announce at the head of a full and crowded page of titles and references. First comes a list of nine volumes in the field of dramatic theory, theatre criticism and cultural history of which he is author, including works the titles of which figure on every self-respecting book-list produced today for students of dramatic literature the world over: *A Century of Hero-Worship; The Playwright as Thinker; Bernard Shaw; In Search of Theater; The Dramatic Event; What is Theatre?; The Life of the Drama; The Theatre of Commitment;* and *Theatre of War*. Then come the titles of nine plays, all written since 1970, one of which in particular—*Are You Now Or Have You Ever Been*—is well known to British audiences from its premiere at the Mermaid Theatre in London and from its recent broadcast (only last week) on Radio Three, and which incidentally was earlier this year running in New York to great acclaim. The next section then catalogues a miscellany of books of which he is editor or author/editor, including the greatly respected and much consulted anthology of *Scrutiny* criticism, entitled *The Importance of Scrutiny,* as well as that best-selling and disturbing account of the hearings of the notorious Un-American Activities Committee, entitled *Thirty Years of Treason.* Then comes a list of those widely used anthologies of drama in translation, including the six volumes of *The Modern Theatre,* the four volumes of *The Classic Theatre,* the three volumes of *The Modern Repertoire,* and a volume of Italian plays. Thereupon, he is further identified as the translator and editor of twelve plays by Bertolt Brecht, five plays by Pirandello, and a play by Eduardo De Filippo, as well as a volume of satirical songs by Wolf Biermann. And then, to put the final flourish to this astonishing variety of endeavour, there comes the titles of eight long-playing albums which he has recorded, either as a reader or a singer, including selections of songs by Brecht and Eisler, Prévert and Kosma, and Biermann.

Yet this breadth of interest is emphatically not at the expense of depth of penetration. Take, for example, his genial enquiry into the nature of drama entitled *The Life of the Drama,* that work of his which, perhaps more surely than any other, will endure to occupy the attention of students of drama for generations to come. On its publication in 1964, the *New York Review of Books* described it as a radical new look at the grammar of theatre, "a work of exceptional virtue . . . central, indispensable," adding that it was clearly founded on years of thought and experience and written with a clarity which testified to the completeness of that preparation. And as one traces that preparation back over the preceding years, one discovers how perspicacious were the words of that reviewer (who, incidentally, was Frank

Kermode, now King Edward VII Professor of English at Cambridge). The book itself had grown out of the Charles Eliot Norton Lectures which Eric Bentley had delivered at Harvard University in the course of the academic year 1960-61—though it is entirely characteristic of him that when he heard a tape recording of what he had said, he promptly decided that this was an object lesson in How Not To Do It, and at once set about totally revising it. These were the years when Eric Bentley was occupying the Brander Matthews Chair of Dramatic Literature at Columbia University, the senior chair in its subject in America, to which he had been appointed in 1954 at the age of 37. During the early years of his tenure, he had pondered many of the ideas upon which his Harvard lectures were based, and had pursued them through several drafts. Yet this was not the only nor perhaps even the most important factor contributing to their maturation. They had also been nourished by the experience of four intensive years of theatrical journalism between 1952 and 1956, when he had been dramatic critic of *The New Republic,* a job which he held simultaneously with his academic post at Columbia and which itself left a rich deposit in two full and lively volumes of collected dramatic notices: *The Dramatic Event* and *What is Theatre?*

And finally, in one's search for the actual point of origin of these same lectures, one comes to 1948, the year in which Eric Bentley was awarded a Guggenheim Fellowship to take him to Europe with the declared aim of writing the book which, sixteen years later, in fact became *The Life of the Drama.* But as the one year of the Fellowship extended to three, Bentley found himself involved among other things in directing plays at the Abbey Theatre, Dublin, at the Schauspielhaus in Zurich, at the Teatro Universitario in Padua, and at Max Reinhardt's castle of Leopoldskron in

Salzburg. Such then was the rich compost which nourished the Harvard lectures and eventually brought forth the book.

As one plots the career of Eric Bentley, however, there is—as with all good plots—a twist to it. Although so much of his life and work had related most immediately to the American and indeed the New York scene, his Guggenheim award of 1948 betokened not a first encounter with Europe but a return. He was in fact a child of industrial Lancashire, born in Bolton in 1916, son of a businessman and one-time Mayor of Bolton who had been prominent in Liberal and in Chapel circles, and of a mother of unusual musical gifts. He was that thing which, in the twenties and thirties before the days of comprehensive schools and local authority grants, carried such rich overtones of meaning and social significance: a scholarship boy. A scholarship took him from elementary school to grammar school; and from there he went as an Open Exhibitioner to University College, Oxford. The school's records of these years reveal much that was anticipatory of later things: in the fact, for example, of his playing Malvolio and Macbeth and Pompey the Great in a succession of school drama productions, and playing them—according to witnesses—with an assurance rare in a schoolboy; even though, as Macbeth, he is also remembered struggling to avoid asphyxiation as he stood at a witches cauldron prepared by an overzealous lab staff! He was, and still is, a gifted pianist, remembered still today for his performance as solo pianist with the school orchestra in a Beethoven piano concerto. To round out the picture, it is reported of him that although he did not particularly distinguish himself as a sportsman, he was judged to have been an excellent instructor of his house Physical Training Team.

His Exhibition was in History, but in the event he read English and, tutored by C.S. Lewis, to whom he owed much, he graduated in 1938. As an undergraduate he gave a lot of time and effort to those issues, both political and cultural, which figured prominently in the thirties, especially the pacifist cause; but he also found time to work with the OUDS—the Oxford University Dramatic Society—and was among other things a memorable Sir Toby Belch. He then moved on to postgraduate study. What happened then is cryptically conveyed by an entry in the Catalogue of the United States Library of Congress, which makes reference to the existence of a typescript entitled "Psychology and the critic of literature: a chapter in twentieth century thought," and carrying the endorsement "Written in 1938-39, accepted in the latter year as a BLitt thesis by Oxford University, revised in the years 1939-41, accepted for publication . . . but never published." Only two fragments (it records forlornly) have ever appeared.

From Oxford he moved to Yale, and in 1941 took his PhD in Comparative Literature with a dissertation which was later published under the title *A Century of Hero-Worship*, though readers in this country will be more familiar with it under the title of *The Cult of the Superman*. (One way, incidentally, of instantly augmenting your list of publications and at the same time confounding the bibliographers is to publish the same book under two different titles, one for the States and another for the U.K.—enquiries as how best to do this, please, to Eric Bentley who has done it more than once!) Following Yale he taught literature and history at a number of different places in the States, including a three year period at the University of Minnesota; and out of these years came two other influential books: a monograph on modern drama entitled *The Playwright as Thinker* (unless you bought the book in London when it was called *The Modern Theatre*), and a study of *Bernard Shaw*.

It was of course during the years when he was professing his subject at Columbia, between 1954 and 1969, that he wrote most of those theoretical commentaries which have so firmly established his reputation as one of the world's most influential drama critics, an achievement marked also by his receiving the George Jean Nathan Award in 1966. But the ten years since he relinquished his Chair in 1969 have seen a new and exciting and as yet incomplete achievement: as a creative dramatist in his own right. His work has included the three dramas published together under the title of *Rallying Cries;* three other separately published plays with titles *A Time to Die, The Red White and Black,* and *Expletive Deleted;* and, most recently, a further volume of *Three Plays,* one re-creating the trial of Oscar Wilde, and the other two being re-visions (and the hyphen is important) of plays by the nineteenth-century German playwright Heinrich von Kleist.

Nor has he lost the zest which he had in great measure as a young man for taking a public and determined stand on particular issues of the day which he considers important or challenging. In recent years, for example, he has forthrightly and courageously come out on a whole range of contemporary issues, of which his devastating open letter to Grotowski in 1969, and the interview he gave in 1974 to the periodical *College English* are but two of many instances.

One may therefore say with all truth that as a sensitive and perceptive commentator on the whole range of classical and contemporary drama, as an academic critic of enviable erudition and experience, as an influential force in the living theatre of two continents, as a pioneering translator and interpreter of Brecht and Pirandello, as an original dramatist of new and disturbingly modern power, and as a polemicist of stubborn courage, he has created a unique role for himself not only in the world of the theatre, but also in what one may call the theatre of the world—a role which he plays with consummate skill and much dry wit.

My Lord and Chancellor, I present to you Eric Bentley for the degree of Doctor of Letters, honoris causa.

[University of East Anglia, Norwich, England, 5 July 1979]

REPERTORY MEMORIES

BY ROBERT BRUSTEIN

Sometimes when young folk ask me whether there was any early response in the theatrical community to Eric Bentley's demand for serious theatre in America, this oldtimer sits back in his Barker lounge, lights up a pipe, and tells the following story of two post-World War II companies:

It was 1949, and I had just completed my first and only student year at the Yale School of Drama. Bentley had recently published *The Playwright as Thinker,* a startling revelation to those just discovering that the stage might have a purpose beyond the need to entertain. Strange foreign sounds were swimming in our heads: Strindberg, Brecht, Pirandello, Wedekind. These were playwrights whose names were mentioned in Alois Nagler's Theatre History course, but students didn't have to read them, and it was rare when their plays found their way onto the Yale stage—or any other American stage, for that matter. We were having enough difficulty trying to smuggle a production of Odets into an environment where Congreve, Oscar Wilde, Pinero, Coward, Philip Barry, and S.N. Behrman were the reigning favorites of the teachers and the models for aspiring writers at the School.

Under the circumstances, there was only one possible course open to dissidents: we founded our own theatre. Since there were seven of us, we called it Studio 7, each contributing about $500 and two other commodities available only to youth—inexhaustible energy and invincible arrogance. Leasing the Provincetown Playhouse in Greenwich Village for the summer, we set about developing a season of plays—naturally directing, acting, designing, and constructing everything ourselves, as well as making repairs on that tiny ramshackle jewel box associated with so much early theatrical experimentation.

Managerially, the two guiding spirits of this venture were Al Hurwitz, a Yale costume designer who later became a schoolteacher, and Gene Wolsk, who later became a Broadway producer. Other ex-students involved were Eldon Elder as scene designer, John Stix as director, three Yale actors, and one more who doubled as business manager. Well, we had a stage, and access to other young talent, but no idea what to stage. When we asked Professor Nagler for suggestions, he uttered some harsh Austrian vocatives that sounded like "Vocheck by Beekner." Those bizarre noises provided a source of considerable merriment during the summer months. It never occurred to us that what he was proposing was Büchner's *Woyzeck,* because none of us had yet encountered this astonishing work, now recognized as one of the landmarks of world theatre.

Instead of doing "Vocheck by Beekner," we gathered to us a number of nonsalaried, non-Equity actors from Yale, and started rehearsing for a production of Lorca's *The Shoemaker's Prodigious Wife.* It featured another fellow-student, Boris Sagal, in the cast playing the Mayor. When

18

Boris (later a movie director) left us in mid-passage for a paying job in *The Beggar's Opera,* he was replaced by a Chaplin-like ex-Yalie (later an opera director), Frank Corsaro. Essentially a puppet play, this work was mild and amusing enough, but drew small houses. The Village audiences were more interested at that time in a rival company at the Cherry Lane Theatre called the Interplayers, run by Gene Saks and featuring the young Kim Stanley, which was doing considerably more experimental work, notably Gertrude Stein's *Yes Is For a Very Young Man.*

After the Lorca, we did a Strindberg, the first production of *The Father,* I believe, ever produced in New York, though (possibly inspired by our effort) it was done on Broadway the following season starring Raymond Massey and Mady Christian. Our production, directed by John Stix, featured Ward Costello and Anne Shropshire as Adolphe and Laura. On that tiny stage, the fury of the performances literally shook the canvas walls. I played the part of Nöjd, pulling on a forelock as I expressed doubts about the paternity of a child fathered on a local girl, and, later, the Doctor, when another actor left the cast. We had hit our stride with this one, and begun to develop an audience. As a final production—performed without me, since I had left the group to reconcile some love problems—Studio 7 did Wedekind's *Earth Spirit.* I can't remember if we had a second season, but the two theatres at the Provincetown Playhouse and Cherry Lane constituted the beginning of the postwar off-Broadway movement.

I also assisted at the birth of the postwar resident theatre movement which began inauspiciously enough in summer barns and civic centers. My company was located in a town hall in Unionville, Connecticut, about twenty miles from Hartford. It had another numerical title—Group 20—having been initiated by twenty young people from New England colleges, most of them from Wellesley. I joined the group in 1950, its second season, after putting in a year of graduate school at Columbia, studying with Lionel Trilling, Joseph Wood Krutch, Maurice Valency, and later (a large lecture course in Elizabethan drama) Eric Bentley. I had been informed about this theatre by one of its members, an Amherst chum named James Maxwell, and its company aims and aspirations excited me. Led by two Wellesley women, Betty Ann Metz and Betty Hart, with Michael Shurtleff as its resident director, Group 20 was devoted to evolving an acting ensemble capable of performing an eclectic repertory of world theatre. Nobody was paid, but all of us received free board—as well as free rooms, in the basement of a nearby abandoned bank. We slept on cots and awakened each morning dripping with moisture. Within a week, our clothes were moldy and our shoes were green, so we moved our sleeping quarters upstairs to the less humid offices of the building.

None of us cared much about physical comforts for we were having an exquisite time in that lovely environment. There was swimming nearby, and the nights were thick with a velvet texture permeated by the scent of flowers. We rehearsed and performed incessantly; no union rules regularized our hours. And on our day off, we went to Hartford to see a movie, or listened to Berlioz at full volume through the speakers mounted on the Town Hall stage. Our repertory that summer was pretty tame—S.N. Behrman's *Amphitryon 38, The Play's The Thing, The Philadelphia Story, Rain,* and *Volpone*—though (*Rain* excepted) I see now it was pretty unusual for the period and the area. Under Bentley's influence, I had become the resident malcontent, vocally disdainful of these tepid offerings; but since I had been given choice roles, my acting ambitions usually won out over my intellectual disapproval.

We rehearsed each play for two weeks and performed it for two weeks, which was pretty much routine summer stock procedure. The difference was that instead of jobbing in actors (or stars) for separate productions, we played everything ourselves. The way we grew in skill and confidence through this experience convinced us that ensemble company work was the process of the future. And when Group 20 moved to an outdoor Wellesley amphitheatre in 1953 and turned into an Equity company known as Theatre on the Green, we had the opportunity to demonstrate this process to a wider and more responsive audience, drawn from the Greater Boston area. By this time, Group 20 was being managed by Alison Ridley, the daughter of the Shakespeare scholar, M.R. Ridley, and had taken on a decidedly English coloration. The company ranks had been enlarged with the addition of such actors as Fritz Weaver, Michael Higgins, Peter Donat, Ellis Rabb, Bill Ball, Louis Edmonds, Nancy Wickwire, Sylvia Short, Tom Clancy, Tom Hill—and later, when we joined forces with the defunct Brattle Theatre, Rosemary Harris, Jerry Kilty, and such visiting artists as Max Adrian and Barry Morse. Some of these people were English, many others were English-trained, primarily at the Old Vic School. So aside from occasional American plays such as *The Crucible,* our schedule was largely composed of plays by Shakespeare, Shaw, Goldsmith, and Sheridan. Like later resident theatres—the Guthrie, say, or the American Conservatory Theatre—our classical summer company was an attempt to transplant the English repertory system in American soil.

This meant that our acting models were essentially the reigning classical English artists: Olivier, Peggy Ashcroft,

21

Richardson, Gielgud, Scofield, Joyce Redman. As a comic character actor, I played Bottom, Jaques, and Sir Anthony Absolute imitating Robert Newton's flamboyant Pistol in Olivier's *Henry V* (though John Barrymore's snorting cadences also sounded in my ears in classical roles). Our directors—among them Eliot Silverstein, Jack Landau, Alison Ridley, Benno Frank, Jerry Kilty, Ellis Rabb—primarily functioned to coach the actors and decorate the stage with graceful designs and choreographic patterns. Since Bentley's one-man effort to introduce Brecht to America had not yet reached the ears of theatre people, bold staging concepts were still a thing of the future. It was considered imaginative if a director could do Shakespeare in modern dress or bring an antique automobile on stage in a play by Shaw.

Still, if our work had no political thrust or metaphorical color, we had nevertheless stumbled on the concept of collective theatre in a nonprofit structure, which was essentially a socialist idea. The commercial stage at the time being largely monopolized by new American works with pickup casts hoping for long runs, our concern for acting the classics in a sequential schedule with a resident company was a comparatively radical impulse—in structure if not in substance. Later, when some of the people associated with Group 20 split off to form their own acting companies—Jack Landau at the American "Young Vic," Ellis Rabb at the APA, Bill Ball at the American Conservatory Theatre—the idea took root and spread, though it usually remained English-influenced instead of aiming towards an indigenous American style, with schedules dominated by English classics rather than the international repertory. The formation of the Guthrie theatre in the early sixties institutionalized the Anglophile leanings of American resident companies which for many years seemed like spinoffs of the Old Vic, Bristol, the Nottingham Playhouse, and, later, the Royal Shakespeare Company and National Theatre.

Meanwhile, Joe Papp was experimenting with a virile, muscular, rowdy approach to Shakespeare in Central Park; André Gregory was employing avant-garde techniques in classical plays at the Theatre for Living Arts in Philadelphia; and when I went to Yale in 1966 to become Dean of the School and start the Yale Repertory Theatre, we tried to apply the collective company idea to a more ambitious range of plays. Under Bentley's influence, our model became not the English repertory system but rather the Berliner Ensemble, with Bertolt Brecht as our resident playwright. Most of those odd-sounding foreign names (including "Vocheck by Beekner") eventually found their way onto our stage, and they were joined later (in New Haven, Cambridge, Minneapolis, Washington, and elsewhere) by others even stranger, such as Andrei Serban, Andrzej Wajda, Liviu Ciulei, Lucian Pintilie, Krystyna Zachwatowicz, Tadeusz Rozewicz, and Heiner Müller. We even did the premiere of a play by Bentley himself—*Are You Now Or Have You Ever Been.* In a further development of considerable interest, the American avant-garde, which for years had been inventing new performance techniques for the stage, began to turn its attention to the classics, with the result that the classical repertory in this country is now in process of total transformation. A Richard Foreman *Don Juan,* a Robert Wilson *Alcestis* and *King Lear,* a JoAnne Akalaitis *Endgame,* a Serban Chekhov cycle, a Lee Breuer *Lulu* and *Oedipus (Gospel) at Colonus*—these were a far cry from our stumbling early efforts with Strindberg at the Provincetown Playhouse and the English classics at Wellesley's Theatre on the Green.

Meanwhile, over three hundred resident theatres had taken root in various American cities and, although not many remained faithful to the repertory company ideal, they represented another significant extension of the kind of work begun in the late forties and fifties. Eric Bentley's influence on this had grown increasingly distant after he gave up weekly reviewing and subordinated critical writing to playwriting and performing, but his insistent critical demand for a serious art theatre in *The Playwright as Thinker, In Search of Theater,* and his collected reviews from *The New Republic,* was surely one of the early clarions of the movement and the inspiration for its international coloration.

ERIC BENTLEY
... AND ME

BY RICHARD GILMAN

A man is walking alongside me whom I recognize from a few photos I'd seen on dust jackets or in the papers. He's taller than I'd imagined, a lot taller than was Brecht, after whom he's vaguely and, it occurs to me, as a sweet sort of tribute modeled his appearance, to the extent anyway of wearing his hair in bangs. It's a beautiful late summer afternoon and Commercial Street, the main drag of Provincetown, is crowded with strollers, some of them going back and forth, as in a Mexican *paseo*. A celebrity alert is in effect, and to me he's one of the biggest celebrities of all.

As he pulls ahead of me I tell the people I'm with who he is and that I've decided to introduce myself to him. So I do. I rush forward, step in his path and say, "Mr. Bentley, it's a pleasure to see you here." Then I tell him my name and add, "I've admired your work for a long time."

Not that long, if the truth were known. This was the summer of 1962. I had been writing about the theater only since the fall of the previous year, having been asked, on the strength of an approval of my style, a review of some new translations of Ibsen and, I suppose, a faith in my capacity to learn, to be the drama critic of *Commonweal.*

I was an unlikely choice. I hadn't formally studied drama or theater, my only practical "experience" lay in having acted in some nondescript plays in school and summer camp, and until a few years before this time I hadn't any particular interest in the stage. In this respect I resembled the great majority of my intellectual contemporaries, for whom drama, as we'd encountered it in this country, was an art distinctly inferior to fiction or poetry. We might of course make an exception for a Shakespeare or a Chekhov, but we saw their work more as literature than as theater (the way they're still seen by English or Comp. Lit. departments) and, besides, they survived from a past that had somehow been able to spawn a true dramatic art; it no longer existed, we thought in our airy sophistication, seeing so-called "modern" drama as pretty much a wasteland.

So what I wrote about and thought about too, when I started to do those things professionally, were poems, stories and novels, as well as general cultural ideas. It may be too much to say that Eric Bentley's books, especially *The Playwright as Thinker,* singlehandedly made me open my eyes to the esthetic and intellectual possibilities of the stage (seeing *Waiting for Godot* in 1954 played a big part in my awakening) but his writing was surely among the chief propulsions I had at the time.

He was what we didn't then call a "role model," and whether or not my becoming a drama critic was an accession to the culture I haven't any doubt that Bentley had the same kind of revelatory effect, an effect like a clearing of vision, light entering where murk had been, on many others besides me: students of the arts, ordinary literate persons and even, presumably, in time, hardened theater professionals.

Is it surprising that the latter group put up the strongest resistance to letting themselves be enlightened? I didn't read *The Playwright as Thinker* when it was first published in 1946, for that was during the extreme phase of my unconcern for theater, but some years after I had read it and was so greatly inspired, I did a little research into the book's contemporary reception.

It was scarcely a publishing "event," though it got a few respectful, and one or two laudatory, notices. The responses it mostly aroused within the theater universe and its satellite world of journalistic theater coverage ranged from the scornful to the shocked to the appalled or, at best—maybe the worst—the condescending. (If I remember rightly, the reaction in the academy wasn't all that much warmer.)

I'm taking some liberties with the actual language of what we might call the establishment rejoinder to *The Playwright as Thinker,* but the burden of it was this: how can this man's approach be right, how can playwrights be thinkers, when everyone knows that they're *feelers,* they deal in emotions not ideas, don't they? Well, don't they?

No they don't, not the way you mean. More than any other critic (Francis Fergusson added to the work of demolition and reconstruction, but Fergusson was much narrower) Bentley gave to the theory and observation and potential practice of theater in this country—he certainly gave it to me—a means of overthrowing so wrong-headed and baneful a distinction.

Mind and body, thought and feeling, ideas and emotions—such crude and injurious antitheses have a long history of causing intellectual blight in America, nowhere more flagrantly and debilitatingly than in the theater. In his quirky way Edgar Allan Poe was the first to hint at the malady, Henry James (whose drama criticism is still too little known) refined the diagnosis and prescribed for its cure, and Bentley carried the understanding into our own time and expanded it.

The points he was making in *Playwright* and that he elaborated on in the writing that was to follow are, in essence, that drama is, or has been, an art as dense or supple or reverberant or mysterious or vigorous or disturbing as any other; that like other artists dramatists *think*, in the ways proper to their art; that thinking in art is the process by which raw, unmediated emotion, with its treacheries and deceitfulness, its inducing of blindness, is made present to the mind, placed, explored and brought into relation with both experience and imagination, brought, in other words, into *consciousness*.

When Pirandello said that what was "new" about his plays was that in them he had "convert[ed] intellect into passion" (he might equally well have said that he had bound them together, made each an aspect of the other) he may have been overstating his originality—in their different ways he had had great predecessors—but the remark and the action it described were accurate and startling enough in the conditions of the theater in his day.

Intellect and passion had always been complementary, reciprocal, but the received wisdom of the theater, even in its admiration for the "classics," persisted in seeing them as contrarieties. This is what lay behind Walter Kerr's infamous dismissal of *Godot* as a "philosophy lesson" not a play, and it's what lay behind the established opinion, widely disseminated in my youth (and still hanging on here and there) that, for example, Ibsen was all intellect or "ideas" and no passion, Strindberg all brute feeling and no mind, and Chekhov, well, the comfortable, silly notion had it, he was neither passion nor thought but some drowsy, moody, "bittersweet," wispy thing in between.

Pirandello, Ibsen, Strindberg, Chekhov, Brecht, to a lesser extent Shaw—these were the playwrights of the modern era whom Bentley's book rescued for me from obscurity, misreading, obloquy or, maybe deadliest of all, the academic. In its pages, too, I came for the first time upon the great neglected nineteenth-century ancestors (all Germans as it happened): Kleist, Grabbe, Büchner supremely; and dramatists I'd only known as novelists or poets: Zola, Yeats, Lorca. For that matter the book introduced me to theoreticians and practitioners I hadn't known or had barely heard of—Appia, Gordon Craig, Antoine, etc.—and also critics—Stark Young, Shaw and Beerbohm in that aspect of their careers. I was educated by this book.

In time I was able to see that *The Playwright as Thinker* had faults: a somewhat jerry-built structure, occasional opacity, some loose ends, mistakes of judgment or interpretation here and there, a few errors of fact. But when my first infatuation had cooled down and I was able to see these things I put them all down, and continue to ascribe them now, to the circumstances under which Bentley wrote. He was an explorer, a pioneer, and such people by definition don't have accurate maps and precise instruments but must work their way through the terrain partly by touch, a feel for what is there, an openness to what may surprisingly be there, a sense of the relation of things come upon to the previously known. Errors, distortions, omissions, even blunders are inevitable.

Even so, the book holds up remarkably well, and though *The Life of the Drama* may be a better book—certainly it's better organized and more assured—it can't displace

29

Playwright from the center of my affections. Something else occurs to me, which is that the book seems to have served, as Bentley said *Brand* and *Peer Gynt* did for Ibsen, as the "quarry" from which he drew the materials for most of what he would later write.

Over the years I've read just about everything Bentley has published, having had to catch up with the books that appeared during the time of my indifference to the theater. I haven't always been persuaded (the book on Shaw, for example, didn't convince me that its subject had done quite what Bentley said he did) and I've sometimes found myself dissenting from some theoretical propositions—about the nature of melodrama, for instance. But I've been wonderfully instructed, made wiser about drama and the stage.

I think of that series of chronicles he published in the fifties—*In Search of Theater, The Dramatic Event, What is Theatre?*—his weekly criticism between covers, along with some occasional pieces. Has there ever been in America journalistic reviewing so supple, witty, deep and unaccommodating? His was the chief voice of reason in—or about, or against—the American theater during those years; he was its tireless, learned policeman, as Shaw described one of the critic's tasks.

I start to reach for the books, which I always keep on a shelf near my desk, but then I realize that I don't need to refresh my memory, for it can offer me any number of exemplary pieces. I think first of "Trying to Like O'Neill," still the shrewdest estimate I know of our (alas!) best playwright. Then they start crowding up: "Doing Shakespeare Wrong"; "The China in the Bull Shop" (a witty tribute to Stark Young, a predecessor at the *New Republic*); "Craftsmanship in *Uncle Vanya*"; "The

Stagecraft of Brecht"; "Tennessee Williams and New York Kazan" (a finely balanced assessment of the playwright and an equally astute evaluation of the director's virtues and delinquencies); "The Broadway Intelligentsia" (mostly the people who think playwrights are feelers); "Is Drama an Extinct Species?" with its prescient remarks on film as threatening to surpass the stage in esthetic interest.

When it came time for me to write my own book, *The Making of Modern Drama,* I was dismayed to find myself with the impulse to quote Bentley on every other page. So I did a *volte-face;* falling deeply into the Anxiety of Influence I kept shutting him out of my mind. Although Eric wasn't old enough to be my biological father, spiritually, intellectually he was my progenitor and if I couldn't kill him, even metaphorically, I could at least keep thrusting him away. Still, hard as I tried to do this, I remember my editor commenting mildly on the frequency with which comments of Bentley's did turn up in my text, and my replying that there simply were cases where I wasn't able to say better, or with any degree of originality, what he'd already said.

Eventually the times outdistance us all, so it isn't surprising that in recent years Bentley has dropped away from what we call "developments" in the theater, or they've skipped beyond him. Then too, much of his energy has gone into his own plays and performing: the critic stepping down into the arena after watching it for so long with an eye nothing escaped. Politics have occupied him more directly than before, political reality, whose presence in drama had been one of the uncomfortable truths he had unearthed and laid before a theatrical world which would much rather not have seen it.

Though my political values aren't that far from his, I don't share all his particular positions and I sometimes find myself irritated by his diatribes. But he's earned them, and it's all right. Everything's all right. He's seventy now and I want to tell him, and as many readers as I can garner, how much he's meant to me. With all the awards our self-congratulatory theater is forever bestowing on itself, there ought to be one for him. But, then, he'd probably turn it down; in his high-pitched, hesitant voice he'd say something elegantly wry, maybe paraphrase Brecht to the effect that any institution that needs heroes is in bad shape. Well, we were in bad shape and we needed him.

II
DRAMATISTS

THE WILD DUCK AS A PORTRAIT OF THE ARTIST IN TRANSITION

BY ROLF FJELDE

The Wild Duck is the most elusive of the entire group of Ibsen's so-called realistic dramas, and designedly so. It is as evasive as Hjalmar Ekdal is to being pinned down; it refuses accommodation to a clearly dominant set or direction of values; it is the work of the final cycle closest to fulfilling Wallace Stevens' line that "A poem must resist the intelligence/Almost successfully." From appearing to be a relatively simple, even cynical retraction of didactic and messianic tendencies in the preceding four plays—Ibsen's corrective self-criticism—it becomes, under continued examination, more and more mysterious, as versions of the truth erode other versions, and key facts—Hedvig's paternity, the disability of Gregers's mother, the benign or malign character of Haakon Werle, the circumstances of and responsibility for the original, actionable transgression of boundaries in the forests—are displaced from knowledgeability. Indeed, if the play asserts anything, it would seem to insist that, given the degree of opacity of human being to human being in this world, let the benefit of the doubt be on the side of caring about what we cannot take for granted—the feelings of a rejected child, the multiple significations of the wild duck.

Of the many perspectives *The Wild Duck* affords on its arrangement of material, the one I would like briefly to emphasize here is both integral to the peculiar power that the play exerts, and yet too often neglected in its larger implications: namely, its symbolic reflection of Ibsen's own self-liberating progress as an artist. Although Ibsen's dramatic actions and thematic interests in the first four plays of the cycle are in fact allusive and far-ranging, it was their issue-oriented content that gave them immediate impact among audiences and readers and ensured their author's controversial international fame. That property of the initial quartet of dramas was undoubtedly focused and reinforced by Georg Brandes's "Inaugural Lecture" of 1871, which was then incorporated the following year in the first volume of *Main Currents in Nineteenth-Century Literature,* a book which Ibsen described in a letter to its author as "one of those works which place a yawning gap between yesterday and today."[1] In the text of the "Inaugural Lecture" one finds the pronouncement that Ibsen, then in the throes of completing the immense ideological summation of *Emperor and Galilean,* appears to have seized upon as a strategy of advance to his next stage of development: "What keeps a literature alive in our days is that it submits problems to debate."[2] If this was to be the path to a living, contemporaneous drama that would have the stature of serious literature, then the evidentiary submission of problems—whatever else the play might contain—would have to be as clear, defined and detailed as possible. Logically, inevitably, photographic naturalism became the ostensible style of *Pillars of Society* in treating the "problem" of business ethics; of *A Doll House* in dealing with inequities in marriage; *Ghosts* in confronting parental responsibilities to truth and to children, even to the brink of euthanasia; and *An Enemy of the People* in challenging environmental pollution with Dr. Stockmann's evolutionary argument against the democratic dogma of majority rule.

After nearly a decade of inciting thought on such questions via a technique that meticulously reproduced the surfaces of modern life—of trying his luck as a "photographer," as he had bitterly phrased it to Bjørnson after the disappointing critical response to *Peer Gynt*—Ibsen found he could no longer suppress his inherently poetic vision. The fifth play in the series, in effect, cracked the photographic plate and imprinted the realistic action with patterns that were not easily reconciled with strict verisimilitude. *The Wild Duck* is thus a pivotal work that represents simultaneously the thinking through of a crucial artistic reassessment and the universalizing disguise of that reassessment within a work of complex, humanistic art. It is one of the earliest examples of that twentieth-century phenomenon throughout the arts, not least in drama—e.g. Pirandello's *Six Characters*—that finds its characteristic expression by taking the medium itself as its subject matter.

The setting that dominates the play, spanning four of its five acts, is the Ekdal studio apartment with its huge skylight, symptomatically a room originally designed for an artist, but currently occupied by a photographer. It is thus a precise replica of the predicament, described above, of the playwright's own career. Moreover, in its twofold division, it simulates a kind of scenic model of the artist's mind. Downstage is a practical, utilitarian foreground for eating, entertaining, discussing the success or failure of incursions into the world, and doing one's professional work, i.e. taking photographs—in short, a spacialized persona comprehending various kinds of interactions with what's "out there." Upstage lies a mysterious, evocative background that the inhabitants of the studio, all save the chief negotiator with prosaic actuality, Gina, instinctively gravitate toward, full of flotsam and jetsam of past human culture and saving remnants of a diminished natural wilderness. The pragmatic foreground is composed around an old-fashioned portrait camera, with its attractive, warmly shellacked wood, black bellows and tripod, as well as its outlying vials of chemicals and retouching tools—the mechanism by which objective reality is reproduced with minimal modification; the numinous background is attuned to the hidden (it should always be concealed or obscured from the audience), charismatic source of meaning identified with the wild duck.

From this angle of approach, the two principal *external* settings apart from the Ekdal home can be aggregated together as the essential reality outside the artist's mind, the chief categories of being-in-the-world with which that mind must cope. That outer dimension is comprised of two planes of experience: the salon and home office in the Werle mansion, and the disorderly apartment occupied by Relling and Molvik—high society and the lower depths. Again, symptomatically, when the artiste manqué Hjalmar ventures into each of them, in Act One and between Acts Four and Five, he returns humiliated, prompt to reassert his uncontested status of command among his own in the studio and the loft. His chagrin stems not merely from the fiasco of his attempts at outward adjustment, of his very presence, in the two exterior settings, but as well, on the psychodramatic level, from the low esteem accorded art in the social, "real" world. In the salon, a piano interlude—Schumann or Grieg, one supposes—is regarded as synonymous with tedium or torture by the competitive worldlings; and an album of photographs on display proves of absorbing interest to the artist alone—otherwise it functions as the nineteenth century equivalent of a coffee table ornament, a mere morsel of entertainment, an item of consumption that is "so good for the digestion" to page through.[3] In the lower depths, on the other hand, art effectively ceases to exist. The failed doctor and the spoiled priest have enough to do just keeping body and soul, their two professional concerns, together.

That the play incorporates a sense of frustration with the inability of art to penetrate the external world and be recognized as such when constricted within Brandes's issue-oriented, social engineering formula is borne out by the fact that no play after *The Wild Duck* adopts a problem play format, even as a vehicle for larger world-historical and/or mythic content. A second impetus toward a reconstituting of method may well derive from Ibsen's suspicion that, by yielding to a reductive, utilitarian role, he was merely being used for others' ends, since what characterizes both levels of the world of actuality beyond the studio/loft is manipulation. From the bastion of worldly power, Haakon Werle has provided Hjalmar with his occupation, much of his income, his wife and possibly even his child with a stealth that deludes Hjalmar into believing that he has attained each through the exercise of his own productive, or reproductive powers. Relling, in a complementary and far more ironic role, has supplied the *geistliche* counterpart to these basic familial props by manipulating Hjalmar—or, comparably, the photographic naturalist?—into the impossible dream of achieving a great invention in photography, elevating it into both a true art and a science, which then becomes the buoying life-lie that keeps him afloat.

As a result Hjalmar has lapsed into a hollow, inflated, albeit deludedly content shell of a human being, alienated from his true self and knowledge of his factual circumstances in nearly every department of his life. And just as Ibsen at this time was turning away from *théâtre utile,* the writing of plays aimed instrumentally at the reformation of society, the Ekdal family group, Hjalmar included, like emblems of contemporary urbanized sensibility, living boxed up in cities while starved for deeper, richer veins of consciousness, turn instinctively toward the loft, that setting identified so strongly with Hedvig, who finds it not a materially diminished realm at all, but a source of endless fantasy and enchantment which she has secretly named "the depths of the sea."

What Hedvig, her father and Old Ekdal have done with the loft is best described by a phrase J.R.R. Tolkien uses in discussing the role of fantasy in literature: they have sub-created a Secondary World, apart from and independent of the Primary World ruled by considerations of acquisitive opportunism and practical utility, i.e. Werle and Gina, respectively.[4] The Primary World exists in historical time; the world within the loft is a domain where time has had a stop. The Primary World is a place where poaching timber from state land has long, life-determining consequences; the Secondary World of the Ekdals' sub-creation is one where such consequences can be, or persuasively appear to be, abolished, through a compensatory, life-enhancing free play of the imagination. The objects and creatures gathered inside, moreover, in their odd juxtaposition, exhibit the quality Tolkien deemed imperative for successful fantasy: arresting strangeness.

That quality extends as well to the origin of the loft's objects. They were left there, we are told, by an old sea captain known only as "the Flying Dutchman." The name evokes the fifteenth-century legend made familiar via Heine's poetry and Wagner's opera, wherein a timeless curse, everlasting till Judgment Day, associated with the sea, is counterposed to a land realm bound to time, and wherein the legendary action, also situated in Norway, portrays another daughter, likewise misunderstood, who goes down precipitously of her own will, like the ship, the Flying Dutchman, and its cargo in the depths of the sea. It is as if the salvaged contents of the loft, like the maimed, mysterious Wild Duck that rules it, have been recovered out of that same sea—just as Ibsen had once written in an early article of criticism,[5] that mythic ideas must be drawn up intact from the sea-depths of the collective consciousness of the race, to be examined and speculated upon as an acceptable, even essential, phase of their consistent development. The Secondary World of fantasy, Ibsen is proclaiming through the vernacular symbolism of his art, must be identified with and derived from the legendary and the mythic; and the claims of the latter, for which the modern psyche is starved in the positivistic contemporary foreground of science, technology and utilitarian realism, are no less rightfully compelling than the claims of society reflected one-sidedly in Brandes's program for serious literature.

With this restoration of balance, this declaration of artistic independence, fantasy and myth are once again openly admitted to the Ibsenian stage, instead of being intricately and ingeniously disguised in the realistic actions, characters and settings, as in the immediately preceding plays of the cycle. Ibsen's outworn luck as a photographer reunites him with his true vocation as a dramatic poet, and the lyric

Pegasus shot out from under him, in Bjørnson's dismissive phrase, is reborn in *The Wild Duck* with hooves that strike an authentic, if more subdued fire. We find it again, appropriately, in the primordial, ghostly white horses of Rosmersholm, a place that bears resemblance to a fairytale castle in some enchanted kingdom where children never cry and grownups never laugh; in the mesmerizing Stranger who rises up like a merman out of a watery grave to claim a lady obsessed with the sea as his bride; in a soignée belle's erotic fantasies of a gifted writer as a vine-crowned Dionysus whose death will emblazon a rebirth of tragedy in a trivialized society; in a master builder who has constituted himself as an omnipotent god capable of direct contact, mind to mind, with a spirit choir of helpers and servers swarming in attendance. These and other such fantastic elements in the later plays are neither psychologized away nor credulously affirmed; rather, they are phenomenologically bracketed, presented "as if," to be tested, interpreted and incorporated within each individual's cognition of the humanly possible. For in between *An Enemy of the People* and *The Wild Duck,* Ibsen sets forth a new goal to replace Brandes's dictum: that "In these times every piece of creative thinking should attempt to move the frontier markers."[6]

Eric Bentley has reminded us that Ibsen was a realist on the outside, a fantasist inside, while Wagner, his early contemporary in innovation, was a fantasist outside, a realist within; and he notes, in *The Playwright As Thinker,* that on the whole the former combination worked better, in giving us "supple strength, fine irony and rich polyphony" in plays like *The Wild Duck.*[7] But Ibsen, by these means, accomplished at least two additional things. He gives us, first, the full and true measure of the world we inhabit more accurately than the pure realists, a world where fantasy, or its equivalent, sits as the interior steersman setting a course incalculable by realistically calibrated estimations of motive and behavior. He was wise enough to recognize that whereas reason and science had their considerable areas of authority—witness those irrefutable analyses of the town's polluted waters—a dangerous fantasy or, more profoundly, a destructive myth could be countered only by a more adequate, humane and compelling fantasy or myth. In that holistic sense, his works remain a collective survival manual and basic training course in the efforts of the race to read and anticipate itself.

But Ibsen's legacy is not restricted to those works alone. The fertile equation factored out in *The Wild Duck,* its unique blend of romanticism, realism, naturalism and symbolism, constitutes the far from exhausted potential of an artistic method he has bequeathed to his successors. Those who study the Ibsen canon in the conventional magpie manner, gleaning techniques for how to develop a character, build a scene or render a social problem stageworthy are guilty, as Dr. Stockmann might say, of setting the intakes of the life-giving waters too low. The greater part of the major plays, that appear so canny, so intricately and ingeniously wrought—and indeed are, in product and result—could only have been achieved in process, shaped by the deep, ulterior currents of the active unconscious, bearing the formal, interpersonal structures on inspired confluences of metaphor and symbol, fantasy and myth. There is, in fact, no more finely honed poetic drama concealed as prose than Henrik Ibsen's—*drama,* one must emphasize, where the medium of the poetry is words always propulsively bent toward defining human lives and destinies. The sooner that truth is generally recognized in exegesis and production, the more fruitfully his pioneering example will enable others to add his full repertory of expression to their own, empowering enrichments of style that proceed, not from mere prowess in technique, but from a changed and amplified vision of the range of human potential—just such a vision as animates the self-reflexive form of *The Wild Duck.*

Notes

1. *Quoted by Eric Bentley, ed., The Theory of the Modern Stage* (Baltimore, 1968), p. 381.

2. *Ibid.,* p. 388.

3. Henrik Ibsen, *The Complete Major Prose Plays,* tr. Rolf Fjelde (New York, 1978), p. 400.

4. J.R.R. Tolkien, *The Tolkien Reader* (New York, 1966), p. 37.

5. Henrik Ibsen, "Professor Welhaven on Paludan-Müller's Mythological Poems," in *The Drama Review,* XIII, 2, p. 46.

6. Henrik Ibsen, *Letters and Speeches,* ed. Evert Sprinchorn (New York, 1964), p. 214.

7. Eric Bentley, *The Playwright as Thinker* (New York, 1955), p. 106.

IBSEN, STRINDBERG, AND THE NEW WOMAN

BY EVERT SPRINCHORN

" 'There is one who will be greater than I,' said the aging Ibsen, pointing to a picture of Strindberg."[1]

The anecdote is apocryphal and seems to have originated with one of Strindberg's disciples. However, Strindberg was unquestionably the only dramatist, in fact the only writer, whose provocative presence made the Norwegian giant look to his laurels. By the early 1890s, when Ibsen is supposed to have made the remark, Strindberg was in the prime of his creative life, the untamed genius, full of surprises, and still exploring unknown territory.

On his part, Strindberg felt he was living in the inescapable shadow cast by the daunting figure of Ibsen. There was a difference of twenty-one years in their ages, and in some ways Ibsen was to Strindberg a tyrannical and distant father, a figure not to be loved nor a model to be imitated, but a master who had to be challenged and overcome.

He had first come under Ibsen's spell in 1869, when as a twenty-one-year-old student at the University of Uppsala, he had read *Brand*, the poetic drama about a priest who sacrifices everything for the sake of an ideal, and who, having lost son, wife, and congregation, perishes in an avalanche, regretting nothing and holding on to his principles to the very end.

Like so many other readers at that time, the young Strindberg was bewildered by the drama. His imagination and his rebellious nature were fired by the uncompromising idealism of Brand, who, like Kierkegaard, put the claims of the religious conscience above all social and religious concerns, but he failed to grasp the full import of Ibsen's existential thought. In his autobiography he described the effect the drama had had on him.

> It cut itself off from Christianity only to hold on to its horrifying asceticism. Brand demanded that one be obedient to the old teachings, teachings that no longer had any validity. He ridiculed the modern striving for humanitarianism and compromise, although he ended by commending "the spirit of compromise." Brand was a pietist, a fanatic, who was sure he was right though all the world was against him. John [Strindberg] felt close in spirit to this egoist, an awful man and wrong to boot. No halfway measures, just push ahead, down with everything that stood in your way. Why not, when you alone were right? His delicate conscience, which ached with every step he took because he felt he was treading on his father or his friends, was numbed by *Brand*. All the bonds of love and regard for others were to be broken for the sake of one's "cause."[2]

In the late 1860s and in the 1870s impressionable readers came away from *Brand* convinced that one's life could have no significance unless one deliberately dedicated it to a higher cause, an ideal. "Ibsen's *Brand,*" said Strindberg, "put an end to the spirit of the 1860s, stirred the serious-minded younger generation, awakened it from its aesthetic dreams and vacuous existence, demanding action and commitment." The older generation of poets with their aesthetic outlook had no understanding of *Brand,* but

> for those of us who had young blood in our veins, it ransacked the corners of our hearts. We found ourselves confronted by a new religion that demanded a life of commitment. What the cast-off religion of Christianity had asked of us was faith. Brand demanded sacrifice. The concept of duty with its accompaniment of suffering sprang to life before our eyes. Here was the voice of Savonarola raised in an age that worshipped art and beauty. But the voice neglected to show us the way forward. We were left troubled, dissatisfied, waiting for answers.[3]

Two years after he read *Brand* Strindberg dealt with the questions it had raised in his mind. In his first important play, *Master Olof,* he pitted a religious idealist against a practical politician, Olof the Lutheran reformer against Gustav Vasa, the ruler who in the sixteenth century forged the Swedish nation out of warring factions: the arrogant nobility, the rebellious peasants, and the possessive clergy. The young Olof believes that the new church can win the hearts and minds of the people, uniting them in the cause of justice. He learns that he has simply been Gustav's tool, and unwittingly he has served the state and not the church. By sowing dissension within the Catholic Church, he has enabled Gustav to appropriate it. To save his life at the end of the play, Olof must swear allegiance to the crown. And he does so. The true idealist in the play is the communist Gert, who goes unrepentant to his death, damning Olof as a renegade.

The difference between Olof and Brand marks the difference between their creators. Brand would let the world perish as long as his ideal remained pure and inviolate. Not so Strindberg's Olof. He would have shared Burke's view that the individual may be foolish but the species is wise. For Strindberg the higher principle that energizes the individual is not a lofty, abstract ideal, but the survival of the race. "The race advances at the expense of the individual?" reads one of his notes for a revision of *Master Olof.* "The race equivalent to genus—the concept—the idea."[4]

In Ibsen's view the great man counted for more than the mass of humanity, the individual's perfection for more than life itself. It was the fanatical idealism, obvious in *Brand* and implicit in most of his plays, that fascinated his readers. Combined with his well-known skepticism, this romantic faith in the ideal constituted the Ibsen enigma, which was perfectly captured, Strindberg thought, in Julius Kronberg's portrait of the Norwegian poet and dramatist, painted in 1877, when he had just been awarded an honorary degree by the University of Uppsala. Writing as an art critic for a Stockholm newspaper, Strindberg praised Kronberg for not letting his palette overwhelm the great personality who rightly should be seen as dominating the canvas.

> One's first impressions, which are always worth taking note of even if they do not contain the whole truth, are somewhat paradoxical—jarring, disturbing. Here on canvas is the Paradox himself: the prophet in gold-rimmed spectacles. . . . The face is that of Brand, the broad, high forehead of the fanatic, the stern mouth of the witness to the truth, whose lips have never actually uttered those truths his hands have set down on

paper, the cold, steely glance that never wavered even when he stood face to face with the Spirit of Compromise itself—there you have Ibsen, the zealous skeptic, the devotee of disbelief, standing before us as the completely self-assured, firmly determined—doubter. . . . This is the great genius wearing a white neckerchief and clad in a poet's cape, draped to follow the lines of the conventionally posed figure, holding pen and paper, all according to the custom. Yet the figure awes and jars, repels and attracts. It helps to know perhaps that Ibsen is a man who loves to hide his true self and that he would prefer to be seen in a ridiculous light than to be recognized as a great man. Who doesn't remember the appearance of the famous poet when he visited Stockholm a few years ago?—in his velvet jacket, white vest with black buttons, collar in the latest fashion, an elegant stick in his hand, and a fleeting, ironic smile in the corner of his mouth, as he made his social rounds, always avoiding any serious conversation.[5]

In November 1879 Strindberg's novel *The Red Room* was published, and a few weeks later Ibsen's drama *A Doll's House* came off the presses. Depicting the seamier side of life in Stockholm, on all social levels, the novel shocked readers with its cynicism and realism. It not only gave an unvarnished picture of reality; it also tacitly denied that there was any higher purpose or ideal. Ibsen's play proved to be even more controversial in picturing sympathetically a woman who abandons her husband and her young children for the sake of an ideal, putting her individuality and self-perfection above family and social conventions. Here was a woman who had read *Brand* and taken its lesson to heart (as had the woman who sat as model for Nora).

49

Strindberg's reply to *A Doll's House* was *Sir Bengt's Wife,* a play with a historic setting but with modern views on marriage, medieval chivalry substituting for nineteenth-century idealism. It was the first of his sex dramas, and in it he attempted to discard the last of his romantic fantasies. He described himself as ridiculing "with a light touch woman's whimsical notion that marriage was utter bliss and sought to reduce those unreasonable demands laid on husbands by Ibsen in *A Doll's House.*"[6]

Strindberg dealt more thoroughly with the woman question in 1884 when he canvassed the sexual mores of his time in a collection of short stories. In both the preface to this volume, entitled *Married,* and in one of the stories, unabashedly entitled "A Doll's House," he took Ibsen to task. The wife of Strindberg's redaction falls under the spell of a recruiting feminist and, after reading Ibsen's play, realizes that she too has been only her husband's plaything and housekeeper. She grows decidedly cool towards him, whereupon he too reads the play and points out to her how little it applies to their marriage. This rational approach has little effect. But when he decides to live like a bachelor, she soon hungers for the pleasures of the marriage bed and comes to realize that the kind of "miracle" that Nora dreams of belongs in fairy tales.

In place of miracles Strindberg offered in his preface specific and practical suggestions that would improve relations between the sexes. Among these were giving women the right to vote, the right to the same education as men, the right to pursue any occupation, the right of any woman to keep her own name when married, and the right to a separate bedroom so that she could possess her own body even in marriage.

These are the proposals of the man who was to win notoriety as a misogynist and opponent of women's rights, while Ibsen, the saint of the feminists, denied at the end of his career that he had "consciously worked for the women's rights movement." "I am not even clear," he said, "just what this women's rights movement really is."[7]

This paradoxical state of affairs had as much to do with class and politics as it had to do with sex and marriage. By the time he came to write *Married,* Strindberg had made himself known as an antiestablishment agitator with socialist sympathies, whereas Ibsen had for a time in the 1860s and 1870s given support to the political right, the extreme right, in his characteristically contradictory way. The women's rights movement also had its contradictions, which Strindberg was quick to see. It was associated with liberalism or progressive politics in the minds of most people, but the feminists themselves were definitely part of the establishment and did not want to undermine it. Quite the contrary: they wanted to become an active part of it.

What happened in the early 1880s when Ibsen published *Ghosts* and Strindberg published *Married* revealed the true allegiances of the various parties. The establishment voiced its disapproval of Ibsen's shocker because it dealt with three forbidden subjects: syphilis, incest, and euthanasia. Yet Sophie Adlersparre, a leader in the woman movement, could courageously defend the play in an article "What Are the Ethical Conditions of Marriage?" on the grounds that *Ghosts* pictures the moral chaos that ensues if the marriage institution is not accepted as a spiritual union of equals. On the other hand, she could not bring herself to defend Strindberg's realistic proposals in the preface to *Married* for improving relations between the sexes. She belonged to the establishment, and Strindberg did not.

The members of the ruling class simply refused to buy copies of *Ghosts* or to stage it. They turned their backs on it in embarrassment. With *Married,* it was different. They confiscated it and brought Strindberg and his publisher to trial, charging them with blasphemy for ten lines in the book that derided Jesus and the Christian ritual. Strindberg had substantial reasons for believing that it was through Mrs. Adlersparre, whose husband was a member of the Riksdag, that the government took action against him. The feminists joined with the political right and the state church, both of which were more anti- than pro-feminist, to punish Strindberg. It was perfectly clear in literary circles that indicting Strindberg's publisher for a few questionably sacrilegious utterances was a legal subterfuge; Strindberg was being arraigned for his political radicalism.[8]

No wonder, then, that Strindberg, facing trial, saw the feminist movement as a devilish ruse on the part of the upper-class against the socialists. Women, he pointed out, emancipated themselves so that they could become part of the bureaucracy of the ruling class, serving as secretaries and clerks, and running offices if not holding them.[9]

The trial embittered Strindberg and understandably changed his attitude toward the feminists. From now on they were the enemy. Although he was acquitted, he found it difficult to find publishers for his new works, and he took to writing some of them in French in the belief that sooner or later he would have to leave Sweden.

The situation was ironic. The advocates of women's rights tried to silence the man who drew up a liberal platform of rights for women, while embracing the man who was almost indifferent to their cause and who refused to specify what rights women should have. The irony vanishes, however, in the light of Strindberg's criticism of *A Doll's House*. In the preface to *Married*, when Strindberg interpreted the stocking scene as Nora offering herself to Dr. Rank, the feminists probably shook their heads at Strindberg's abysmal ignorance and insensitivity. When he described Nora's husband as straightforward and aboveboard compared to Nora herself, who eats macaroons on the sly and keeps secrets from her husband, they must have sighed in despair, recognizing that Strindberg was a lost cause. And when he said that it is not true that the husband treats Nora like a doll, "but it is true that she treats him like one," they would have smiled grimly and let the remark pass. But when Strindberg went on to say that the basis of the marriage institution is sexual, that its purpose is the perpetuation of the race, that a childless woman is not a woman at all, and that the ideal of the feminists is a hermaphrodite with more than a touch of lesbianism, he went too far. And yet he went even further. He said all the talk about women's rights emanated from a very small circle of over-cultured, improperly educated women—women who had sex in the head and not in the body. The woman question was only a question for those idle ladies of the upper-class who had time to worry about it. It did not concern farmers' wives at all. No Noras among them, because they lived in close contact with nature, took sex casually, and were kept busy tending their families and carrying out their daily chores.

The feminist concern with the "ideal"—with the "miracle" that was buzzing in Nora's bonnet—had, said Strindberg, little or nothing to do with the real problem. The inescapable fact in his view was that love was an irrational force. "If man and wife have taken a fancy to each other, then the best guarantee for a happy marriage exists, because love is a force of nature, surviving intellectual prattle, overwhelming the conscious will of the individual, and defying all imaginable tempests, all conceivable vagaries."[10]

Although he got several things wrong, his critique is still the most penetrating examination of *A Doll's House*. He saw more deeply into Nora's character than did the actresses, playgoers, and critics of the time. He saw that Nora was an hysterical type, easily going to extremes. Ibsen drew her that way, but the feminists apotheosized her as a saint, and actresses often chose to present her that way, barely plumbing the deep subtext of the play, serving up a tract rather than a complex characterization, reducing Ibsen's living woman to a propagandist's puppet, and thus leaving Ibsen open to the stricture, still heard today in drama classes and newspaper reviews, that the steel-strong, independent Nora of the last act has nothing in common with the twittering and flighty Nora of the first.[11] Strindberg understood Nora's character and saw that the division in her soul was the result of over-refinement. She was a badly brought up, spoiled woman, deceitful because she had to play a part forced on her by society and hysterical because her education had filled her mind with romantic ideals that could not possibly be fulfilled, "a romantic monstrosity," as Strindberg called her, "a product of that beautiful philosophy known as idealism, which tries to make human beings believe they are gods and that the earth is a little heaven."[12] The truth was that *A Doll's House,* like most of Ibsen's plays, did not concern itself with emancipation, "but with the claims of the ideal."[13]

Not greatly concerned about women's rights but obsessively interested in human destinies, Ibsen would have appreciated Strindberg's analysis of Nora if it had not been for the badgering, arrogant tone of his remarks and the underlying thrust of his criticism. The gulf that separated the two dramatists was not their views on rights for women, which would have kept them merely at arm's length, but their opposed views on nature and culture. "My Rousseau-istic point of view," said Strindberg, "which takes nature as the norm, won't allow me to join the modern idealistic gallants who make women over into angels and men into devils. We should be human beings—men and women—and then there would be equality between the sexes."[14] Unlike Strindberg, for whom accommodation to nature was the desired goal, Ibsen wanted to overcome nature. Life was worthwhile only if one pursued the farthest star and dreamt the impossible dream. Perhaps only obsessed, neurotic people could devote their lives to the realization of such dreams and hopes, but to Ibsen they were, in the final analysis, the privileged ones. They changed the world instead of adapting themselves to it.

Among the first jottings for *A Doll's House* is this:

There are two kinds of moral law, two kinds of conscience, one in man and a completely different one in woman. They do not understand each other, but in matters of practical living the woman is judged by man's law as if she were not a woman but a man.[15]

Ibsen left open to question whether the two laws were inborn in the sexes or were the result of social development. Either way, he believed that the conflict could be resolved by making sex subsidiary to mental activity and spiritual communion in marriage. Instead of being husband and wife, the marriage partners would be comrades who voluntarily submitted themselves to the same moral law.

Adopting a line of thought that was supported by nineteenth-century science, Strindberg maintained that such arrangements were abnormal and generally unsustainable. He might have accepted something like the unisex ideal before 1884, if it were possible to achieve it through education. After the 1884 trial, however, he abandoned the liberal platform he had laid out in the first volume of *Married* and took to arguing that it is because of biological differences that there is one law for men and another for women. It was ludicrous to think that "one could raise woman to man's level by giving her the same kind of education."[16] "Nature has given women uteri and men testicles. Let me see [them] emancipate [themselves] from that!"[17]

Strindberg buttressed his position by citing Darwin and Herbert Spencer. The latter, in his "synthetic philosophy," one of the first attempts to incorporate evolutionary theory into a comprehensive philosophical system, provided Strindberg with just the sort of evidence he required. There were indeed, implied the English Aristotle, two kinds of law or behavior, one for each sex, and both made by nature. Under this natural dispensation, women have a special instinct for caring for children and an innate capacity to please and to conceal their true feelings. They are easily awed, respect power and authority, and, while quick to perceive the direct consequences of an act, they have difficulty dealing with abstract questions. And so on, in a stereotyped list of female characteristics.[18]

Having secured his position on scientific grounds, Strindberg went on to write a series of plays that dealt with the conflict of the sexes, the emancipation of women, and the faddishness of comradeship. In *The Father* (1887) he offered a psychological explanation for the sexual conflict, attributing it in part to Christian teachings in which the ideal woman was asexual. The harmful result was that men divided women into two distinctly separated categories, sexually immaculate mothers and whorish mistresses, the one protective and caring, the other challenging and destructive.

Similarly, men had to assume for women the roles of boys to be cared for or lovers to be devoured. In the marriage bed, the boy at his mother's breast is transformed into the aggressive lover, the mother becomes a whore, and the sexual embrace turns into an incestuous nightmare. Viewing the sexual antinomy as arising, in part, from medieval Christian attitudes tended to undercut Spencer's biological explanation by placing it in a historical and social framework. As always, Strindberg probed more deeply in his plays than in his essays and tracts.

As Strindberg saw it, comradeship was a shying away from the horrible implications of the sex act. In his next play, *Comrades,* he ridiculed this feeble attempt to transform marriage into an asexual union, a business partnership. The plot, naturally, is an inversion of what goes on in *A Doll's House,* with the husband being treated like a doll by his wife. She almost succeeds in getting him into a female costume and dancing for her as Nora danced for Torvald. The "greatest miracle" is revealed to be a man who can dominate his wife. The husband here makes the sacrifice, letting his wife win first prize with one of his paintings, and he is the one who walks out at the end, saying that he can pick up a comrade at the nearest bar; at home he wants a wife. A doctor speaks as *raisonneur* and in one of the drafts of the play blames Ibsen's idealism for bringing modern marriage into a state of confusion. "Give us back," he says in a speech that glances at no less than four of Ibsen's plays,

> some of the joy we had, you who preach the joy of life. Give us the cheering Spirit of Compromise and send the trolls home. They came down from their misty heights with mountainous demands and hotel bills for expensive ideals and made life dark and unpleasant.

Give us the sun again, a little bit of sunshine, enough to
see that this old planet still holds on to the old heavens.
Not the whole sun, just a bit of it.[19]

Ibsen certainly observed the development of Strindberg's
thoughts on women, and for much of the time he was ahead
of them. Since he was not a doctrinaire feminist, he could
agree with much of what Strindberg had to say. There was,
however, that impassable gulf between them: Ibsen was at
heart an idealist, Strindberg, in the 1880s, a realist.

As the young rival who had had to bear the wrath of the
feminists for his outspoken comments, Strindberg went out
of his way to challenge and irritate the silent Norwegian.
Ibsen was no longer the "Paradox"; he was a hypocrite who
lacked the courage of his convictions, who would not come
out from behind his characters and say what he really meant.
He was a bad Darwinist, working against the good of the
species by, for example, letting Mrs. Alving in *Ghosts* tolerate
incest. He was an outdated thinker, reviving the
androgynous ideal of the early romantics, and in truth an old
man who in the midst of his male menopause had turned
from the misogyny of his youth, as expressed in *Love's
Comedy,* to the fashionable feminism of *A Doll's House.* Above
all, Ibsen was an aesthete who valued his artistic reputation
and his social position more than all the ideas put forth in his
plays, and that was why he never stood by them.

In his brash satire on Stockholm society, *The New Kingdom*
(1882), Strindberg poked fun at a famous tastemaker, a
writer and critic, who is fatuously proud of his Ph.D. and his
honorary awards (six of them), who collects pornographic
pictures, who is researching an article on syphilis, and whose
conscience is troubled by the knowledge that he is the father
of an illegitimate child. Although Strindberg was writing

about Stockholm, Ibsen might have been struck by the curious resemblance of this cultural arbiter to himself. He had just the year before written about syphilis in *Ghosts,* had an illegitimate son, an honorary doctor's degree, and was the orgulous possessor of six (!) medals.

Strindberg followed this jibe with the sustained attack on *A Doll's House* in *Married,* which riled Ibsen so much that he would not allow his name to appear along with Strindberg's on a list of sponsors for a memorial for J.P. Jacobsen, a Danish writer whose works Ibsen admired. To the embarrassed collector of contributions, Strindberg replied, "Keep my tenner, and cross off my name."[20]

(Ibsen's huffy reaction was typical of him. In 1869, feeling insulted by a remark Bjørnson was rumored to have made, Ibsen refused to contribute to a journal for which Bjørnson was being considered as co-editor. The Jacobsen incident reveals an essential difference in the personalities of the two dramatists.)

Three years later, in *The Father,* Strindberg wrote a poetic speech for the Captain in which there is a pointed reference to Ibsen as a sleepwalker who dreamt he was the great awakener of men's consciences.

Ibsen did not reply directly to Strindberg's censure and mockery. He bided his time until 1890 when he wrote *Hedda Gabler* and emulated the Swedish misogynist in painting a full-length portrait of the modern unmotherly woman. Strindberg's Miss Julie was representative of the type, neurotic and sexually anomalous because she had been raised as a boy by her aggressively feminist mother. Thekla in *Creditors,* written in the same year as *Miss Julie,* 1888, was another version of the new woman, emancipated from the old sexual mores, revelling in her freedom, taking the initiative in sexual encounters, brazen, cynical, amoral.

Like *Creditors, Hedda Gabler* is a *comédie rosse,* then the latest
fashion in Parisian drama, wickedly sophisticated, morally
subversive, a comedy of manners for an age in which
everything was being questioned. Turning the tables on
Strindberg and beating him at his own game, Ibsen took his
principal character, Hedda herself, from one of the stories in
Married called "Upon Payment." Strindberg's heroine
Helen is the daughter of an army officer. Her mother died
when Helen was a child and she was reared in a man's world.
Her arrogance, pride, and self-command scare off admirers.
Her sexual nature is ambiguous; her figure is not very
feminine; and the sex act both fascinates and nauseates her.
A well-educated woman, she plays the piano, tries her hand
at poetry, and serves briefly as lady-in-waiting to a countess.
After her father dies, she meets a docent, a philosophy
teacher specializing in ethical theory, who believes that a
proper modern marriage should be a communion of souls in
which both parties surrender their individual personalities to
the unisex ideal, according to which "the man shall cease to
be a man, and the woman cease to be a woman." This
addition to the marriage contract leads to the husband's
being barred from Helen's bed on the wedding night.
Subsequently, Helen endeavors to work for the women's
rights movement by getting her husband into politics. She
has sexual intercourse with him only "upon payment," that
is, when he does something for the "cause." And always she
is careful not to get herself pregnant.

Coming to his senses, her husband realizes what his ethical
system has led to.

> It had become shameful to be a mother, to have a
> gender, to be reminded that you were female.
>   That was it. Working for heaven on earth, for the
> higher things, for humanity—that was the ideal, so they

said. No! For vanity's sake, for their egos, for publicity—that was the fact.

. . .

And this woman—what was she working for? For progress? For the redemption of mankind?

No. Against progress, against freedom and enlightenment.[21]

The husband in this story was modeled on L.H. Åberg, docent in philosophy at the University of Uppsala, author of three pamphlets defending the moral basis of *A Doll's House* and *Ghosts* by arguing that a marriage without a union of souls was no better than prostitution.[22]

Although a play as complex as *Hedda Gabler* springs from many seeds, Strindberg's story provided some germinal ideas.[23] Virtually all the points mentioned in my outline of the story found their way into Ibsen's drama. But more surprising than the close parallels are the conclusions that Ibsen reaches. How much substance was there to Strindberg's repeated charge that when the spiritual ideal comes into conflict with the physical purpose of marriage, the outcome was destructive, and that consequently comradeship was a fruitless ideal and feminism a reactionary movement? Strindberg was sure that women were seizing power in the western world, but what type of woman was taking command? "One cannot be certain," he wrote in an 1887 essay, "that evolution is moving towards mother-power. Are these mothers who are ruthlessly pushing ahead? No, on the contrary, they brazenly cry out that they do not want to be mothers."[24]

One of Ibsen's notes for *Hedda Gabler* states that a main point to be made in it is that all women "are not made to be mothers."[25] Yet in the play itself Ibsen out-Strindbergs Strindberg in displaying the negative force of the unmotherly woman who can find no creative outlet for her energies and intellect. *Hedda Gabler* provides absolute confirmation of Strindberg's view of the modern woman as an agent of regression, not leading humanity to enlightenment but preventing it from moving forward. Pacing her rooms like a caged animal, her sexual instincts thwarted by her psychological makeup and her fear of scandal, a prudish aristocrat envying the bohemians, with a man's mind in a woman's body, and hating the baby that is growing within her, Hedda is the incarnation of the darker impulses of human beings and a living example of the dire consequences of repression. Overflowing the high wall of inhibitions built up in her over the years, her emotions burst forth in a crescendo of cruelty and destructiveness. First she deliberately and gratuitously insults her husband's kind aunt; then at the end of Act Two she coaxes the alcoholic Løvborg to drink, fully aware of the danger to him. At the end of Act Three she burns Løvborg's manuscript in which he had pointed the way to a better future for mankind. And finally she uses her father's pistols, symbols of her heritage, to destroy Løvborg, to kill herself, and to eliminate the baby inside her body. So much for loving-kindness, for motherhood, for progress, for humanity—all tossed aside in one grand, selfish gesture with which she could make a mock of the world that had imprisoned her. No wonder that Strindberg believed that his works had spawned her.[26]

A few years later in a speech delivered to the League for Women's Rights, Ibsen declared, "It is up to the mothers . . . to awaken a sure sense of *culture* and *discipline*. This feeling must be awakened before it will be possible to raise the people to a higher level. It is the women who shall solve the human dilemma. As mothers they shall solve it. And *only* in that capacity can they solve it."[27]

If this was not bearding the lioness in her den, it was definitely a rebuff to one element in the feminist movement. It is right in line with Strindberg's thinking and underscores the implications of *Hedda Gabler*. The unmotherly woman is hostile to progress and enlightenment, however cultured and educated she may be. Hedda burns the manuscript that outlines the means by which people can be elevated to a higher spiritual plane, or at least describes what life on that higher plane would be like. It is left to the motherly Thea and devoted Tesman, Hedda's husband, to piece together the manuscript from the notes that Thea has kept and treasured as if they were her child. Though neither she nor Tesman have the insight that Hedda has, it is through them that the future will be built.

That manuscript with its vision of the future is the essentially Ibsenian element in the play. In contrast to Strindberg, Ibsen insisted on the necessity of an ideal that would serve as God and the Kingdom of Heaven had served the Christians, a challenge and a hope. After *Hedda Gabler*, Ibsen reasserted the "claim of the ideal," showing in *The Master Builder* a man—not a woman—attaining the heights he had reached in his youth and losing his life in the process. In his very last play, *When We Dead Awaken*, Ibsen echoed the final moments of *Brand*. Again his alter ego dies in pursuit of the ideal, an ideal that had been lost sight of during those years when he had written realistic plays and, as in the case of Gregers in *The Wild Duck*, disparaged the bearer of the ideal as a neurotic bungler.

For Ibsen, the individual who mattered had to make a choice: either a committed life on the heights or a drifter's existence in the lowlands; either a life of sacrifice for one's dream, indifferent to the suffering caused to oneself and others, or a life of sensual indulgence, meaningless and empty; either a life of the soul or a life of the body.

As Ibsen worked on his play, Strindberg began his *To Damascus* trilogy, at the end of which his alter ego also climbs a mountain. There in a monastery he hears the words that sum up the meaning of his experiences, words that come as a firm denial of Ibsen's teachings.

"Don't be exclusive. Don't say 'Either—or'; say, 'Both—and.' In a word, or two: humanity . . . and resignation."[28]

Notes

1. James Huneker, *Iconoclasts,* New York, 1905, p. 141. Huneker's source was Emil Schering, Strindberg's German translator.

2. *Jäsningstiden,* in August Strindberg, *Samlade skrifter,* ed. John Landquist, 55 vols., Stockholm, 1912-20, vol. 18, p. 355.

3. "Den litterära reaktionen i Sverige," written in 1886. *Samlade skrifter,* vol. 17, p. 208.

4. Per Lindberg, *Tillkomsten av Strindbergs Mäster Olof,* Stockholm, 1915, p. 65.

5. "Konstakademiens utställning 1877." *Samlade skrifter,* vol. 4, pp. 169-70.

6. *Författaren.* In *Samlade skrifter,* vol. 19, p. 192.

7. Ibsen, *Letters and Speeches,* ed. Evert Sprinchorn, New York, 1964, p. 337.

8. See Carl Snoilsky's letter of October 21, 1884, quoted in Göran Söderström, *Strindberg och bildkonsten,* Stockholm, 1972, p. 100.

9. Letter to Bjørnson, c. 12 October 1884. *August Strindbergs brev,* ed. Torsten Eklund, 15 vols., Stockholm, 1948— vol. 4, p. 352.

10. *Giftas. Samlade skrifter,* vol. 14, p. 27.

11. See Evert Sprinchorn, "Ibsen and the Actors," in *Ibsen and the Theatre,* ed. Errol Durbach, London, 1980, pp. 118-30.

12. *Giftas. Samlade skrifter,* vol. 14, p. 24.

13. "Kvarstadsresan," *Samlade skrifter,* vol. 17, p. 23.

14. Letter to Jonas Lie, 30 August 1884, *Brev,* vol. 4, p. 312.

15. Henrik Ibsen, *Samlede Verker,* Hundreårsutgave, eds. Francis Bull, Halvdan Koht, and Didrik Arup Seip, Oslo, 21 vols., 1928-57, vol. 8, p. 368.

16. *Författaren. Samlade skrifter,* vol. 19, p. 174.

17. Letter to Bjørnson, c. 12 October 1884, *Brev,* vol. 4, p. 352.

18. Strindberg, "Likställighet och tyranni," (1885) in *Samlade skrifter,* vol. 17, pp. 99-100.

19. *August Strindbergs dramer,* ed. Carl Reinhold Smedmark, Stockholm, 4 vols., 1962-70, vol. 3, p. 487.

20. Michael Meyer in his biography of Ibsen says this story is "of course completely untrue" (*Ibsen,* New York, 1971, p. 649). It is nothing of the sort. Meyer's anti-Strindberg bias blinds him to the evidence, which is all on Strindberg's side. Strindberg did contribute to the memorial, Ibsen did refuse. The evidence: Strindberg's letter of 12 June 1885, *Brev,* vol. 5, p. 101; the correspondence between Edvard Brandes and Alexander Kielland, June and July 1885, in *Georg og Edv. Brandes Brevveksling med Nordiske Forfattare og Videnskabsmaend,* eds. Morten Borup, et al., 8 vols., Copenhagen 1939-42, vol. 5, pp. 206-7; and the letter from Georg Brandes to Carl Snoilsky, 19 June 1885, in *Carl Snoilsky och hans vänner,* ed. Ruben G. Berg, 2 vols., Stockholm, 1917-18, vol. 1, p. 328. Also, the critic and literary historian Johan Mortensen accepts Strindberg's version without reservation (*Strindberg som jag minnes honom,* Stockholm, 1931, pp. 51-2).

21. *Giftas, Samlade skrifter,* vol. 14, pp. 336-7

22. Ulf Boëthius, *Strindberg och kvinnofrågan,* Stockholm, 1969, p. 339.

23. The influence of Strindberg's story on *Hedda Gabler* was first remarked by Sten Linder, *Ernst Ahlgren*, Stockholm, 1930, pp. 253-4. Oddly, although Strindberg claimed that *The Father* and *Creditors* had left their mark on Ibsen's play, he said nothing about "Upon Payment." See the comments by Mary Sandbach in her translation of *Giftas, Getting Married*, New York, 1972, pp. 376-7.

24. "Sista ordet i kvinnofrågan" (1887), in *Samlade skrifter*, vol. 54, pp. 274-5.

25. Ibsen, *Samlede Verker*, vol. 11, p. 508.

26. Ibsen almost certainly read Strindberg's major works. From a friend in common Ibsen received in 1898 a copy of *To Damascus, Parts I and II*, and Ibsen replied, "Give [Strindberg] my warmest and most sincere thanks for his new book and tell him that he has given me a truly great and unexpected joy with this evidence of his friendly thoughts toward me. As you know, I have his portrait always before my eyes in my study, and he lives in my thoughts through his works, which I always buy and read as soon as they appear." (Letter to af Geijerstam, October 4, 1898, in *Henrik Ibsens brev 1845-1905. Ny samling.* Ed. Øyvind Anker (*Ibsenårbok* 1979) Oslo, 1979, p. 457.

27. Ibsen, *Samlede Verker*, vol. 15, p. 417.

28. Strindberg, *Samlade skrifter*, vol. 29, p. 359.

EROS, PRIAPOS, AND SHAW

BY JACQUES BARZUN

Thespiae was the place in which Eros was most worshipped. The Thespians used to celebrate games in his honor on Mount Helikon.

Keightly's *Mythology*

The widespread thought-cliché about Shaw's plays and Shaw himself is that they lack passion, by which is meant sexual passion. As such, the works and their author may be interesting to connoisseurs of ideas, historians of culture and the drama, but they are bound to leave unmoved everybody else—the really human human beings.

Oddly enough, this judgment is made by intellectuals, the only people who write out their opinions and lecture others ex cathedra. It is they who have created the figure of Shaw as a Puritan, emotionally wanting to the point of being but a thinking machine, brilliant—yes—and irresistibly funny, but not destined for enduring fame among playwrights, because lacking the power to understand and represent the throbbing heart of mankind.

The verdict is in fact a convention of the stage: so brainy a man cannot have a heart. The locus classicus of this line of thought occurs in Lord David Cecil's paraphrase of Max Beerbohm's opinion of Shaw and his work: "There was something essentially unesthetic about it; and something inhuman. Shaw cared more for ideas than for people; Max was the reverse. If Shaw realized Max's feelings about him, he did not mind. He had the virtues of his inhumanity: he was not at all touchy."[1]

Little Max had not the excuse of being at a distance from the man and guessing only from the writings. He knew Shaw and was even indebted to him for the post of drama critic on the *Saturday Review*. But why blame Beerbohm when so many other critics spontaneously agreed with him? It is the fate of singular geniuses to engender a conventional view, a plausible simulacrum of the true figure, which the attentive biographer must first destroy before he can attempt a faithful portrait.

This preliminary labor entails the explanation of many things, the reorientation of the common mind upon the evidence, and the straightening out of faulty logic. Under the strain of taking all this in, the common mind tends to be suspicious and it soon snaps back into its old groove of belief. That is why conventional opinion persists in spite of scholarship and critical biography. Machiavelli, Swift, Diderot, Berlioz, Nietzsche, Shaw continue to lead double lives.

But that is no reason for giving up the muscular role of Sisyphus. Let me begin with the fallacy that because one cares about ideas one cannot care also about people. Chesterton has a characteristic tilt at this absurdity when he scouts the notion apropos of Sherlock Holmes. Popular prejudice readily believes that so wonderful a reasoning animal must be immune to love. Chesterton retorts: "You might as well say that he could not be expected to have much appetite for lunch because of his proficiency in mathematics."[2] One could also reply on Holmes's behalf, "it isn't the emotion of love I resist, it is the complications that arise from it and that are due mainly to the other party's *ideas.*"

We start out, then, not with two possibilities, but three: the individual who is in fact devoid of human feeling—"inhuman" in Beerbohm's sense; the one who suppresses his feelings so as to avoid trouble; and the one who has feelings like everybody else and does not suppress them, but has an additional set of feelings whose presence bewilders the onlooker and blinds him to the existence of the first set.

Shaw, as all ought to know, was not afraid of the complications attendant on love affairs. He breasted them with ardor early and late, from persecution at the hands of the impossible Jenny Patterson to infuriation at those of the super-impossible Mrs. Pat Campbell. But these facts, which negate the thesis about the asexual idea-monger, do not settle the important issue that the Maxes of the world have raised without quite knowing it, the issue whether an artist's "caring about people" affects the truth to life and aesthetic quality (whatever that may mean) of his productions.

So let us for the moment push back Shaw into the niche of the marble faun, inhuman and uninterested in the warm bodies around him, and on this contrary-to-fact assumption look at the plays. An author's earliest should, on the basis of the supposed "heat exchange" between life and works, display the greatest amount of feeling. And so they do in Shaw: Blanche in *Widowers' Houses,* Vivie in *Mrs. Warren's Profession,* the two women in *The Philanderer* are charged with feeling, and their behavior toward parents and lovers are as sharply observed and rendered as one could wish.

But with the exception of Julia in the third play, these heroines—if that is their proper title—are not moved by one feeling exclusively. They are not love incarnate like Racine's Phaedra, they are modern selves with *several* strong desires. And these emotions they volubly express—hate, jealousy, curiosity, anger, domination, respectability. Is it not the very lifelike complexity of these human beings that confuses the critic, who expects on the stage what he would scorn in a novel—a character with but a single motive?

It would be easy but tedious to take that critic by the hand through all of Shaw and point to the father in *Misalliance,* the love-sick boy poet in *Candida,* the nearly adulterous pair in *The Devil's Disciple,* the strong-minded charmer Mrs. George in *Getting Married,* the unconscious flirt Gloria in *You Never Can Tell,* the proper-practical Nora in *John Bull's Other Island* and expatiate on the accuracy in variety of all those portraits of amorous people. And think of the exquisite treatment of Liza's feeling for and against Higgins—a masterly foreshadowing of the relation between patient and analyst.

In all the plays, moreover—at least up to *Heartbreak House*—it is sexuality that is at work, with or without the glow of romance. Not only is that "new" subject openly discussed in *Mrs. Warren's Profession,* but the plays offer discoveries about it. For example, in *Widowers' Houses,* Trench, in the middle of his quarrel with Blanche, suddenly sees "that all this ferocity is erotic"—the words are in the stage directions, following a four-line description of "her flush of undisguised animal excitement." In *Mrs. Warren,* Frank Gardner, acting as if he were Vivie's "little boy," cuddles with her provocatively. In *The Philanderer,* passionate pursuit of "sexual objects" is the theme. All three plays are suffused with eroticism that turns into violence in words ("I could kill him") and even into the uncompleted act of shooting.

At that date, this linkage of love and aggression is something new on the English stage. In others of the plays, notably *Candida,* we are shown the strength of sexuality in its maternal guise; Morell and his wife are bound together by his filial dependence, to which she responds in a manner not wholly pleasing to see. In *Arms and the Man,* Bluntschli ends by acknowledging and succumbing to the unconscious passion he has been subject to. For passion in Shaw is what the word rightly means—a suffering, caused by a force that overtakes and for a time overwhelms the normal self. This view is not only the classical view, it is also the modern view on which Shaw bases his philosophy of evolution. The Life Force is nothing if it does not grab its agents and make them do its work. *Man and Superman* makes the point in words which it takes a reviewer's sophistication to misunderstand and call sexless.

This failure to see what is there is due to an expectation that is not fulfilled. What the misreaders look for is Eros in traditional guise—the cherub with gossamer wings and little arrows that he implants with a tender smile. What Shaw depicts is Priapos, the son of Aphrodite like Eros, but by Dionysus the noisy and riotous. (Comedy itself began with his band of revellers, the *komos.*) Priapos is the god of fertility, "protector of those who keep sheep and goats." In Theocritus he is prayed to for delivery from "love." And he is, says the mythologist, "rarely portrayed without his indecent symbol of productiveness."

In being priapic more often than erotic, Shaw is also mid-Victorian. Let me explain. The term I have just used must, again, be taken strictly: Queen Victoria reigned for 64 years from her accession in 1837. The mid-point of her span is therefore 1869, when Shaw, aged 13, was just reaching adolescence. His ideas and feelings were formed, in the usual way, by what his mind took in between that date and his 25th year, that is, the early 1880s. Now, there is no profounder error in the heads of twentieth-century people than the belief that the mid-Victorians denied the importance of sexuality in men and women, and therefore knew nothing about it. On the contrary, they were ever-conscious of it and assessed its power all the more justly for their efforts at containment.

These efforts, begun well before Victoria, had a political purpose: to smother the revolutionary impulse by an inner check on the expression of all feeling. This test of "respectability" would generate a social pressure more effective than any police force. But it is no accident that the people's acceptance of the first modern police force—Sir Robert Peel's "bobbies"—coincided with the self-repression and shortly produced the most law-abiding nation in the world.

Of course, the containment of instinct, and of sexuality above all, needed continual warnings, and Victorian literature is full of them. The standard Victorian novel is about seduction and its consequences. *Adam Bede, Silas Marner, Richard Feverel, The Return of the Native, The Lady in White,* and most explicitly and vividly, *Our Mutual Friend,* testify to the irresistible power of sex. It is noteworthy that in the last-named, Hexam's priapic obsession is balanced by the two nonchalant, amoral figures of Lightwood and Wrayburn, who seem drawn from an Oscar Wilde dialogue thirty years ahead of time.

What we find in these great novels was echoed or anticipated in the little ones, by means of which all of the middle classes from top to bottom were indoctrinated. Nor

72

was the teaching only indirect. For example, after the so-called Northumberland Street affair of the early sixties, in which a Major Murray shot and killed one Roberts, who had pursued Murray's wife for many months, the newspapers "explained" what could cause so violent a sequence of events among civilized folk. The *Times* said: "It is when such fascination, whether designed or not in the quarter from which it comes, has worked upon a man and endowed some object with an absolute supremacy, and when the man's mind is completely carried off and drained into the excesses of one swollen passion, that [murder will ensue]. . . . In this case we have the romance of uncontrolled passion." But the editorial significantly adds: "Some people, as soon as they hear that word, expect something great, refined, and sublime; but this is not at all necessary for romance. . . . All that is necessary is that there should be *strength* in it."

That element, which obviously stands for the potency of sex, could be indulged by those who also had social power, whether based on rank or wealth—or paradoxically, on the lack of them. At the same time as the respectable must resist what another newspaper account called a "particular craving, . . . a tormenting want that creates a void within," the classes above and below the solid core of society might give rein to their passions, fill their hungry void. It was understood that the high aristocracy—e.g. the notorious Marquis of Hertford—could not be held to the common standard; wealth, title, an old name made one independent of respectability. So did the Bohemian life and the anonymous condition of the lower classes. Thus in Thackeray it is Lord Steyne who blandly and with immunity corrupts Becky Sharp; again, it is the artists and writers who (like Dickens) go in for liaisons with actresses or over to Paris for a sexual holiday; and it is the urban and rural poor who—as retrospective sociology tells us—keep up with relative freedom the ancestral cult of Priapos. Meanwhile, London throughout the nineteenth century was the world center of prostitution.

All this can be read at sight if one is not hypnotized by Lytton Stracheyism. And so there was really no need of the recently devised category of "Other Victorians" to teach us that sexuality did not vanish from human consciousness for 64 years.

In Shaw's young mind these commonplace realities were modified, complicated by circumstances. He was a genius, to begin with, and saw things like no one else—though he knew how others saw. This double vision was strengthened by growing up in the no-man's land between the respectable and the "not quite." He could thank his feckless, drunken father for giving him this observation post and his strong-minded mother for showing that a ménage à trois was a relation no more standardized than an ordinary marriage. Her case was certainly stranger than George Eliot's, yet was carried off with equal aplomb in the face of surrounding dismay and disapproval.

The lessons for Shaw were numerous and clear, the main one being that society's need to make lives uniform was continually defeated by human variation. It followed that the idealized copy of social norms on the contemporary stage was false. When, in addition, the revolt against respectability began to gather strength in the 1880s, Shaw was ready with his complex characters and his peculiar obsession with sex.

He was of course not alone in showing up the well-intentioned pretense, later called hypocrisy or misplaced idealism. All over Europe, science, literature, and social thought were in a kind of conspiracy to tear off the seven veils of respectability and revel in the exposure of mankind's unedifying nakedness. Ibsen in *Ghosts,* Charcot at the Salpétrière, Zola and his fellow Naturalists, Krafft-Ebing in Vienna, Nietzsche in his solitude, Edward Carpenter and Gide speaking for homosexuals, the feminists demanding freedom, including free love—all cooperated unwittingly to bring on at the turn of the century the first, the true and original sexual revolution. The attack was explicitly on "morality"; art and science were substituted for the Decalogue, the new goal being the finer, saner life beyond good and evil.

Though this destruction of an ethos seemed to start all at once, its early agents can be found throughout the century. In the 1820s and '30s, Blake, Shelley, and Gautier—to name only three—had expressed the sexual side of the Romanticist demand for a full knowledge of man's nature, and Shaw's high regard for Blake and Shelley is significant. The nineties as a whole have rightly been called a time of Neo-Romanticism.

Between the two Romantic periods the final debate on evolution had accustomed the public to take for granted the animal functions of man and give up the duty of concealing or repressing them. Soon "advanced" minds drew some obvious conclusions about "love," which the experience of medical men confirmed. Infant sexuality—among other facts—was observed and recorded well before Freud. In the sixties, some physicians—Dr. Allbutt, Dr. Garrett (a woman)—began to give private lectures on physiology and sex, including contraception, which Herbert Spencer, George Eliot, and Bertrand Russell's parents attended.[3] The progress made by hygiene, the growth of interest in sports, the surveys of urban degeneration[4]—all exhibited or contributed to a new respect for the body, and with this a reasoned contempt for the dominant taboo.

The very scope and strength of this movement may cause surprise that Shaw was not caught up in it as actively as some other artists. He lived a "respectable" bourgeois life and the exhibition of sex in his plays is not naturalistic; it is seen in vivid touches of the sort illustrated above and inferred from the characters' awareness of the pervasive *élan vital*. What is more, at every turn Shaw inveighs against the romantic view of life: is there not here a paradox, not to say a flat contradiction?

It might help to unravel this tangle if among the emotional attitudes of the 19th century one distinguished three overlapping tendencies. The early Romanticists aim at completeness and put love and genius at the core of their vision of life. To recur to myth, love in their sense is Eros and Anteros embracing each other, not denying Priapos, but making him the powerful servant of spiritual union.[5] In the Victorian resistance to revolution *and* Romanticism, love is split into romance (the blossoms, the sweetness of first love) and lust, the ever-present fiend. Finally, the Neo-Romantic naturalists rehabilitate, even glorify, Priapos, and condemn repression in the name of science and individual liberty.

In this sequence it is against romance that Shaw directs his crusade. The prettification of the feelings that arise when two people fall in love angers him because it is dangerous to them and to society. Yet the stage, which he regards as the chief instrument of sex education,[6] keeps teaching by example the false attitudes of romance. So in his plays he shows couples with minds not only free of the romancy figments but so conscious of them that they talk both like lovers and like critics of love, shrewd observers of the priapic Life Force.[7] In this portrayal he was only a little ahead of his time. By 1920, for good or ill, the intelligent—thanks to Shaw and others—had acquired precisely that self-consciousness about their feelings of love and urgings of sex.

Outside the plays, Shaw often overdid the debunking and very likely confused his readers. He points out, needlessly, how uncomfortable it is for lovers to walk with their arms around each other's waist. True, but the discomfort is evidently nothing to those who do it, as one may see on any street: they want to be close. Again, he says that for love and sex one woman or man is so much like another that the belief in the unique beloved is but one more illusion of romance. True when we reflect how the jilted recover and find a new flame, but false when we recall (as Shaw himself does) that "a thick ankle" can effectually cast out desire.

To sum up, when Shaw says *romantic* he derives the word from romance, not Romanticism. What he covers with ridicule and scorn is the sentiment on the pink greeting-card, in the facile storybook, on the sentimental and melodramatic stage. But to fall in love, to feel driven by desire, to idolize and idealize the object of one's passion—these events of human life Shaw regards with the same awe and delight as the Romanticists, seeing in passion even more than the romancers see, for the outcome of love is creative evolution, the birth of new genius and new departures.

I predicted the need for a great deal of explaining. There is still some distance to go as we move on from the first to the second half of the charge that in Shaw's plays feelings are absent and ideas in excess. This second impression is due, most often, to his verbal gift. "Exhaustive literary expression" (as he termed his aim) causes some people to lose their footing as in an undertow; they then ascribe their loss of balance to ideas above their heads. A self-observant witness on this point is the interviewer who wrote in 1939: "While Mr. Shaw does not seem to speak with particular rapidity, the steady and rhythmic flow of his polished and oftentimes glittering phrases is so succinct and covers so much ground in such a short time that it is out of the question for anyone but a court stenographer to get down anything more than the substance.''[8]

''So much ground in such a short time'' is the key. If Shaw had this effect on an experienced reporter by mere impromptu talk, one can gauge the result of the prepared speeches in the plays. The audience, caught up in the dramatic situation, easily follows the ''retortive backchat'' but flounders in the periodic harangues. The same thing comes about in Shakespeare, of course, but there the excuse is that the language is archaic, and poetry besides. That is plausible, but I suspect that the rapid flow of ideas bewilders equally in both playwrights. In both, too, the audience gets the drift and stays in its seats for the rest of the action. Only, in Shaw the substance (to echo the reporter) has to do with contemporary issues and this leads to saying afterwards that what should have been a play was in fact a discussion.

Now it is true that the theatrical renaissance of which Shaw was a principal agent was grounded in the discussion of ideas. Ibsen, Strindberg, Tolstoy, Galsworthy, Wilde used the stage to argue, as was inevitable when one outlook on life was embattled against another. An entry in Tolstoy's diary for 1893 puts it plainly: ''A work of drama . . . consists in presenting people of the most diverse characters and situations, putting before them and confronting them with the need to solve a vital problem not previously solved by people, and making them act and observe in order to find out how this problem can be solved. It's a laboratory experiment. I would like to do this in my next drama.''[9]

That next drama was *The Light That Shines in Darkness*, which it is interesting to reconsider as being a piece of scientific work. By comparison, Shaw prefers ''art'': he puts the "problem" and its solution in his prefaces instead of his plays. But a lengthy preface naturally confirms the unreflective in their belief that here is a playwright interested solely in problems and solutions, of which he has half a hundred on tap. And yet the candid reader who goes from preface to play without a break is bound to exclaim at the end, "How in heaven's name does the first piece help me to understand the second?" For the preface ranges over all the social, moral, religious, artistic, and economic subjects that *might* have a bearing on *some* of the points raised by the drama. Shaw has only given his reader the background of knowledge and thought that stands behind—way behind—the action. To understand the play one must scrutinize the characters, who in the end do not solve any social problem at all, sometimes not even their own. One must make up one's mind, as in any play, about right and wrong behavior and this without benefit of a moral. Indeed, most of the plays do not conclude, they stop; and what the audience has had is not a laboratory demonstration but a confidential look at a set of emotions and perplexities—the roof lifted off the house next door, where thinking people live and are troubled.

That last clause no doubt contains the difference between the plays of Shaw's time and those just preceding: trouble leading to thought. For all plays whatsoever are full of ideas, but when the ideas are conventional they appear not as ideas but as bare fact or sheer feeling. In melodrama and sentimental comedy the purity of the heroine, the avarice of the mortgage holder, the attitude of the parents toward the impecunious suitor, and his own well-advertised notions of honor, deference, and proper ambition are so many ideas. In tragedy, the accepted moves of war, empire, love, and betrayal are also ideas, and all are regarded as inevitable. It is only when any of these is turned upside-down that the public, also convention-ridden, thinks it is being fobbed off with brain-products instead of heart throbs. When Shaw in *The Admirable Bashville* has Cashel Byron say: "Two things I hate, my duty and my mother," he rudely wakes up the sixth row, whence the reviewers file out to write that here is a man bent on injecting ideas into literature.

In fairness, one must add that Shaw is usually not content to upset or invert only one convention in one play. His capacity for "covering much ground in a short time" is not purely verbal, it is also conceptual and imaginative. Not that he peoples his plays solely with iconoclasts and reformers, but that the situations he hits upon bring out of ordinary types actions and responses that they themselves did not expect—a common result of sudden shock and the very foundation of high comedy.

This double artistry—in language and in plotting—obviously adds to the confusion here being unraveled. Take by way of comparison the three comedies of Oscar Wilde other than *The Importance of Being Earnest,* whose status as a farce conceals the multiplicity of original ideas. In the other comedies Wilde is trying to liberalize the Victorian code of sexual morality. A woman with a past, or a seducer, or an illegitimate child is shown to possess merits that outweigh "the fault," and indeed make it irrelevant—nobody's business—in the encounter that the play presents. Wilde's contribution to this new morality was considerable and it is now unjustly overlooked. But his success then was not due to his brilliant dialogue and memorable aphorisms; it was due also to his hammering away at one stock attitude in each play. His characters, drawn from high society, all learned the new principle in unison, like a beginners' class being demonstrated before the parents in the stalls. They left edified and modified. Today that very simplification has killed the life out of all these plays except *Earnest;* whereas Shaw's continue to occupy the stage in England and America, in Germany and behind the Iron Curtain.

To be sure, Shaw's way with ideas was the opposite of Wilde's studied nonchalance and aristocratic hauteur. Ideas were to Shaw a passion: "my intellectual interests . . . have been so much more lasting and dignified than the more primitive and fleshly interests that I can conceive no better paradise than one in which they have developed into passions and become ecstatic"—this from a letter written in his 67th year.[10] From the start, it is plain, both forms of passion existed side by side and were transmuted into scene after scene of the best plays. Anyone who sees or reads the second act of *Major Barbara* or the baiting of Mangan in the last act of *Heartbreak House* and who does not feel the adrenalin flooding his arteries must be deficient in imagination—or in adrenalin.

One readily grants that what stirs the imagination varies with human temperament and also with education. The sob story that moves the simple to tears moves the sophisticated to laughter. And among the artistically cultivated there is a further division which sets apart two groups that for want of better terms might be called the sensual and the sensuous. Milton invented this last word so that he might define poetry as "simple, sensuous, and passionate." It was his type of poetry he had in mind, but whole ranges of art and artists could be classed under the description—Shelley and Blake, for example, Delacroix and Berlioz, Mozart and Stendhal. The other, the sensual class, would include Keats, Ingres, Balzac, Wagner, and Oscar Wilde in his fables and dialogues. A clearly contrasting modern pair is Henry James and Proust, who reach a similar end by the sensuous and the sensual path respectively. The second group create by imagination like the former, but they do not appeal *through* the imagination; they move the senses first and then reach the inner nerve. In many, perhaps most, people the senses are nearer the surface and ready to be struck; imagination in them needs to be primed; they respond to red heat but often fail to perceive the white.

That is what happens when Shaw—or Milton—appears deficient to these otherwise good judges: where is the bared flesh, the lush decor, the smell of blood? The word Puritan comes pat to resolve the difficulty. For "Puritanism" read "sensuous passion" and the difficulty *is* resolved. The historical Puritans were without question passionate people. They were fierce about political, religious, social, and economic ideas. They loved music and poetry and produced great literature. They hated the theatre because it offered, then as always, the alluring spectacle of sexual irregularity. When Shaw gave his third collection of plays the title *Three Plays for Puritans,* he shared all these passions, including hate of the contemporary stage for its wrong-headed sexual teachings. And by the title of the book he warned his readers that the violent conflicts in the plays would be settled by other standards than those of sensual romance.

A last misjudgment of the plays springs from the merit mentioned above—the literary expression, or rather, expressiveness—with which Shaw endows one or more of his main characters: "it isn't lifelike—people don't think and talk like that." One might answer, "Well, Shaw does," but that would be quibbling. The real answer is that this artificiality is inherent in literature and particularly in theatre. True, most modern plays begin with casual chat that sounds "real," but unless the pivotal remarks that come later are carefully, artificially put together, no play, no characterization, no suspense, no intelligible outcome is possible.

As to the characters, it is undeniable that their knowledge of themselves and of others, and the readiness with which they talk of their motives, are—and cannot but be—pure artifice. This is especially true in comedy and one must remember that Shaw, despite his passion and his seriousness, is writing comedies. He writes them in the classical tradition; he is the modern Molière and Aristophanes, where also you will find the point of the piece exhibited in long, self-aware declarations and arguments. Think of the *Misanthrope:* Alceste and Philinte, Alceste and Célimène carry on virtually scholastic debates about life in society, hypocrisy and truthfulness, the pleasures of company and of retirement. In Aristophanes' *Clouds,* the father's complaint and the philosopher's retort come in long speeches. The Greek audience in fact expected one *very* long speech from the chorus, about contemporary issues related to the play; the Greeks had a word for it: the parabasis.[11]

It satisfied the deep human desire for a sermon or a lecture, which reminds us of the religious roots and instructional bent of the theatre that Shaw kept recalling all his life. What makes instruction good theatre (and vice versa) is opposition, conflict between equally plausible views, and in that department Shaw is supreme. He never sets up a straw man or gives all the good arguments to one side. He always knew by what a short margin one position is better than another and how that difference variously strikes various temperaments; nor does he let his private preferences stand in the way: in *Heartbreak House,* Shaw the teetotaller has Captain Shotover defend rum even while making a Shavian point.

If one thinks of some of the plays written since Shaw's death in 1950, one may fall into the trap of supposing that the drama has got away from artificiality by getting rid of long speeches and overt argument. The fragmented colloquialism of Tennessee Williams and the repetitious monosyllabism of Beckett or Pinter may seem faithful representations of real life. That is not so. Nobody ever talked that way. The new trick is even more artificial than the former explicitness; the speeches are contrived to the last degree—first, to establish a mood and "plug" a symbol; then, to give the actors some clue to the coherence of their parts; and lastly, to promise something capable of holding an audience. What is more, the art in these delicate structures relies heavily on the previous art that it seems to reject, for it counts on the listener's supplying, between the lines, certain critical views of life, love, society, wealth, sex, and self. And these views, without which the spare dialogue would be gibberish, are largely derived—translated, so to speak—from the propaganda initiated by Ibsen, Strindberg, Pirandello, and Shaw.

It remains only to say a word about Shaw's relations with others in private life; we must see what his alleged lack of "interest in people" amounted to. The *Letters,* now in their third volume edited by the incomparable Dan Laurence, afford the best means of passing judgment. In them we see Shaw in touch with hundreds of people—friend, foe, and stranger—giving them without stint his attention, advice, and help through influence or cash. At times it seems that the whole world is at his door or clinging to his coat tails. For someone who "did not care for people," the position is remarkable.

What are we to make of a man who, burdened to the limit by his own multifarious work, takes time to comfort the bereaved—e.g. Lillah McCarthy during and after her separation and divorce; support his relatives (mother, sister, Irish cousins); assist fellow authors (Frank Harris, Granville-Barker); back up his often incompetent helpers and hangers-on (Henderson, Hamon, O'Bolger); take part in efforts to save victims of mistreatment (Casement, T.E. Lawrence), patch up or prevent quarrels, failures, missteps, and follies—in short, behave towards all with undeviating fairness and, when attacked, never retaliate or hold a grudge, however brutish the opponent?

Reading these letters makes one feel again and again that here is saintliness in action, and it is this, naturally, which gives rise to the impression of not caring for anybody—for anybody *in particular*. Shaw lacked *partiality*. Just as in his plays he could see that everybody was in the right, or nearly, so in life he could see why those whom he dealt with acted as they did. In return he treated them, not according to their deserts, but according to their best selves, realized or unrealized.

The truly best understood this conduct and repaid it with gratitude and affection, the others with resentment. The common weakness is wanting to be loved "for oneself," as an exceptional being. It is part of one's self-regard and it goes with the assumption of romance about a unique beloved. Shaw, the Great Facilitator, was consistent in not feeling that way, about himself or others. His pluralism (as it were) reminds one of the old saints, who could be combative yet loving; one thinks, too, of Jesus the man, who also made light of kinship and friendship in their usual restrictive form. Shaw manifestly loved his neighbor in that Christian sense. Liking the neighbor was something else, which in any case excluded the conventional utterance of unfelt sentiments. His mind was clear of cant, as Dr. Johnson recommended. The result was that people did not feel "caressed" by his friendship or attention, no matter how concentrated it was on their individual good. Some, like Beerbohm, probably felt the reverse—ruffled and neglected.

Such people are within their rights when they express their distaste and even disapproval of the Shavian character. They are culpably wrong when they impute to it a lack of humanity or speak of Shaw's "cold-hearted sympathy." That oxymoron springs, once again, from blindness to the role of imagination. It is inconceivable, for example, that Shaw "the uncaring" could have been guilty of the treatment that the "loving" Max Beerbohm inflicted on Grace Conover: he fell in love with her, proposed to her and was engaged, wanted the fact "kept a dead secret," postponed marriage more than once, broke off indecisively, having in ambiguous letters kept her dangling for six years.[12] Where in this course of behavior is the warm concern for other people that Shaw is said to lack?[13]

Pairing these incidents in two lives is not meant to glorify Shaw at the expense of his quiet detractor, whom it is also important to "understand." But the contrast may suggest how unfeeling a person can be from lack of a certain imagination, the kind that respects individuality so fully that it can cherish and succor without effusiveness. Indeed, it is not so much Max who is to be censured as his biographer, who mindlessly writes of Shaw's "inhumanity" and grants him only the allied merit of not being touchy. Chesterton, who knew his Shaw at first hand, found more fitting words: "It is not easy to dispute violently with a man for twenty years, about sex, about sin, about sacraments, about personal points of honour, about all the most sacred and delicate essentials of existence, without sometimes being irritated or feeling that he hits unfair blows or employs discreditable ingenuities. [But] I can testify that I have never read a reply by Bernard Shaw that did not leave me in a better and not a worse temper or frame of mind; which did not seem to come out of inexhaustible fountains of fairmindedness and intellectual geniality; which did not savour somehow of that native largeness which the philosopher attributed to the Magnanimous Man."[14]

With that epitaph and his plays rightly read, Shaw's humanity needs no defense. It is the unregenerate critics and biographers who need a re-education in the science of man and the use of words.

Notes

1. *Max: A Biography,* London, 1964, 166.

2. "On Logic and Lunacy" in *Essays,* ed. John Guest, London, 1939, 328.

3. *The Amberley Papers,* ed. Bertrand Russell, 2 v., London, 1932, I, 513.

4. The recruitment of soldiers for the Boer War in 1899 brought out massive evidence of physical defects and debility, which were seen as signs of "degeneration." Max Nordau's book of that title (1893) had prepared the public for concluding that modern life was destroying body and mind.

5. The German ideal of the *schöne Seele* depended on many qualities, among which the capacity for passion was only one. Corresponding ideals, without a special name, inspired French, Italian, and other romanticisms.

6. Bernard Shaw, *Collected Letters 1911-1925,* ed. Dan H. Laurence, N.Y., 1985, 455. See also Shaw's approval of *Lady Chatterley's Lover* as providing excellent instruction for the young. (Remark to General Smuts, quoted in Colin Wilson, *Bernard Shaw,* N.Y., 1969, 267.)

7. The continual spoiling of good criticism by the loose and ambiguous use of *romantic* justifies, I think, the neologism *romancy,* which I use here for the first time.

8. *New York Herald-Tribune,* June 25, 1939; repr. in *The Independent Shavian,* vol. 23, No. 1, 1985, 3.

9. *Tolstoy's Diaries,* ed. and trans. R.F. Christian, 2 v., N.Y., 1985; entry for May 5, 1893, I, 322.

10. *Letters,* op. cit., 813.

11. In *The Clouds,* a "conservative" play, the parabasis covers some four and a half pages expounding the author's view of his originality and of his predecessors and contemporaries in Athens. This "address" as we have it was rewritten after the failure of the play on its first appearance.

12. *Max,* op. cit., 119 ff., 224-25. See also the petty trick Max played on Shaw at a public dinner. (*Letters,* op. cit., 451).

13. One of the curiosities of biography is the tendency to attack the strong and excuse the weak. David Cecil writes apropos of Max's engagement: "Yet his virtues and his weakness alike combined to make him hesitate before breaking with her. He felt to do so would be dishonorable and he shrank from the unpleasantness the breach would involve." (*Op. cit.,* 221).

14. G.K. Chesterton, *Autobiography,* London, 1936, 227-28. "The philosopher" is Aristotle.

A PARAGRAPH BY SHAW

BY STANLEY KAUFFMANN

Shaw on Dickens (Ungar, 1985) contains everything substantial that the former wrote about the latter, although it could not possibly include every comment on Dickens by Shaw. The book, edited by the invaluable Dan H. Laurence aided by Martin Quinn, contains one item that struck me especially. On 2 January 1912 Sir William Nicoll, the editor of *The Bookman,* wrote Shaw that he was planning a Dickens Centenary Number for which, say Laurence and Quinn, "he was asking representative authors to favor the journal with short notes on: (1) personal recollections of Dickens; (2) indebtedness; (3) evaluations of his novels. . . . " On 4 January 1912 "Shaw's replies were hastily penned on the reverse of Nicoll's letter." Facing the printed page in the book is a photographic reproduction of Shaw's holograph replies, in that handwriting that seems much too careful for a man who wrote so much.

The reply to (1) was "None." (Shaw arrived in London six years after Dickens died. He did, however, know Dickens's daughter, Kate Perugini.) The ten-line reply to (3) calls Dickens "one of the greatest writers that ever lived. . . as ignorant of Art and Philosophy as a cave man. Compared to Goethe he is almost a savage. Yet he is, by pure force of genius, one of the great writers of the world.''

It is Shaw's reply to (2), one long paragraph, that fascinates. Here it is:

> Obviously a great deal. My works are all over Dickens; and nothing but the stupendous illiteracy of modern criticism could have missed this glaring feature of my methods—especially my continual exploitation of Dickens's demonstration that it is possible to combine a mirror like exactness of character drawing with the wildest extravagances of humorous expression and grotesque situation. I have actually transferred characters of Dickens to my plays—Jaggers in *Great Expectations* to *You Never Can Tell,* for example—with complete success. Lomax in *Major Barbara* is technically a piece of pure Dickens. It is not too much to say that Dickens could not only draw a character more accurately than any of the novelists of the XIX century, but could do it without ceasing for a single sentence to be not merely impossible but outrageous in his unrestrained fantasy and fertility of imagination. No combination of phonography and cinematography could reproduce Micawber, Mrs. Sparsit, and Silas Wegg from contemporary reality as vividly as Dickens; yet their monstrous and sidesplitting verbal antics never for a moment come within a mile of any human utterance. That is what I call mastery: knowing exactly how to be unerringly true and serious whilst entertaining your reader with every trick, freak, and sally that imagination and humor can conceive at their freest and wildest.

I've quoted this paragraph in its entirety because of its entirety.

First, let's look at the date and what Shaw was in the midst of at that time. On the evening of New Year's Day, 1912, *Fanny's First Play* had opened at the Kingsway Theater, having been moved from the Little Theater, and one can safely assume that Shaw was involved in refining the production before and after that move. On 2 January he wrote a long letter to the composer, Rutland Boughton, criticizing in technical detail a toccata that Boughton had sent him. In the first week of January he wrote to Pinero that he had begun a religious sketch "something like *The Sign of the Cross.* " This of course was *Androcles and the Lion,* which was finished 6 February 1912. During January he also answered a questionnaire from *Le Monde Illustré,* with a much longer response than the one to Nicoll, on the subjects of war in general and Italy's recent invasion of Tripoli. These facts are selections only from the sum of what was occupying Shaw just then—at the age of 55. Yet he found time to turn over Nicoll's letter and dash off some answers. (It took me 15 minutes just to copy that paragraph.) The facing photograph shows only three corrections in the passage quoted. After "this glaring feature of my" he inserted "methods— especially my." After "to combine" he scratched out a word. In the last sentence, after "to be," he scratched out a word or two.

Next, a look at the prose. Much less has been written about Shaw's prose than about his dialogue although, even excluding the five early novels, there is more prose than dialogue. Examine the structure of Shaw's paragraph. It begins with a four-word incomplete sentence, a flat reply to the question. That flat reply then serves as a launching pad for the upward flight of "my works are all over Dickens" into a sentence full of small arcs that form a large arch. That long second sentence is followed by a shorter sentence starting with "I" to vary the tone. Then a short declarative sentence, about Lomax, for a breather. Then two long sentences, in Victorian prose at its best, full of music and free of fat, touched with Shaw's recurrent tickle of alliteration ("fantasy and fertility"), and ending with a seeming full stop. But there follows a one-sentence cadenza, a commentary on what he has already said, taking it to a calm, summary height with a surge of feeling and of postulate combined. In that sentence, note the phrase "trick, freak, and sally," itself cumulative in rhythm, alive with a freshness all the more telling because it is tossed off en route. The real test of the paragraph's structure is the one that can always be applied to Shaw's prose: try reading it aloud. It flows musically. It comes out vocally. It actually invigorates you to speak it. This, too, is a kinship with Dickens, one that Shaw doesn't point out.

Shaw boasts—one can't say "admits"—that he has taken characters from Dickens. Elsewhere he has specified others. One facet of this influence that he doesn't specify is the theory of nomenclature. Dickens hardly invented the idea of characterized character names: it's an ancient practice. Shaw uses the recognizable Dickensian flavors, double distilled. In *On the Rocks,* to take a later instance, a play set in 10 Downing Street during the year 1933, some of the cabinet people are Viscount Barking, Sir Dexter Rightside (Foreign Secretary), Sir Bemrose Hotspot (Admiralty Lord), and Sir Broadfoot Basham (Police Commissioner).

But, to a more subtle aspect of the subject, what does it mean to say, as Shaw does, that he "transferred characters" from Dickens to his plays? We all know instances of subsequent use of characters by later writers—Sherlock Holmes, for prime instance—but that facile adoption is neither perceptible nor possible in a Shaw. More than mere mimicry is involved. If we try to follow the "transfer" process imaginatively, it may come out something like this. Dickens wrote a lawyer named Jaggers; Shaw needed a lawyer, whom he chose to name Bohun. (Pronounced "Boon," by the way.) Shaw wanted comparable effects and resonances from Bohun, so took Dickens's process of emphasis as his guide. It was impossible to give Bohun the same diction as Jaggers, both for reasons of period and of personal touch. But he could apply the same prisms of view, as nearly as he could, to his own observations and experience and to his own structural needs in the fourth act of his comedy. Shaw, then, has two sources where Dickens had only one: he can draw on Dickens's art and on his own perceptions. Thus the Shaw process has a touch in it of what Wilde calls the critic's advantage over the artist, or rather what makes the critic's work "more creative than creation." Shaw partakes of that critical process by creating *on* creation, then combining it with an originating artist's use of raw life.

But the apex of the matter, which would apply if Shaw had never consciously "transferred" a character from Dickens, is summarized in the last sentence of his paragraph. Shaw says that mastery, in this aspect of art, is the ability to be "unerringly true and serious" while entertaining your reader with the "freest and wildest" imagination and humor. (Like Dickens, Shaw almost never uses this method in a major character, a protagonist. Bohun could be conceived by that method but not the hero, Valentine, high-spirited though he is.) If more of Shaw's critics understood that idea of mastery, more Shaw criticism would be worth reading. It would at least meet Shaw on his own ground, instead of nattering about frivolity or a mixture of realism and cartoon.

For an example of this mastery in practice, where inevitably it is interwoven with other masteries if it is to succeed, look at *The Doctor's Dilemma*. Consider the four "supporting" doctors. (The other important characters, including the two doctors, Ridgeon and Cullen, are handled otherwise.) First, their names: Cutler Walpole, the obsessive surgeon; Sir Ralph Bloomfield Bonington, the smiling dispenser of reassurance; Leo Schutzmacher, the hardheaded Jew; Blenkinsop, the financial failure of the lot. Each of these descriptively tagged characters supplies his own relatively narrow range of colors in the play, and each of them is entailed in the play's most serious elements, in which he functions by means of his own narrow, essentially comic temperament. In a program note for the first American production of *The Doctor's Dilemma* in 1915—which stipulates that he was "nursed on Dickens" and forcefully rephrases some of the matters in the paragraph quoted—Shaw states that the play is "an exact record" of the scientific matters it treats, that it is "also a sermon, a tragedy, a comedy of manners, and a romance. . . . And . . . it is all the things it is, all the time." But the four doctors named above are not all these things. Each is only what he is, as defined early, and is brought recurrently into contact with the motions of the play to be precisely what he is, thereby to dramatize some aspects of the medical profession and to give the motion of the play a dependable springboard. Each is reliably, almost endearingly, predictable.

Here is the key to the "mastery" that Shaw hails in Dickens and of which he is an heir. These four doctors have no contradictions of character, no ambiguities or paradoxes.

They are not charade characters, as in medieval mysteries, because their attributes, confined though they are, are graphically real, come from the world as we know it. They are not caricatures because, however they may be extended, all proportions are precisely maintained. But, for the comic master, they provide a chance to take realistic observation and amplify it with imagination, as one might take a veristic photograph of an odd angle of reality and blow it up. Contrasted with principal characters, who must have all the contradictions and paradoxes of human nature appropriate to them if they are to bear the centrality of the drama, those four doctors are vivid reminders of human frailties that, in a sense, constantly threaten the central figures. We see here the Dickens mastery that Shaw loves; and we can also discern a larger mastery shared by both of them: the ability to use that minor mastery as a strand in a grand and multicolored fabric.

These notes of mine, I repeat, grow out of one paragraph "hastily penned" on the back of a questionnaire.

SHAW AND THE MARRIAGE IN DIONYSUS

BY MICHAEL GOLDMAN

In any good performance of Shaw, there's a kind of elation, a bounding, contagious exuberance, which many critics have associated with Shaw's acknowledged master, Mozart—who taught him, he said, the art of "writing seriously without being dull." The energy is so indefatigable, however, that it has struck other members of his audience as merely mechanical, like Yeats's image of Shaw as a sewing machine ceaselessly chattering away. The motif I will be discussing here presents a kind of focal point for the exuberance in Shaw's art, a kernel around which the energy accumulates and which helps generate it. It also implies a dramatic method, that is, it has a great deal to do with the way Shaw's images and actions and even his jokes are meant to work in the theater. As such, it may help us to see the Shavian gaiety not as a kind of superficial or incidental charm, but as profoundly reflective of his dramatic vision. I call this motif the Marriage in Dionysus, and I want to spend most of my time tracing its operation in one play, *Major*

Barbara, which in many ways is Shaw's most self-conscious exploration of the bases of his art.

I

Shaw's heroes are men and women who stand in a superior relation to the sources of real power in their worlds. Caesar, for example, prevails because he understands logistics, strategy, and the men under his command better than his enemies—he also understands his enemies better than they do themselves. Most crucially, he understands the difference between real and illusory sources of power. His soldiers win, not, as the Egyptians believe, because they have seven arms each, each carrying seven spears, or because the blood in their veins is boiling quicksilver, but because Caesar has trained them into an efficient fighting force. Indeed, part of the pleasure of any play by Shaw comes from watching false notions of power scattered and put to flight by those who know where real power comes from.

One spectacular image for this relation to power is the great crane that swings above the stage throughout the second scene of Act Three in *Caesar and Cleopatra*. The crane may well strike a reader, and perhaps even a viewer, as conclusive evidence for that favorite invention of Shaw's detractors, the "unserious" artist, a man supposedly willing to be entertaining at any cost. In the midst of a battle on which the course of world history depends, the characters take time out to investigate a machine which couldn't have existed in 48 B.C. For of course the crane is a staggering anachronism, a steam engine. Actually the image is deeply to

Shaw's purpose, not least in its power to irritate us by seeming frivolous.

The point of the steam engine is that it can get things done ten times as effectively as other methods of utilizing power, and this, as the dialogue makes clear, is why it fascinates able and hard-working men like Rufio, Britannus, Apollodorus, and Caesar. The crane stands out among the machines of Egypt because it makes a superior use of power. Likewise, Caesar stands out among ordinary men. He is a master of reality where others are ruled by superstition and illusion.

Shaw frequently uses stage devices of this sort—the motor car in *Man and Superman* is another example. Enry Straker's car becomes an emblem of the Life Force itself, which sweeps Jack Tanner this way and that to his uncomprehending wonder, but as in *Caesar and Cleopatra* the practicable stage machine is used to produce an exhilaration, a comic pleasure which comes from watching a superior relation to power in action. Similarly, St. Joan's relation to the new forces of nationalism and Protestantism is beautifully emblematized in the third scene of her play, when Dunois is waiting for the wind to change so he can attack Orleans. Joan arrives, the wind suddenly changes, and the scene ends in a climax of excitement. This is the third of Joan's "miracles," but the point of the scene is caught in the activity of its dominating prop, the large pennant which indicates the direction of the wind. The miracle is not a mere sign—God is on our side—but a logistical necessity. The wind must be blowing right for the military genius of Dunois to seize it, just as Joan is the religious genius who can seize the winds of doctrine at this moment in European history to effect a revolutionary change. Joan and Dunois can't do their work in a vacuum. The wind is a source of power they must use.

II

All these props are associated, then, with an elating feeling of what it's like to handle and wield power in a radically more efficient way. It is the joining of the individual to a deep source of such power—the commitment to the superior relation—that I am calling the Marriage in Dionysus. In Shaw, it is both a process which certain characters undergo and an experience for the audience. Like many comic playwrights, Shaw sometimes ends his play with a wedding or a promise of one. Far more significantly, some form of what the Cambridge anthropologists called a *gamos* or sacred marriage is present in most of his plays, though it doesn't necessarily come at the conclusion. It is not, however, usually a literal marriage, but a wedding of individual will to a source of higher power. The most literal instance of this is Jack Tanner's surrender to the Life Force, his marriage to Ann Whitefield at the end of *Man and Superman*. A much richer example is that of Barbara and Cusins setting their hands to the massive capabilities of Undershaft's war machine at the end of *Major Barbara*.

I have already suggested that the case of *Major Barbara* is particularly instructive; among other things it makes clear why one may legitimately connect the name of Dionysus with the central processes of Shaw's art. In *Major Barbara* Shaw invokes Dionysus repeatedly, and in a manner that makes his relevance to the meaning of the play and to Shaw's work in general unmistakably plain.

Major Barbara begins with an acknowledgment to Gilbert Murray:

> The Euripidean verses in the second act of *Major Barbara* are not by me, nor even directly by Euripides. They are by Professor Gilbert Murray, whose English

version of *The Bacchae* came into our dramatic literature with all the impulsive power of an original work shortly before *Major Barbara* was begun. The play, indeed, stands indebted to him in more ways than one.

Murray, of course, was a good friend of Shaw's, and Shaw regularly turned to him for advice on classical matters. In fact, Shaw read *Major Barbara* to Murray in draft, and it's possible that he took some of the suggestions for revision that Murray made to him.[1] But the debt to Murray, as Shaw's acknowledgment suggests, is deeper than this. It is considerably deeper, I think, even than the well-known fact that Adolphus Cusins is recognizably modelled on Murray. Far more important is Murray's significance for Shaw as a student of Greek religion and a translator of Euripides and especially of *The Bacchae,* the play about Dionysus so extensively quoted at the very center of *Major Barbara's* middle act.

Let me start with the passage itself:

> One and another
> In money and guns may outpass his brother;
> And seethe with a million hopes as leaven;
> And they win their will; or they miss their will;
> And their hopes are dead or are pined for still;
>> But whoe'er can know
>> As the long days go
> That to live is happy has found his heaven.

>> Is it so hard a thing to see
>> That the spirit of God—whate'er it be—
> The law that abides and changes not, ages long,
> The Eternal and Nature-born: these things be strong?
> What else is Wisdom? What of Man's endeavor,
> Or God's high grace so lovely and so great?

> To stand from fear set free? To breathe and wait?
> To hold a hand uplifted over Fate?
> And shall not Barbara be loved for ever?

This is Murray's translation, with two slight alterations. In the second line, Shaw has made Cusins substitute money and guns for Murray's "gold and power," a reasonable updating that doesn't change Euripides' meaning and rather improves on Murray. The other change is called attention to by Undershaft:

> **Undershaft.** Euripides mentions Barbara, does he?
> **Cusins.** It is a fair translation. The word means Loveliness.

Murray had written "Loveliness."

But what is the Euripidean context of this gracious hymn to loveliness and the fulfilled life? The *Bacchae* is a play about the coming of Dionysus and the worship of Dionysus to Greece, particularly the city of Thebes. Dionysus is a new god and naturally he is viewed as subversive by representatives of the state and established religion. He is worshipped with music and song; his converts form a group of dancing, singing, ecstatic revellers. Dionysus brings peace and joy to his followers; he can also bring them visions and superhuman strength. But his power is terrible. The subject of the *Bacchae* is Dionysus' revenge on the people of Thebes, who have at first refused to worship him. He does this through the very Dionysiac power that brings his worshipers delight. He converts and then destroys them with his power. His greatest enemy is Pentheus, king of Thebes, and he punishes him by, first, luring him out to watch the Theban women, now converted, in their revels. In their hallucinated ecstacy, the women, among whom is Pentheus' mother, mistake Pentheus for a sacrificial animal and tear him to pieces. The act of dismemberment marks the climax of the play.

The chorus of the *Bacchae* is composed of women, privileged followers of Dionysus who have accompanied him to Greece from Asia and who sing throughout the play about the power and glory of the god; they celebrate the pleasures of his worship and thrill to the vengeance he wreaks on Thebes. Now, the chorus Cusins quotes is spoken just after Dionysus has hypnotized Pentheus and persuaded the young king to go off with him to the hills around Thebes to see the Bacchic revels, to go off, that is, to his horrible death. Pentheus and Dionysus leave the stage and the Bacchae sing the hymn, from which Cusins quotes, to the loveliness and happiness of the life that their worship has brought them. The chorus, then, is, like Euripides' play itself, a hymn to the Dionysiac power, a power that is at once lovely in its possibilities and the current of energy it conveys, yet terrible in its destructive potential. Terrible, particularly, to those who think they can safely ignore it.

What use should we make of all this classical information? Out of context, the excerpt evokes only the peaceful pleasures of Dionysus worship, a happiness and wisdom far superior to thoughts of money and guns. But the full meaning of Dionysus in Shaw's play need not and should not come to us by a process of literary source-hunting. It is, rather, actively present in *Major Barbara,* in this scene, in this passage. The sense of a religious connection with a source of raw power that is needed to produce loveliness but that also can be horribly destructive is carefully worked into the dialogue between Cusins and Undershaft. As they discuss Cusins' version of Euripides, it is Undershaft who makes the really Euripidean point about the doubleness of Dionysus, the real raw power at the source of life:

I think, my friend, that if you wish to know, as the
long days go, that to live is happy, you must first
acquire money enough for a decent life, and power
enough to be your own master.

In the course of the discussion that surrounds the
quotation from Euripides, both Cusins and the Salvation
Army are explicitly identified with the worship of Dionysus.
Later in the act, Cusins calls Undershaft, "Dionysus." Not
only are Cusins and Undershaft identified with the god, so is
Barbara. ("Dionysus and all others are in herself.") More
importantly, like the other two, she is identified with a power
that lies beneath all religions. Like Dionysus', it shows us a
divine madness that gives one superhuman strength:

> **Undershaft.** Would anyone else than a madman make
> [cannons]? . . . Can a sane man translate Eurip-
> ides? . . . Can a sane woman make a man of a waster
> or a woman of a worm? . . .
> **Cusins.** You mean Barbara is as mad as we are?

They are three of a kind, a Bacchic triumvirate.

This returns us to Cusins' substitution of Barbara's name
for loveliness. It is scarcely innocent on Shaw's part. Is
Barbara loveliness? Certainly, she's lovely, but especially in
the double-edged sense in which loveliness is the subject of
the choral ode, loveliness as a projection of a terrible power.
Barbara's power is acknowledged also in the title of the play
and perhaps even in Shaw's choice of her name (foreign—in
the Greek sense of barbarous—and thus potentially
dangerous, like Dionysus himself. The easy joke that it's
funny to find a military title attached to a woman's name
becomes more trenchant in this light).[2]

III

Having, I hope, justified the use of Dionysus in my formula, I'd like now to discuss some of the ways the play brings home a sense of marriage to a deep source of power both as an experience for the audience and a subject for reflection. I shall take as my main instance that prop out of which so much fun and festivity is made in the second act, Adolphus Cusins' big drum. Let me pause first to put it in dramatic context, because it's useful to remember where Cusins' entrance with the drum comes in the play. Earlier in the second act, Shaw has held together the details of his vivid portrait of life in the Salvation Army shelter by building his action out of a series of linked serio-comic power struggles that suggest a hierarchy of increasingly superior uses of power leading up to the power Barbara wields through the Army. The pivotal figure here is Bill Walker. He's able to impose his will briefly with his fists. He isn't conventionally afraid of hitting a woman, so he knocks down Rummy Mitchens and bloodies Jenny Hill's lip. He's thus a challenge to the Army's authority. Soon he will be matched against Major Barbara, but before that we have a sense of a relation to power similar to Bill's but significantly superior:

> Hit a girl in the jaw and only make her cry! If Todger Fairmile'd done it, she wouldnt a got up inside o ten minutes.

Fairmile is superior not merely because he's physically stronger, but because he's got better control of his power. He knows where and how to hit. Later, Fairmile will accept Bill Walker's spitting in his eye in true Christian fashion, not by simply turning the other cheek, but by praying for

105

him—taking good care to kneel on Bill's head while doing so. The fact of power is kept before us as a source of laughter.

But what Todger does to Bill physically is as nothing to what Barbara does to him mentally, and the confrontation between them is the climax of the first part of the act. It's a good example of one of Shaw's favorite kinds of scene—an encounter in which some superior figure sails over the difficulties posed by a hard-breathing, conventionally powerful opponent with an ease that turns the opponent's own energies against himself and leaves him bewildered. Major Barbara uses this kind of moral judo against Bill:

> **Barbara.** What's your name?
> **Bill** [*insolently*] Wots thet to you?
> **Barbara** [*calmly making a note*] Afraid to give his name. Any trade?
> **Bill.** Oo's afride to give is nime?
>
> . . .
>
> **Bill.** Aw dont blieve in your Gawd, no more than you do yourself.
> **Barbara.** [*sunnily apologetic and ladylike, as on a new footing with him*] Oh, I beg your pardon for putting your name down, Mr. Walker. I didnt understand. I'll strike it out.
> **Bill** [*taking this as a slight, and deeply wounded by it*] Eah! you let maw nime alown.
>
> . . .
>
> **Barbara.** Whats your trade?
> **Bill** [*still smarting*] Thets nao concern o yours.
> **Barbara.** Just so. [*Very businesslike*] I'll put you down as [*writing*] the man who—struck—poor little Jenny Hill— in the mouth.

Bill [*rising threateningly*] See eah. Awve ed enaff o this.
Barbara [*quite sunny and fearless*] What did you come to us for?
Bill. Aw cam for maw gel, see? Aw cam to tike her aht o this and to brike er jawr for er.
Barbara [*complacently*] You see I was right about your trade.
[*Bill, on the point of retorting furiously, finds himself, to his great shame and terror, in danger of crying instead.*]

The scene continues in this vein, and finally, after Bill is worked over by Barbara to the "point of breaking down," we hear the drum.

Thus the appearance of the drum marks the high point of Barbara's power as a Salvationist. The drum, which will now be on stage throughout the rest of the act, catches the comedy and the seriousness of Cusins' devotion to Barbara and to the vital force he honors in her and in all the religions he collects. He and Barbara kiss over the drum, "Evidently," Shaw remarks, "not for the first time, as people cannot kiss over a big drum without practice." As so often, what looks like a bit of parenthetical Shavian cuteness is dramatically central. The kiss over the drum was a very effective and funny moment in the original production. The fact is, it *can't* be done without practice, and when you see it you enjoy the expertness the practice has created, the skillful complicity of the lovers in handling this funny and tender accomplishment. Once again, skill is needed, a superior control, to manage the large and awkward instrument and make it conform to their desires. At the same time, the image makes us think of the kiss itself in connection with the big drum, and we sense the festive, explosive power of both.

The suggestiveness of the drum grows as it sits on stage during the dialogue between Cusins and Undershaft, which includes the chorus from the *Bacchae* and deals with power, religion, love, Euripides, Dionysus, and how to win Barbara. Their colloquy starts with a reference to the drum, leads to Undershaft's announcement of his gospel of money and gunpowder, and contains Cusins' assertion that he is a sincere Salvationist. When he declares that the Army has revealed "the true worship of Dionysus" to him, he concludes by playing a "thundering flourish" on the drum.

At the end of the act, when Undershaft has given his check to the Army—indicating where a power even greater than Salvationism lies—an "immense rejoicing" breaks out, accompanied offstage by a full band and onstage by Cusins on the drum, as he acknowledges Undershaft as Dionysus:

Dionysus Undershaft has descended. I am possessed.

To the Greeks, of course, Dionysus was a late-arriving god who manifested his power by converting other religions to his own. The parade marches off to the beat of the big drum, playing a tune from Donizetti that the Army has converted to its own purposes, now converted again to the service of Dionysus Undershaft.

In the last scene of the play we come to the god's own lair, the heavenly city of St. Andrew Undershaft. The stage setting is designed to illustrate Undershaft's relation to power, the meaning of his gospel:

> . . . *The crest of a slope . . . where the high explosives are dealt with. . . . Across the crest runs an emplacement of concrete, with a firestep, and a parapet which suggests a fortification, because there is a huge cannon . . . peering across it at the town. . . . Several dummy soldiers more or less mutilated, with straw protruding from their gashes, have been shoved out of the way under the landing. A few others are nearly upright against the shed; and one has fallen forward and lies, like a grotesque corpse, on the emplacement. . . . Down on the emplacement*

*behind the cannon is a trolley carrying a huge conical bombshell
with a red band painted on it.*

As we realize from the jokes about carelessness with
matches and the discussion of how explosives are made, the
characters in this scene are literally sitting on a powder keg.
And somewhere out in Manchuria, not dummy soldiers but
real ones are being blown to smithereens by Undershaft's
latest success. What we get in this scene is not of course a plea
for munitions manufacturing, but a dizzying trio on the
theme that power exists and that individual life can partake
of it, wed itself to reality. Or rather, that trio, more subtly
and articulately than the drum, makes us feel the excitement,
the process of the wedding. It is not a moral or political
conclusion the play offers us, though it stimulates and colors
our moral and political thought, but the feeling of how
elating it can be to make contact with reality.

Cusins makes his decision. He is selling his soul for
"Reality and power." All that remains is for the third
member of the Bacchic triumvirate to make up her mind.
And of course she does, for she loves Cusins and has found
her place and her work. She will be about her father's
business. "Oh for my drum!" Cusins has cried, and now
Barbara cries, "Glory Hallelujah!" and kisses him.

Cusins. My dearest: consider my delicate health. I
cannot stand as much happiness as you can.

Barbara. Yes: it is not easy work being in love with me,
is it? But it's good for you.

Barbara, loveliness, Dionysus, dangerous power, the power
that makes the wars and revolutions and religions of the
world—the play has fused their meanings. Undershaft strikes
the Dionysiac note once more in the last line, "Six o'clock
tomorrow morning, Euripides."

109

This is what I mean, then, by the Marriage in Dionysus, the felt and celebrated union of the individual will to the vital sources of power in the world. More than a recurrent motif, it is a central vibration, a great energizing impulse in Shavian comedy—whether or not it is explicitly the subject of a play, as in *Major Barbara* and *Man and Superman.* The Marriage in Dionysus, for example, is what Vivie Warren opts for when she rejects all other alliances as prostitution and waste. It is beautifully expressed in the climactic image of *Androcles and the Lion.* Just as the Christians enjoy a relation to power that is superior to that of the Romans, so the gentle tailor who has a way with animals can dance gracefully and safely with a beast that terrifies an emperor. And thus the unforgettable "silhouette" of that play: Androcles waltzing with his lion before the astonished Roman crowd. In later plays like *Heartbreak House,* the marriage can become parodic. We feel its failure to take place with full efficacy, as when Ellie Dunn "marries" the nodding Captain Shotover—and the dynamite he has been storing to destroy the enemies of vitality is exploded not by the "mind ray" he has claimed to be working on, but by an accident of war.

Awareness of this motif can have a bearing on performance as well as criticism. Remembering its presence in Shaw may help those actors and directors who are afraid of Shaw's intelligence and long speeches and of what critics who could neither do his day's work nor think his night's thought still like to call his "bloodlessness." The key to Shaw is festivity, energy shared generously with the audience, contact with a dangerous but lovely source. When Joan, at the end of her play, exclaims, "O God that madest this beautiful earth, when will it be ready to receive Thy saints?" too many actresses concentrate only on the pathos of the second half of the line. But "beautiful earth" is equally important, and it is crucial to the final moment of the play. For what animates all Shaw's saints and heroes, as it animated their creator—is an impulsive love of beauty, a beauty specifically of this earth.

Notes

1. For the biographical facts about Murray's relation to *Major Barbara,* see Sidney P. Albert, " 'In More Ways Than One': *Major Barbara's* Debt to Gilbert Murray," *Educational Theatre Journal,* XX (May, 1968), 123-40.

2. I am not the first to suspect some kind of critical significance in the play's references to Dionysus and Euripides. Cf., e.g., Margery M. Morgann, *The Shavian Playground* (London, 1972), p. 138; Charles Berst, *Bernard Shaw and the Art of the Drama* (Urbana, 1973), p. 166 n. 17; Maurice Valency, *The Cart and the Trumpet* (New York, 1973), pp. 257-58; and J.L. Wisenthal, *The Marriage of Contraries: Bernard Shaw's Middle Plays* (Cambridge, Mass., 1974), pp. 66-67, 68, 74. An unshakable academic reflex compels me to point out that Wisenthal's "marriage" refers to the union of dialectical opposites, rather than the kind I describe. More to the point, Wisenthal agrees with me that "power" is a central subject of *Major Barbara,* but he takes the word in the sense of "control or command over others," whereas I think Shaw primarily has in mind the meaning accorded it in the physical sciences, as in "electrical power," i.e., the capacity to produce energy. Wisenthal also, very interestingly, suggests Ibsen's *Emperor and Galilean* as a possible source for the religio-Dionysiac elements in Shaw's play.

BENTLEY ON PIRANDELLO: FORTY YEARS LATER

BY ANNE PAOLUCCI

When I first read *The Playwright as Thinker* (The World Publishing Co., Meridian Books, New York, 1946) there was little in the critical literature on Luigi Pirandello to make one pause and take notice. At first it seemed ironic to me that the only truly exciting new words on the Nobel Prize winning Italian dramatist came from Eric Bentley—a critic who was neither Italian nor committed unconditionally to the academy. Italian critics had dealt with Pirandello's work in a traditional manner, following the accepted categories and trying to make something out of characters who eluded definition on stage, themes that were not clear statements, and language which seemed often excessive and distracting—melodramatic even. The few who had dealt with Pirandello in English suffered pretty much the same difficulty.

Criticism for the most part had missed the point; Pirandello's novelty eluded standard interpretation; the very things that made him strikingly new were often interpreted as

113

excesses (e.g. too cerebral, etc.) Bentley was the first to give Pirandello immediate standing as an author who was innovative and creative in a way that defied familiar critical molds. He brought Pirandello's work—particularly the plays—into the spectrum of existing European drama. His initial comments aroused interest and whetted the appetite for the plays themselves. By focusing on Pirandello's revolutionary handling of the stage—a critical theme that has since been explored in many and different ways—Bentley provided the best introduction possible to those extraordinary plays. For the first time in this country we began to look at the playwright who had, a generation earlier, made a large impact on the theater world with the Pitoëff production of *Six Characters in Search of an Author*. In America no one was really sure about Pirandello yet; although he had visited the United States with Marta Abba and had seen a number of his plays staged, his audience was limited. It was Bentley who provided the foundations on which future critics were to build. He made Pirandello's plays accessible as important theater as well as important literature. He did this first by placing Pirandello in a critical position that was unassailable, making comparisons with other modern dramatists and emphasizing his novelty and his insight of the stage. Even today, at a distance of almost forty years, Bentley's pages are fresh and intriguing—a provocative assessment of Pirandello's special genius. Time has proved Bentley right on target.

In the few paragraphs he devotes to Pirandello in *The Playwright as Thinker,* Bentley isolates the single most important feature of the new playwright: "The quintessence of Pirandellism is [the] peculiar relation of intellect to feeling." He knocks down the charge of "cerebral" and shows that everything is translated into human responses of

114

the most immediate kind. He glosses over the constantly repeated critical notion of "relativity" and tries a different approach: "Ostensibly Pirandello's plays and novels are about the relativity of truth, multiple personality, and the different levels of reality. But it is neither these subjects nor—precisely—his treatment of them that constitutes Pirandello's individuality. . . . Another and deeper Pirandello awaits discovery." In short, it is Bentley who first warns us that the discovery of the real Pirandello requires that "relativity . . . be set on one side." And he goes on to point out that "there is actually nothing in the plot of *Right You Are* to indicate that there can be no correct version of the story. The unusual thing is that we do not know what it is. . . . The truth, Pirandello wants to tell us again and again, is concealed, *concealed,* CONCEALED! It is not his business to uncover the problem and solve it for us. . . . The solution is the problem. . . " (148-149).

How different from the metaphysical arguments used for and against Pirandello by so many critics and scholars right down to our own day! Bentley tears away the heavy structure of academic criticism and shows us the way to *feel* the novelty in Pirandello. He is not afraid of unconventional strategies and ignores the familiar categories. He approaches *Right You Are* with no formal preconceptions at all. For that reason he is able to grasp the Pirandellian oscillation between theater and non-theater, character and mask. He even questions the so-called *pessimism* of Pirandello:

What a pessimist Pirandello is! says someone. Certainly. But again the point of Pirandello is not his philosophy—of relativity, personality, or pessimism—it is his power to conceal behind the intellectual artillery barrage the great armies of fighters and the yet greater hordes of noncombatants and refugees. Pirandello is a pessimist. So also must many of the people of Europe be, people who have lived through the extraordinary vicissitudes of the twentieth century, uncomprehending, passively suffering. . . . Pirandello, like Kafka, like Chaplin, speaks not for the aware and class-conscious proletarian but for the unaware, in-between, black-white-cotton—coated scapegoat. (151)

For the last two and a half pages of his eight-and-a-half-page discussion of Pirandello, Bentley departs even more radically from conventional critical analysis and provides us with a "note to the director of [*Right You Are*]" which is more enlightening than anything that could be said in a straightforward critical appraisal of action, character and theme:

Make a marked distinction between the enquirers into the story, who are a sort of chorus representing what Pirandello regards as the Mask and the three "real People" involved in the domestic tragedy. The Three are typical people of a middle-class tragedy in that they express grief and arouse pity without terror. Note how Pirandello's initial descriptions of the characters and his subsequent stage directions stress alike the genuineness and acuteness of their sufferings. (151-152)

He underscores—still in the guise of improvised stage directions—the need to bring out laughter "when perhaps weeping would seem more in order"; the tale must be "comedified." The old theatrical business of "mingling laughter and tears was never more calculated, more intricate, more meaningful, or more depressing than here." The directions finally focus on the dialectical form of the Pirandellian play: "Accentuate then—do not soften—the clashes of sound and color of which the play is composed. If you let it work, you will find the whole thing ultratheatrical" (153).

By not submitting to the programmed analysis which served so well right down to Ibsen, Strindberg, O'Neill and even—in our own time—Arthur Miller, by recognizing the crucial need for a new critical language to deal with Pirandello's new kind of theater—the Pirandellian fragments of idiosyncratic non-character or character no longer of one piece—by forcing us to view the Pirandellian stage as unfamiliar ground waiting to be discovered, Bentley gave Pirandellian studies the only proper direction, the only possible critical course to follow.

Early in the seventies, I wrote my book on Pirandello— *Pirandello's Theater: The Recovery of the Modern Stage for Dramatic Art* (Southern Illinois University Press, Carbondale, etc., 1974)—in which I tried to look at the plays through the spectrum of the contemporary theater. It was dedicated to Bentley because I felt, and still feel, that he was the first to see Pirandello as the Father of the Absurd. I examined Pirandello from a number of angles, comparing *Enrico IV* with *Hamlet* and looking at the "theater" plays from the perspective of the Absurd. I elaborated affinities with Beckett and Ionesco, recognized allegorical resonances similar to those found in the plays of Edward Albee, struggled with concepts which at the time were properly gut reactions and realized that Pirandello deserved a more thorough study placing him at the very center of the Absurd. The whole concept of non-theater, of dialectical inversions (of the kind that Vivian Mercier would insist on in his work on Beckett), of looking at the contemporary theater as "art transcending itself" (to use that provocative phrase of Hegel's) struck me as fertile critical ground. I had merely scratched the surface.

But I also knew that Bentley had provided me with the assurance I needed to follow such a path in dealing with a playwright who, in certain critical circles, was still more in the past than in the present or future.

I had worked with Eric Bentley on other projects in-between. He had asked me in the sixties to translate Pirandello's essay on the history of the Italian theater (it appeared as the Introduction to his *Genius of the Italian Theater,* The New American Library, Mentor Books, New York, 1964)—a task I would not have undertaken except on his insistence. Even earlier we had established communication in connection with a new translation I was preparing of Machiavelli's *Mandragola*—the first to appear since Stark Young's almost a quarter of a century earlier. Through these exchanges over the years, I learned that Bentley was a critic who could draw attention because he didn't create distance between the subject and the audience; he never posed, never assumed the kind of academic posture that discourages communication; he was himself, always respectful of the subject and always conveying a sense of immediacy and discovery. I saw in him the kind of critic I wanted to be, and recognized the affinities we shared even as I found my own style.

Since *The Playwright as Thinker,* Bentley has written much on the modern theater, including the theater of Pirandello. His latest collection of essays, published in 1985 as *Pirandellian Studies I* (ed. Walter J. Centuori, University of Nebraska/Lincoln), brings together samplings that cover almost forty years of critical writing—from 1946 to 1985 (including an original Bentley version of *Enrico IV* set on Long Island with the title *H for Hamlet*).[1] This most recent anthology of Bentley on Pirandello reminds us that Bentley indeed survives all the fads and special interests—Freudian,

Marxist, etc. Like T.S. Eliot and A.C. Bradley, he is able to give the reader the impression of *travelling* the distance with him, of *discovering* in the best Socratic tradition what is true not by statement but by the process of intelligent query. It is the kind of criticism that *lives* and *communicates* beyond its own time.

One does not need to survey the entire literature of Bentley on Pirandello here; enough has been said to convince the reader, I hope, that from the very beginning Eric Bentley had hit on the essential life of Pirandello's theater and was able to communicate that discovery to others.

But he went further, as we know. In addition to critical writings that continued to track Pirandello's special genius through modern and contemporary theater, he also took on the important task of translating the major plays. We know how successful *Naked Masks* proved to be and still is; for the first time, Pirandello's major plays were made available in a popular format for use in the classroom, a publishing event that made Pirandello easily available for production also.

What emerges in the total picture of this truly Pirandellian critic (Pirandellian, certainly, in his unconventional way of handling the subject and in his *organic* conception of the play as an *experience* to be felt and identified with) is a new critical language which is *created by and through the experience of the play itself.* I have never felt so completely inside the Pirandellian world as I do when reading Bentley—even if I disagree with him. It is the same feeling I have for Eliot or Bradley. Such critics keep us riveted to the text.

Bentley's critical language serves as a catalyst for explorations beyond Pirandello. The notion of the "solution as the problem" or the "concealment" of a statement that could explain things takes us imperceptibly to the center of the Theater of the Absurd: where action is cyclical or circular and open-ended; where nothing happens and everything changes; where characters are fragments of a mirror image, states of mind and emotions, attitudes and moments of being which remain unresolved; where language is shattered syntax and hysterical outbursts, refrains and irrational observations, non sequiturs, and verbal extremes of silence and unintelligible rantings.

Pirandello admired innovation. He respected leaps of genius and appreciated what might have seemed to others simply aberrations. In his essay on the history of the Italian theater he reviews the central role played by the Italian theater as it moved ahead from religious forms to the living (seemingly still "crude") forms of a natural environment. He cites Boccaccio and reviews the spirit of "romance" that entered the Italian theater at that time, "a sense of movement." But with Goldoni, Pirandello finds the true genius of the modern Italian and European theater. Like Pirandello the critic, looking at the innovative genius of a Goldoni, Bentley has isolated for us the very heart of Pirandello's new theater, looking forward as Pirandello did, and placing the new experience in the history of the contemporary theater.

Bentley may yet write on Pirandello, but whether he does or not, he will always be celebrated as the first to have discovered the need for a new argument and a new language to help grasp Pirandello and his stage. Through Bentley we have learned to see with Pirandello that the stage is the vehicle for sorting out the masks we all wear, for stripping our familiar selves down to the mysterious core in all of us. We learn to accept the dialectic oscillations that enable us to face the infinite mirror reflections that are the movement from statement to question, from question to infinite suggestivity. And in that knowledge we find the pulse of our true identity.

Notes

1. *Pirandellian Studies* is a journal. The essays will be republished in book form as *The Pirandello Commentaries,* Northwestern University Press, 1986. *H for Hamlet* is available in Bentley's *Monstrous Martyrdoms,* 1985. [M.B.]

WEDEKIND AND WITKIEWICZ (WITKACY)[1]

BY JAN KOTT

1. Wedekind

Frank Wedekind (1864-1918) was undoubtedly one of the most interesting, distinct and characteristic figures to have appeared on the theatre scene of Scandinavia, the Hapsburg Empire and Germany in the period between Strindberg and Brecht. I write "figure" because Wedekind was not only the author of *The Awakening of Spring*, and a cycle of plays about Lulu, but he was also his own legend during his lifetime and after his death. He acted in all of his own plays and he also played many figures from the "Moderna" off stage. What is most important, however, is his place in the history of the new theatre. He began where Strindberg left off (even Wedekind's first wife Frida had been Strindberg's second wife) and he saw the German stage through to the young Brecht. He brought all of Strindberg's mysticisms down to earth and demonized them. One could probably say that

Wedekind is the Strindberg in George Grosz's illustrations of *Ecce Homo*. Everything is outlined in thick expressionist strokes; the means of expression are sharpened to caricature and the grotesque, while the rigors of action and verisimilitude are already completely relaxed. The disintegration of form becomes the method. But this note is not about Wedekind, but about his influence on Witkacy (Stanisław Ignacy Witkiewicz, 1885-1939).

It is remarkable that so much has been written about Witkacy, and that no one has looked more closely into the influence of the Wedekind legend and plays. The first one to note the ties between *The Water Hen, The Awakening of Spring* and *Earth Demon* (this was the title of *Erdgeist* when staged in Cracow in 1904 in Jadwiga Beaupré's translation) was Grzegorz Sinko in a review of the Teatr Wspőczesny production in Warsaw: "In Act Three, the overworked and erotically aroused Tadzio brings to mind characters from Wedekind's *The Awakening of Spring* and especially Hugenberg from *Earth Spirit*. . . . The first scene of *The Water Hen* is distinctly related to the last scene of *Earth Spirit*, in which Lulu ironically provokes Doctor Schön to commit murder: 'Be quiet and kill me here!' She also reminds him, just as ironically, of the words he dictated to a reporter after the suicide of Schwarz: 'You suffer from a persecution mania' " (*Teatr*, No. 11, 25 May 1980).

At almost the same time and independently of Sinko, Daniel Gerould writes (in his monograph, *Witkacy*—Seattle and London, 1981) about the impact of Wedekind's title vamp Lulu on *The Water Hen* and about the fact that Tadzio was undoubtedly taken from the demonic boy Hugenberg, who was sent to reform school for visiting Lulu. In addition to these more obvious details, Gerould also adds the accurate observation about the coexistence of characters from the world of high finance and international crime with decadent

124

artistic circles and intellectuals in the Lulu plays. Witkacy undoubtedly found stimulus in this mixture for his own "joining of art and neuroses, violence and metaphysics."

Here Gerould hits the nail on the head. In many of Witkacy's plays one is struck by the recurrence of this explosive and so theatrically innovative Wedekind combination (frequently repeated by the Expressionists and even Brecht). It suffices to cite the cast of characters from *Earth Spirit* to notice immediately how "Witkacian" a café this is: two doctors, one of them a publisher who has a son, an actor and director of a theatre; one painter; one reporter; one prince; "a traveler from Africa"; one valet; one maid; one coachman; and, above all, two vamps: Lulu and a countess—a great lesbian and artist.

The most "pre-Witkacian" of characters outside of the main figures is Prince Escerny, who finds himself in Lulu's dressing room right after announcing his discoveries at Lake Tanganyika. And here is a sample of the dialogue, which I could swear is from Witkacy:

> **Escerny:** Imagine, madam, that instead of that rabble you have only one viewer, chosen by yourself.
> **Lulu:** I never see anyone anyway.
> **Escerny:** A hunting lodge—you hear the lapping of waves from the nearby lake. In my African expeditions I am forced to apply a quite inhuman tyranny. . . .
> **Lulu:** [*clasps a strand of pearls around her neck while looking at herself in the mirror*] That's a good lesson.
> **Escerny:** What happiness for a woman to have a man completely dependent on her.
> **Lulu:** [*jingling her spurs*] Ah, yes!

After this visit in Lulu's dressing room, Prince Escerny vanishes as suddenly as he had appeared:

> **Lulu:** The prince is travelling.

Rodrigo: [a circus acrobat] To put his kingdom up for auction?

Lulu: He left to discover an unknown tribe of savages somewhere in Africa.

I had always thought that Prince Edgar of Nevermore, who "was eaten by a tiger in the Janjapara Jungle," while "he read the work of Russell and Whitehead, *Principia Mathematica,* to the last" was just one more of Bronisław Malinowski's[2] "doubles," but it turns out that he, too, wandered into *The Water Hen* from *Earth Spirit.*

The Water Hen ends in lightning flashes of bullets and the din of hand grenades. "The world is going to pieces." The world is going to pieces and the revolution approaches in many of Witkacy's plays. It always seemed to me that this approaching revolution originated in his experiences of the year 1917. But perhaps the *Earth Spirit* molded this vision as well. In the second act the painter Schwarz lifts letters from a tray: "News always makes me tremble. Each day I am more and more horrified that the world is headed for inevitable annihilation." Is this not Witkacy? And at the end of that same act "A revolution has broken out in Paris." What kind of revolution? Certainly not the Revolution of 1870. And it has nothing to do with the action in *Earth Spirit.* It is not motivated psychologically or historically. It is introduced on another plane. On a plane of disintegration and annihilation. Just as in Witkacy. Lulu's second husband has just hung himself. He had found out from the publisher Schön that the latter has been "keeping" Lulu for years. On stage is his son, Alva, who is also the vamp's lover:

Schön: [*violently angry*] He had no principles. Nor a drop of morality [he, the husband who hung himself—J.K.] [*He suddenly gains control of himself*] Revolution in Paris?

Alva: Our publishers were struck dumb, as if by a thunderbolt. Everything has come to a grinding halt.
Schön: This will probably allow me to get out of this. If only the police would arrive. Time is now more valuable than gold. [*Doorbell rings.*]
Alva: They're coming . . . [*Schön wants to go to the door*].
Lulu: [*blocks his way*] Wait a minute, there is blood on you.

It is exactly this type of "anti-natural" dialogue, undoubtedly Wedekind's discovery, that was picked up by Witkacy; and the end of this dialogue between the scoundrel, artist, and Lady Macbeth:

Lulu: Wait I'll wipe it. [*She sprinkles perfume on her handkerchief and wipes the blood from Schön's hand.*]
Schön: That's the blood of your husband.
Lulu: It leaves no stain.
Schön: You are a monster.
Lulu: You will marry me anyway. [*The doorbell keeps ringing in the hallway.*]

In the year 1902, after the incredible success of *Earth Spirit* in Berlin's Kleines Theatre, Friedrich Kaysler, one of Max Reinhardt's best actors, said to Wedekind: "You have strangled the naturalist's beast of verisimilitude and have reintroduced the element of play into the theatre." It is from this perspective of Wedekind's role as precursor that one should consider his influence on Witkacy's dramaturgy.

2. *The Water Hen*

The Water Hen is the third "waterfowl" in a play title after *The Wild Duck* and *The Seagull.* Gerould adds Maeterlinck's *The Blue Bird* to this obvious list and one more seagull from Knut Hamsun. *The Wild Duck* plays in symbolic opposites and Chekhov's "seagull" is both a symbol and a stage prop (as when Shamrayev pulls it out of the cupboard at the end of the play). But Witkacy's "water hen" with its metathesis designates if not a profession then certainly special talents and predilections. I can still remember how in Karpowicz's café in Zakopane before the war a member of Witkacy's circle would speak of a certain lady of that group as a "water hen."

3. The "Bag"[3]

Witkacy's experiences from his years in Russia are still a blank spot in his personal and intellectual biography. We will probably never gain access to his personal experiences, but it is possible to recreate his literary, theatrical and philosophical experiences to a certain degree. For Witkacy, who was not yet thirty years old when he arrived in Petersburg, these must have been years of enormous intellectual receptivity. Russia was undergoing a period of great artistic ferment with its many avant-gardes in poetry, painting and theatre. It was then that the Russian Formalist School of literary research was coming into being. The Formalists cast off all geneticisms and psychologisms and examined literature as artifact (as we would say today) and text. The art of the word. One could find the rigor of poetics and arrange an entire system of devices for poetry and even for drama. At that time the novel still eluded the rigors of linguistic and stylistic analysis and appeared to exist only on the plane of "contents," that is, beyond art and form.

This position was most clearly and consistently represented by Gustav Shept (1879-1937), a professor at Moscow University and a scholar of Husserl and Kant. He wielded a great influence on the young, among them Roman Jakobson. He excluded the novel from the terrain of poetics and considered it a rhetorical form. He called it "a contemporary form of moral propaganda" and denied it any kind of esthetic value. Bakhtin writes about this in the essay, "Discourse on the Novel" (in *The Dialogic Imagination: Four Essays,* ed. by Michael Holquist, Austin, 1982, beginning on p. 267). Gustav Shept first published his ideas about the novel in *Esteticheskiye fragmenty* (I do not know the date) and later, in greater detail, in the book, *Vnutrennaya forma slov,* Moscow, 1927. Shept was not alone in his opinions. Victor Vinogradov (1895-1969) expressed similar thoughts in "On Artistic Prose" (1930) and other essays. Earliest of all was Victor Shklovsky (*Vozkreseniye slova,* Petersburg, 1914, and *O Poezii i zaumnon yazyke,* 1916). Vinogradov was probably the first to coin the term "formal hybrid" when speaking of the novel. The phrase was in the air.

The formulation and entire theory of the novel as a "bag" seems to be not so much a result of Witkacy's esthetic assumptions (or perhaps not necessarily) as much as a replica of the earlier opinions of Russian Formalists. The matter seems worthy of closer investigation. Witkacy's theories of "new form" did not spring like Minerva out of his head; their originality lies rather in their garish and brutal formulation in Witkacy's idiolect, that is, the language spoken by Witkacy's scoundrels and water hens.

4. *The Shoemakers* and *The Lower Depths*

About seven years ago I was in Osaka at a performance of Gorky's *The Lower Depths.* The production was traditional, in Russian costume, and at first it made the impression of a Stanislavsky replica. It wasn't until halfway through the first act that I realized something was different. There was no furniture in the basement dwelling. No chairs, no beds, only mats. Or some sort of rags on the floor. And all the actors

129

were lying on the floor or squatting down Japanese style. In the first and fourth acts, Alyosha also squatted. He played a harmonica and mended shoes. Mended shoes and played the harmonica.

In Witkacy's *The Shoemakers* the most stubbornly and imposingly repetitive stage image is that of the shoemaker apprentices mending shoe soles. From the first scene of the first act to the end with almost no stopping. Theatrical interdependencies exist not only on the plane of contents and various "ideolos" but also in certain especially evocative situations and scenes. If Witkacy saw *The Lower Depths* with Alyosha stubbornly mending soles, this image must have stayed in his memory. Perhaps it would be worth asking a few of the actors who remember the prewar productions of *The Lower Depths* (solutions to staging problems were generally applied over and over again during this period) if Alyosha mended shoes on stage (there is no such information given in the text itself).

5. Artaud

In his "First Manifesto of the Theatre of Cruelty," Artaud writes: "We will produce, with no regard for the text . . . a Marquis De Sade tale in which eroticism will be transposed, and allegorically characterized and dressed in a way to make the cruelty violently external and to hide all the rest." Artaud's manifesto is from 1932 and Witkacy had never heard of Artaud. And as far as I know, he never read De Sade either. But there is something amazing in the way Witkacy in many of his plays realizes Artaud's program and his formal "reading" of De Sade.

This is worth mulling over. The "catastrophic" Witkacy (where in the world is this catastrophism now?) is frighteningly passé. "The fumes of meaninglessness" are intolerably burped up even in professional theatre and existential metaphysics no longer send shivers down the spine. Contrary to Witkacy's prognoses, the metaphysical feelings and experiences which religion gives have revived with full force in Europe, Asia, Africa, and in both the Americas, so what has remained of his forecasts? I think that beyond Witkacy's furious theatricality, the most interesting thing in his plays could be the subepidermal presence of the epoch: of the Moderna and the early twenties—the intellectual styles, erotic accents, customs, temptations and taboos, seductive gestures and even costumes. "Through the center door, inside, to the right of the fireplace, enters Sophia of the Abencérages Kremlinska dressed in an automobile costume, with a riding whip in her hand. Behind her also in automobile outfits: Sir Thomas Blazo de Liza, Teerbroom and Oliphant Beedle. Behind them in a cardinal's robe is Dr. Don Nino de Gevach and in the full uniform of the Guard of the Cuirassiers Regiment, Count Tchurnin-Koketayev" (*Dainty Shapes and Hairy Apes,* an early Witkiewicz play of 1922). If I were a director of Witkacy plays, I would spend hours listening to hit songs of the period and looking at old silent films, photos of the stars, and pictures from operettas. What was the most fashionable dance in 1922? The shimmy. And it is exactly to the accompaniment of the shimmy that Nina and Liza ought to return from the "orgy" "in their bathrobes: Nina in blue, Liza in red."

It is probably not too late for a Witkacy retro. I dream about a Witkacy firmly planted in his epoch.

6. A Few More Words About Wedekind and "demonic girls."

Tilly Newes played Lulu at the Vienna premiere (1905) of *Pandora's Box,* the second in the cycle of Lulu plays.

Professional actors performed, but the production was a semiprivate affair, one time only, chiefly at the initiative of Karl Kraus, who also talked the director into having the young debutante Tilly Newes play the role of the "earth spirit." She was not yet twenty and up to that time she had played mainly boys. In this performance, Wedekind played Jack the Ripper, who murders Lulu at the end of the play. As Tilly writes in her memoirs, this was "the role of her life." Wedekind was over forty at the time and he immediately fell in love with his "victim." He sat next to her at supper after the premiere and asked her right off: "Miss Tilly, are you still a virgin?" He apparently put this question to all unmarried women. It seems to me that we are already quite close to some of Witkacy's dialogues.

The day after the premiere, Wedekind sent Tilly a letter, showered her with compliments and raved that she played Lulu "like a madonna." Madonna-like? Why? The riddle was solved by my colleague from Stony Brook, Leo Treitler: like the perverse madonnas of Munch. In *Pandora's Box*, Lulu returns from prison and is almost a professional "water hen." "Like a madonna?" Why? But we have other testimony to the fact that the Moderna was discovering the sexual charms of Lolitas in short dresses and black stockings. Once again we are close to Witkacy and his demonic girls: Iza Kretchborski—"very highbred and rabidly attractive" (*Tumor Brainiowicz*); Amusetta—"blue ribbons in her hair . . . in a light gray dress, tied with a blue sash" (*The New Deliverance*); Piggykins—"a blonde ten-year-old dressed in white with pink ribbons. Beautiful as an angel. Dark, enormous eyes" (*Gyubal Wahazar*); the ten-year-old but already aroused Sophie (*The Anonymous Work*); and (most in the Wedekind mode) Janulka, daughter of Fizdejko—a fifteen-year-old "bovine blonde, quite tall and thin. Pretty and quite spiritual, with something monstrous in her face. That 'something' is accented subtly.'' (Perhaps I am mistaken, but the latter seems to be an accurate portrait of Irena Solska: a perverse mistress of Witkacy's and the most talented Polish actress of the Moderna. Please see the 1926 drawing of Solska signed T.E. which is reproduced in Gerould's American edition —J.K.)

> **Janulka:** [*regretfully*]: So you won't ever love me, Gottfried?
>
> **The Master:** You can be my mistress this very night, but we won't ever love one another. Feelings are only a pretext for Pure Form in life.
>
> **Janulka:** [*cheerfully*] Oh, if that's what you mean, it's wonderful. I was only afraid there might be something ascetic. Because I have a body too, Gottfried, and a very pretty one at that [*rubs up against him*].

This seduction by the young girl has nothing in common (even after inverting the sexes) with the play of high and low in Gombrowicz and with his fascination with young-ness/youth. Kavol Irzykowski, the most sophisticated Polish critic of this period, once wrote about the dressing room of the soul. Wedekind and Witkacy's Eros is a costume for both soul and body, but both of these changes of clothes take place in a theatre dressing room and through use of theatrical props. Perhaps this is that famous decadence.

Earth Spirit begins with a scene in a painter's studio where Lulu is posing for a portrait dressed like Pierrot with a long shepherd's staff. This portrait will later hang on the wall in each of the following acts of both plays about Lulu. Witkiewicz, as we know, ran about the streets of Zakopane dressed like Pierrot. Pierrot was a favorite costume of the Moderna and it is enough to recall the blue Picasso and

133

Wojtkiewicz. Witkacy did not have to remember Lulu. But Wedekind *is* important here and so are the costumes.

In this complex dialectic of anachronism and precursorship, Witkiewicz had no peer among his contemporaries. It was Witkacy's role as precursor that amazed everyone at first, while today his anachronistic side is more interesting. The Witkiewicz of the Moderna has been uncovered several times in the last few years, perhaps most convincingly by Jan Błoński, a noted Polish literary scholar and critic. But it seems that the theatre has still not noticed. The historical, anachronistic and decadent Witkiewicz of the Moderna still awaits his director and appearance on stage. Only Tadeusz Rozewicz presaged this Witkiewicz.

Translated by Lillian Vallee

Notes

1. The Polish version of this paper was published in *Pamiętnik Teatralny*, 1, No. 4, 1985.

2. Bronisław Malinowski (1884-1942), anthropologist and Witkiewicz's boyhood friend. Witkiewicz accompanied Malinowski on his travels to Ceylon and Australia on the eve of World War II.

3. Witkiewicz's term for the novel as a sort of grab bag; a mélange of life's elements. A "bag" is capacious.

"HOW HAPPY COULD I BE WITH BOTH!" BRECHT'S EARLY LOVES

BY MARTIN ESSLIN

How happy could I be with either,
Were t'other dear charmer away!

John Gay, *The Beggar's Opera*

When Brecht—later to become the great renewer of Gay's masterpiece—was confronted with the same situation as Captain Macheath, two women claiming him in marriage, his reaction was quite unlike the Captain's:

Asked whom he wanted to marry, he replied, somewhat cynically but definitely amused: "Both."

This account of one of the climactic scenes of Brecht's early life occurs in a book, which has not hitherto received much attention, containing the reminiscences of the two, by now octogenarian, ladies involved.[1] Read in conjunction with Brecht's early diaries (published in 1975)[2] a much clearer picture of Brecht's early loves emerges. The story is one which, indeed, might well have constituted the plot of a Restoration comedy, with, at its center, a character that has much in common with that great polygamous charmer, Captain Macheath. But, at the same time, it is rich in tragic overtones.

What value has our knowledge of these biographical details for our understanding of Brecht? I am by no means inclined to overestimate it. If Brecht's person and character had not been ruthlessly exploited by the official propaganda machine in the GDR and been distorted into that of a cheap plaster saint, one might well pass over it in silence. Nevertheless the story in many ways illuminates not only Brecht's private, but also his artistic personality and can shed some light on the genesis of one of his most interesting and enigmatic plays—*Im Dickicht der Städte.*

The book containing the reminiscences of the mothers of Brecht's first children is a curious miscellany of memoirs and interviews. Its bulk consists of Paula Banholzer's own narrative of her relationship with Brecht, followed by the transcript of an interview with her, which basically repeats her story in somewhat more colloquial language; and by an interview with Marianne Zoff, Brecht's first wife.

Paula Banholzer, the daughter of a respected Augsburg physician, was fifteen when she met Brecht in the spring of 1916; he was eighteen. She had first noticed him following her on her way to and from school. After first attempts to approach her had failed, he managed to attract her attention in the Augsburg skating rink and by the beginning of 1917 they had become friends. In the following summer he took Paula, whom he had nicknamed "Bittersüss," occasionally translating the word into English as "Bittersweet," and later usually shortening it to Bi, on long walks by the banks of Augsburg's river, the Lech.

Bi, who had originally thought him ugly and unkempt, was fascinated by his conversation:

> He talked about his plans for the future, read to me at times from his work or gave me a small poem he had written. Slowly I started to like him and was impressed by his knowledge and ability.[3]

Bi became a member of the circle of friends (among them George Pfanzelt, Otto Mueller-Eisert, Caspar Neher, Otto Andreas Bezold, Heinrich Hagg), whom Brecht dominated to the point where they appeared to Bi to be his bonded slaves. Together they went for long walks, swam in the river, listened to Brecht singing his poems to the guitar and visited the Augsburg fairground, the "Plärrer," where Brecht was fascinated by the barkers, the waxworks, the merry-go-rounds and their tinny music, acrobats and freak shows, and above all by the "Schiffschaukeln"—the "boat swings" in which a couple could propel itself high into the air, standing up, with the girl's skirts blowing in the wind.

By the autumn of 1918 Bi had graduated from her high school—the Maria-Theresia Schule—and Brecht, who had not yet been called up for military service, was studying at Munich University.

> Gradually the plan and the desire must have ripened within him to possess me wholly. Again and again he talked to me enthusiastically how beautiful it would be if we could spend a whole night together. And I also thought it would be quite nice to spend a night with him in cosy conversation.[4]

The implication here is clearly that Bi, brought up as a Victorian middle-class girl, did not know what spending the night together meant.

The occasion arose—it must have been towards the end of September 1918, for Brecht started his military service as a medical orderly in the Augsburg military hospital on 1 October—when her parents sent Bi out on an expedition to buy black market food in the country, an activity which then—and in the Second World War—was called "Hamstern" (i.e. collecting food for hoarding, as hamsters do in their pouches). The idea was that she should pretend to be spending four days in the country, but in fact, return to Augsburg after two days, leave her bags at the station and go on to Munich.

> When I got back to Augsburg with my "hamster"-bag, Brecht's friend Otto Andreas Bezold met me at the railway station. He took the bag from me, put it in the "Left-Luggage" and deposited me, with many greetings, in the next train to Munich which took off presently. At the Munich Hauptbahnhof Brecht was waiting for me with a face radiating anticipatory pleasure.[5]

After roaming around the streets of Munich, sightseeing, they decided they must find her a room in a hotel.

> We went to the "Reichsadler," a hotel near the Hauptbahnhof. I was afraid to spend the night alone in the hotel. . . . How glad I was to hear from Brecht that he too had taken a room there, which was—what a coincidence!—right next to mine.[6]

Inevitably when she had gone to bed, Brecht appeared. The girl, glad not to be alone, agreed, still in all innocence, that he might lie down in bed beside her. When, after the first amorous approaches, he realized that she did not know what it was all about —

> He no longer made any attempt at seducing me, but took me in his arms and told me the facts of life. For the rest of the night we only had that single topic of conversation, and with a great sense of empathy Brecht told me all. There could be no question of sleep. Our talk lasted till the morning.[7]

The next day, although the sleepless night had given Bi a headache, was spent in roaming around the city. When her headache got worse, they returned to the hotel. She lay down in her bed.

> While I was dosing half asleep he literally took me by surprise, and what is more: in a very clumsy manner. At that time Brecht was 21 years old [almost—he would reach that age on 10 February 1919, just over three months later. M.E.] and had up to that day—as he later assured me—never been with a woman. I am sure he was not lying, otherwise he would not have gone about it so clumsily[8] [*denn sonst hätte er sich nicht so angestellt*].

The German phrase is difficult to translate, it could also mean "made so heavy weather of it." But in the interview with the editors, the transcript of which follows her account, when asked whether she believed Brecht's assertion that he was still a virgin when he seduced her, she replied: "I am sure it was the truth. For no man who has already had a woman can pretend to act so ignorantly" [*so dumm kann sich kein Mann stellen, der schon einmal eine Frau gehabt hat*].[9]

When it became clear that the events of that clandestine expedition had resulted in Bi's becoming pregnant, Brecht immediately did the right thing and asked her father for Bi's hand. The answer was a categorical no. Bi was packed off to the country, a little place called Kimratshofen, in the Allgaeu some eighty miles southwest of Augsburg, where the family knew a trusted midwife, who had been a schoolfriend of Bi's sister. Not only did Brecht write her a daily letter, he frequently came to visit her on weekends, although in that winter of 1919, the first after Germany's defeat, the train service was very slow and he often lacked the money for the bus between the railway station at Kempten and Kimratshofen. He once trudged six hours through the snow to get there.

On 30 July 1919 Brecht's first child, a son, was born and named Frank (after Frank Wedekind) Otto Walter. On 2 August there was a christening party attended by some of Brecht's friends. Otto Mueller-Eisert and Caspar Neher acted as godfathers. Brecht was overjoyed.

But what were they to do with the child? Bi's family was adamant. It must not darken their doorstep in Augsburg. So it was put into care with a local family in Kimratshofen—in the house of a roadworker named Xaver Stark.

Shortly after her return to Augsburg Bi could not stand the separation from Brecht any longer and moved in with an aunt in Munich. This enabled her to participate in Brecht's life which more and more drifted towards the theatre. He took part in performances of his idol, the inspired beerhall comedian Karl Valentin. In 1920 he became a "dramaturg" with the Munich Kammerspiele. Bi met famous actors and actresses, among them Elisabeth Bergner. But she gradually noticed that the relationship had cooled. In July 1921 Bi took a job as a governess in Nuremberg.

Brecht's diaries, which start in June 1920, give the other side of the coin. He had quite a number of other girlfriends. One of them, Hedda Kuhn, whom he had met as a fellow student in 1917 when he started his "medical studies," also thought that he should marry her, but by August 1920 he was tired of her:

> A letter from He. I had not treated her well the last time . . . now she starts to lacerate me. . . . And I, who had grown tired of her, when she lay lazily in my bed and cried. . . . I now feel the fresh wind and the wind blows. . . . . The heavens ought to beat me with a shovel for my inclination towards lying and vanity. When I have the slightest doubt about Bi's innocence, I feel a blow to the bowels and I envy Job, so much does that stinging fly torment me. But when He[dda] goes into contortions uphill and downdale because I lured her out of her shell and left her stranded, I remain as cold as a cattle-dealer. . . . [10]

Another girlfriend, Marie Rose Aman, about whom he wrote one of his best early poems, "Erinnerung an die Marie A.," also appears, around the same time in Brecht's diaries (22 August 1920):

> Before that I went for a walk with Rosemarie, she has opened up and withered, I am leaving her altogether. God bless her![11]

And even Bi had lost some of her attraction for him. On 23 September 1920 he met her and they went to Munich to look for somewhere to live (still with a view to marriage). But—

> She has grown fat, immediately feels my disappointment, becomes sober and heavy. The night is dim, much sleep, without poetry. . . . It gets better in the morning, we roam about after accommodation—things get normal between us—not better. The loveliness has gone somewhat to seed.[12]

141

One of the reasons for his disillusionment with these, and other, girlfriends was the appearance of a new attraction—Marianne Zoff—who had started a two-year engagement as an opera singer at the Augsburg Municipal Theatre at the beginning of the 1919 season.

Shortly after she had made her debut Brecht appeared one evening in her dressing room:

> He came into my dressing room and complimented me. . . . I was surprised. . . . First of all about the appearance of this emaciated little man. He made a thoroughly unkempt impression, with his worn leather jacket, old corduroy trousers and a shabby visored cap in his hand. . . . I wondered why I had not thrown him out immediately, but, at the same time, looked at him not without fascination, as one contemplates an exotic animal in the zoo. I liked his ascetic skull, the thin-lipped mouth moved incessantly, the dark button-eyes were piercing, I liked his thin-limbed pianist's hands. . . . [13]

The friendship between Brecht and Marianne Zoff developed on long walks through Augsburg. Brecht called the dark, almost swarthy, half-Jewish beauty his "Maori woman." But it was a stormy affair. Marianne Zoff had a rich admirer, a middle-aged man called Recht, who was a typical "Schieber" of those times—one of the shady businessmen who speculated in that period of acute shortages of food and essential commodities in buying up scarce goods and immediately reselling them, without ever laying eyes on them, thus shifting them around ("schieben" means to "shift" or "push") and driving prices sky-high. Recht, who was Jewish, highly emotional and given to dramatic outbursts about possible suicide or murder (he carried a sword-stick), had been Marianne's protector for several years, and, when he had money, overwhelmed her with gifts of fur coats and jewelry. She professed to be disgusted by this man, whom she also accused of "perversity," yet she could not tear herself away from him. Brecht's diaries are a harrowing record of the angry scenes between him and Recht, Marianne's endless vacillations between the two men, her disgust of Recht, then, after some emotional scene and threats of violence, her pity for him, who was old and diabetic and had done so much for her. The parallels between this situation of a struggle between two men—one young and poetic, the other an old hardboiled businessman—and Brecht's play *Im Dickicht der Städte* are only too clear.

The situation reached its first climax when Marianne told Brecht on 11 March 1921 that her period had not come. On 13 March he noted in his diary:

> Now I am getting a child by the blackhaired Marianne Zoff, the brown-skinned one, who sings in the opera. I kneel down on the floor, cry, beat my breast, cross myself many times. The spring breeze blows through me as through a paper-stomach, I bow down. A son will be born to me. Again.[14]

The next day Brecht was in Munich and recorded in his diary that Bi was suffering from a vaginal catarrh, proof that she was by no means out of his intimate life. He also notes, in the same diary entry, that Hedda Kuhn has sent him 300 marks towards his expenses for a trip to Berlin. . .

On 21 March Marianne informed Brecht that because of the child she had once again made peace with Recht and would stay with him till June. On 23 March she let him know that she was going to marry Recht in spite of all. But on the following day she rushed into Brecht's room and told him in tears that she was disgusted with Recht and was finishing with him. On 27 March Recht appeared and made a scene during which it turned out that he was unaware of Marianne's pregnancy. When informed of it, he burst into tears. There followed a scene of melodramatic renunciation:

> "It was not vouchsafed to me to make this woman happy. So *you* make her happy!" I was to promise him, that, if she ever left me, as she was leaving him now, to give her up in the same way. He held out his hand, I shook it. . . . [15]

Two or three days later Brecht informed Marianne that he could not afford to marry her. She replied that she could not go through with having the baby without being married. By the end of April she went back to Recht on the understanding that he would marry her.

Brecht, on the other hand, was still keeping alive the hope of marrying Bi. On 13 April he assured her that he wanted it, and she told him that she would be ready for it in three or four years' time. On 28 April Brecht and Bi went to visit little Frank in Kimratshofen.

On 7 May 1921 Marianne had hemorrhages, on 9 May Recht told Brecht that she had been operated on and had lost the child. The suspicion that the operation had in fact been a deliberate abortion tormented Brecht and evoked violent feelings of resentment:

> Never before have I seen through the swindle of whoredom: romantic ideas of love seen so nakedly. So the pregnant whore discharges her load! And this cracked vessel into which the effluvia of all kinds of men have trickled, I wanted to put into my chamber! Hence her violent fear to be left, seen through, unmasked,

abandoned, her desperate hope that she needed a new, incredibly strong situation in order to tear her, at the last moment, away from whoredom, to spirit her away from it, to fight her out of it! Out of my life! Out! Let her now be used by others as their whore, throw her to the others, leave her to R[echt]![16]

But a week later Brecht was already making plans that Frank should be given to Marianne—to replace the aborted child. In July 1921 Bi Banholzer had taken a job as a governess in Nuremberg. One day she received a letter from a girlfriend telling her that Brecht had been unfaithful to her. As a result she tried to forget him and became engaged to another man. She wrote to Brecht to tell him of this step. Whereupon he immediately appeared in Nuremberg and talked her out of her engagement.

Soon afterwards Bi's father died and she returned to Augsburg. Brecht looked after the family and even composed the death notice they placed in the local paper. With Bi's father out of the way, the last obstacles to their marriage seemed to have been removed. They talked a great deal about it. To Bi their course seemed to be set fair.

Yet, at the same time, Brecht's affair with Marianne Zoff continued on its stormy course. Brecht spent more and more time in Berlin. Marianne Zoff had left Augsburg and was now with the opera at Wiesbaden. At Christmas 1921 she visited Brecht in Berlin, and when, shortly thereafter, in January 1922, Brecht collapsed (probably from undernourishment) she gave notice at the theatre and hurried to Berlin to sit by his bedside in the Charité. When letters arrived from Bi she was furious.

On 23 September 1922 Bi accompanied Brecht's father and his brother Walter to the first night of *Drums in the Night* at the Munich Kammerspiele. Marianne Zoff was also present, indeed, as she put it in her interview, "twice over" (in zweifacher Ausfertigung)—she was again pregnant with Brecht's child. Bi was unaware of that turn of affairs, until—

> One morning I was rung up in the office [Bi had taken a job as a secretary with the M.A.N. engineering works in Augsburg] by Brecht, whose voice sounded unusually excited. He pleaded with me not to talk to or receive a gentleman who would shortly telephone me. He would explain it all to me at the weekend when he was coming to Augsburg.[17]

But Recht had already appeared at Bi's home and her mother had let him in. In the end she could not avoid encountering him:

> He introduced himself as a Mr. Recht, Marianne Zoff's fiancé, and informed me that his bride—I would understand his despair—was expecting a child by Brecht. . . .

> I agreed when he suggested we should take the train to Munich straight away. In Munich Marianne Zoff would meet us at the Hauptbahnhof. We would then jointly confront Brecht and remind him of his responsibilities.[18]

In a café in the Maximilianstrasse the confrontation with Brecht duly took place. When he replied to the challenge with the declaration that he wanted to marry both of them, Marianne left the café. Bi remained behind but told Brecht that it was all over between them. But later, when Bi was on her way home to Augsburg, he appeared in the train and developed his plan:

> He told me of his painful situation: that, because of this unfortunate development, he was being forced by

Marianne Zoff to marry her. But he loved only me and could certainly not live with Marianne as he would with me. And no wonder: Brecht succeeded again and after an hour we were reconciled. As the climax of this reconciliation we agreed on a date for our marriage in the very nearest future.[19]

Bi had thought that this had finally put an end to the idea that Brecht would marry Marianne. But, on a day in the autumn of 1922

Brecht finally came out with what had worried him so long. He *had* to marry Marianne Zoff, because she did not leave him in peace. But he wanted to marry only me and that is why he had come up with the following idea. . . .

. . . As Marianne was interested in marriage merely because of the baby, he would comply with her wish. But as soon as the child was born, she would have to consent to a divorce so that he could marry me immediately afterwards.

I eventually agreed and Brecht actually composed, together with Marianne, a contract in which she declared herself ready to divorce him as soon as the baby was born.

Solemnly and with beautiful speeches I was handed a copy of this contract, which I carefully kept.

But now I also asked him that he should come to me in Augsburg immediately after the marriage ceremony. I would meet him at the station.

Brecht promised this without hesitation, and, indeed, came to Augsburg two hours after the time he had mentioned as that of the marriage, on 6 November.

Later I heard that the marriage had taken place on 3 November in Munich and that Brecht had had a

147

shortened honeymoon of three days with Marianne Zoff.[20]

Needless to say, the contract about the divorce immediately after the birth of Marianne's child was, as a lawyer later told Bi, invalid, because "in contravention of accepted moral standards." Nor did Brecht divorce Marianne Zoff after the birth of his daughter Hanne Marianne on 12 March 1922.

Yet Bi remained hopeful. As the months went by, she did meet another man, Hermann Gross, a well-to-do merchant, and informed Brecht, during one of his visits to Augsburg, that she wanted to marry him. Brecht simply could not endure to lose one of his women. So he demanded a confrontation with Gross. For three hours the two men argued about her in her presence. Gross pointed out that he could provide for her, and Brecht, after all, was already married:

> [Brecht] simply said: "Bi knows quite well how she should decide. She knows that I am going to get a divorce to marry her, for she is my bride. . . . It is for Bi to decide and we have to accept what she decides." And once more I decided in Brecht's favor.[21]

But as more time passed without a move from Brecht, and Gross continued to lay siege to her, she decided that enough was enough:

> I sat down and wrote Brecht a long letter, informing him that I had finally and irrevocably made the decision in favor of Hermann Gross.

> I received no reply from Berlin and assumed this to mean an unspoken agreement on his part; today I know that for the first time in his life Brecht, in a matter concerning us, had felt too secure. After another three

148

months had passed I was on the eve of my wedding. Hermann Gross did not want to risk anything and had scheduled the wedding at short notice. Two weeks before the ceremony a phone call came from Berlin. Helene Weigel was at the other end and told me that Brecht wanted to take me, immediately and for good, to Berlin. Everything had been settled.

He had already got me a job with a bank and had taken care of accommodations for both of us and everything else.

Ordering me that I should immediately pack my bags, Helene Weigel ended the conversation, without waiting for my reply. The next day Helene Weigel in person arrived in Augsburg. . . . She talked to me for a long time, but, of course, she did not possess Brecht's persuasive power.

I stayed in Augsburg.

Helene Weigel said goodbye with an astonished expression on her face, when she noticed that I could not be made to change my mind. . . .

Ten days later I married in Augsburg Hermann Gross, the businessman at whose side I could look forward to a bourgeois existence.[22]

The chances are that Helene Weigel whom Brecht had sent as his envoy to stop Bi Banholzer's marriage, was, at that very moment, already pregnant with Brecht's next illegitimate child. Stefan Brecht was born on 2 November 1924.

Brecht's marriage to Marianne Zoff remained intact, at least on paper, for another three years. By that time Brecht and Marianne no longer lived together. Marianne had become attached to the actor Theo Lingen—who later became one of Germany's leading film comics. Marianne left after having found Brecht in bed with Helene Weigel. Lingen wanted to marry Marianne, but Brecht—

> came to see Theo and me and begged us not to ask for a divorce. . . . I had heard that there was another woman who—so I believe—also had two children by him. Not a very pretty person, as far as I remember. Brecht did not want a divorce, because, otherwise he would have to marry that woman.[23]

This mysterious lady with the two illegitimate children by Brecht, who, Marianne Zoff claims, "died shortly afterwards" may be a myth, a conflation of gossip about Brecht's illegitimate children. Yet Marianne Zoff says that although she has forgotten her name, Brecht certainly had mentioned it to her.

The divorce of Marianne Zoff from Brecht finally did take place, on 2 November 1927. He married Helene Weigel on 10 April 1929, when his son Stefan was already four and a half.

Ironically, Frank Banholzer, Brecht's first child, was later taken in by Helene Weigel's sister in Vienna. It was only in 1935, when he was already sixteen, that Bi finally took him to Augsburg and apprenticed him with a commercial firm. Yet even then he could not live in her home, but had lodgings with her mother. When the war broke out he was called up and was killed in action in the Soviet Union in 1943.

When Brecht died on 14 August 1956, Hermann Gross, according to Bi, remarked: "So that dog has died before me after all!" Gross died six months later.

What is remarkable about this story is Brecht's inability to let go of Bi. His diaries show that he very soon tired of some of the girls with whom he was involved. In the case of Paula

Banholzer he simply could not endure losing her, even at a time when he was already involved with numerous other women. Similarly, in spite of his repeated intention of leaving Marianne Zoff to the Shlink-like Recht (Shlink's Malayan race is a transparent metaphor for Recht's Jewishness), he clung to Marianne Zoff long after he had fulfilled his professed intention of divorcing her as soon as their baby had been born in wedlock. Brecht was, indeed, one of nature's polygamists. He followed the same pattern to the end of his life—with Weigel, Elisabeth Hauptmann and Carola Neher in Berlin; with Margarete Steffin, Weigel and Ruth Berlau in Denmark; Weigel and Berlau in the United States, to name but the best known instances—and to the end of his life Helene Weigel was the one who managed these relationships, as she had tried to in the case of Paula Banholzer.

Brecht's cynicism about marriage and divorce also persisted throughout his life. As Klaus Völker reports, in 1954 Brecht told the East German philosopher Wolfgang Harich, with whose wife, Isot Kilian, he had an affair: "Divorce her now, and marry her again in about two years' time."[24] Brecht clearly felt that by then he would be tired of her.

Brecht's polygamous nature shows him as simply unable to resist his sexual urge. That he was aware of this tendency in himself (for which he created the brilliant metaphor of Sergeant "Bloody Five" in *Mann ist Mann,* who loses all self-control over his sexual drive when it rains) clearly emerges from his diary entry of 25 February 1921, at the height of his dilemma about Bi, Marianne and some other women:

Clothes, soap, a sunny apartment, theatre, good food, higher feelings, laziness, people's esteem, a smooth existence, travel, beauty, youth, health, art, freedom? And all of that thrown into the dirt in order to obey a physiological drive, which, as soon as satisfied, seeps away![25]

The conflict between the physiological drives on the one, rational thought on the other hand, which dominates Brecht's drama from Kragler to Azdak, could not have been more clearly stated. The desire for coolness, detachment, distancing, the need for the discipline of a self-denying creed is the obverse side of the enslavement to the physiological instinct. English has no really good equivalent for the German term "Hörigkeit"—of which Brecht speaks in his "Ballade von der sexuellen Hörigkeit" in *Threepenny Opera,* which deals with the situation that was so very much his own: However high-minded and determined to keep himself free from affairs with women a man may be— ". . . vor es Nacht wird, liegt er wieder droben." (Before it's night he's topping her again!)

In looking at all this, of course, all moralizing should be strictly avoided. Brecht, as a true revolutionary, was clearly, like Nietzsche, concerned with a regeneration of the bourgeois moral code. What is open to doubt is merely whether he succeeded in living this new concept of sexual morals without undue exploitation of the women who were his partners in this enterprise.

Notes

1. On the title page and the dust cover this book announces itself as *Paula Banholzer/Soviel wie eine Liebe/Der unbekannte Brecht/Erinnerungen und Gespräche/herausgegeben von Axel Poldner und Willibald Eser,* Munich: Universitas Verlag, 1981. [Paula Banholzer/As

much as Love/The Unknown Brecht/Memories and Conver-
sations/edited by Axel Poldner and Willibald Eser], but in fact
it consists of a longish narration by Paula Banholzer "Bidi
und Ich/Meine Zeit mit Bert Brecht" [Bidi and I/My Time
with Bert Brecht]; a transcript of a conversation: "Willibald
Eser und Axel Poldner befragen Paula Gross geb.Banholzer,
die Jugendliebe Bert Brechts, von ihm zärtlich 'die Bi'
genannt" [Willibald Eser and Axel Poldner question Paula
Gross, née Banholzer, Brecht's love of his youth whom he
tenderly called 'Bi']; the transcript of a further conversation
"Marianne Zoff-Brecht-Lingen erzählt Willibald Eser über
ihre Zeit mit Bert Brecht" [Marianne Zoff-Brecht-Lingen
talks to Willibald Eser about her time with Bert Brecht];
"Gespräche über Brecht" by Herbert Greuel, a director
whose connection with Brecht largely stems from his having
directed some plays by Marieluise Fleisser (another early love
and protegée of Brecht's) in the postwar period; and a
desultory little piece of three and a half pages, "Der
Schauspieler Karl Lieffen über den Regisseur Bert Brecht"
[The Actor Karl Lieffen on the Director Bert Brecht], by an
actor who took part in Brecht's production of *Mother Courage* at
the Munich Kammerspiele in 1950. References to this book
will use the abbreviation SVWEL.

2. Bertolt Brecht, *Tagebücher 1920-1922. Autobiographische
Aufzeichnungen 1920-1954,* Frankfurt: Suhrkamp, 1975. Will
be cited as TB. (All translations are my own. M.E.)

3. SVWEL, p. 22.

4. SVWEL, p. 34.

5. SVWEL, p. 34.

6. SVWEL, p. 35.

7. SVWEL, p. 36.

8. SVWEL, p. 38.

9. SVWEL, p. 122

10. TB, 18 August 1920, pp. 26-27.

11. TB, p. 31.

12. TB, p. 67.

13. SVWEL, pp. 157/8.
14. TB, pp. 91/2.
15. TB, p. 101.
16. TB, p. 118.
17. SVWEL, p. 82.
18. SVWEL, p. 83.
19. SVWEL, p. 86.
20. SVWEL, pp. 87/88.
21. SVWEL, p. 95.
22. SVWEL, p. 98.
23. SVWEL, p. 187-p. 816.
24. Klaus Völker, *Bertolt Brecht. Eine Biographie,* Munich: Hanser, 1976, p. 388.
25. TB, p. 78.

THE BUSINESS DEALS OF HERR BERTOLT BRECHT

BY JOHN FUEGI

When Bertolt Brecht wrote his novel, "The Business Deals of Herr Julius Caesar" (unfinished at his death and first published in 1957), his objective was to reveal the mechanics of how Caesar worked behind the scenes to create an image for the world. "How," Brecht asked, "was this done?" What were the business deals that undergirded Herr Julius Caesar's staggering success? Were they sordid, were they manipulative, were they unethical? And if they were all of these things, what does this do to our perception of the great Caesar of stern visage and laurelled brow? Given Brecht's careful cultivation of his own public persona, complete with uniform and props, one is prompted to direct the questions he asked of Julius Caesar back to himself. What about the business deals or contracts of Herr Bertolt Brecht, running as they do to thousands of pages in a dozen languages? The lines cross and recross, tangle and bewilder; and, as we shall see, the border between business deals and personal relationships is always blurred.

Such a study, one tackling the sheer scale and complexity of Brecht's business affairs, would shed a great deal of light on his relationships with those whose efforts made the construction of "the Brecht oeuvre" possible. If Valentin could speak of having an *Unsinnfabrik* and Erich Kastner could have a *Versfabrik,* such an inquiry must determine what kind of apparatus was necessary for Brecht to produce at the rate he did. How did such a "machine" run? How many employees (is that the right word even?) were required at all times to maintain production levels? Here again, was there a separation between the business/artistic strands and the personal strands of Brecht's life? Did his production method actually require the steady availability of several people (usually women), each willing to respond to his express needs virtually at any time of night or day? What was the effect of these working conditions on the coworkers themselves? For an understanding of Brecht's business relationships in general, and with Weill in particular, it is helpful to survey first the way in which Brecht regularly dealt with contractual matters.

From the published accounts of his friends and/or lovers, there are numerous reports of Brecht insisting that a friendship, a love affair, or even a marriage be undergirded by a formal agreement (*Abkommen*) or a subcontract. As Brecht scholarship moves beyond hagiography to actual biography, it is beginning to be recognized that it was Brecht's practice throughout his adult life to maintain multiple, simultaneous sexual liaisons.[1] During the period when Brecht moved back and forth frequently between his parents' home in Augsburg to various pads in Munich, besides several additional liaisons, he was having particularly intense affairs with Bie Banholzer (with whom he had already fathered a child in July 1919) and Marianne Zoff, a Viennese opera singer. After Bie (then in Augsburg) received a visit from a thwarted lover of Marianne who wanted Bie to break up Brecht's relationship with Marianne, the two women decided to confront Brecht together in a Munich café. They resolved to force him to declare his intentions and decide between them. But when they sat down with Brecht in the café and pointed out the incompatibility of the two intensive liaisons and asked which one of them he *really* wanted to marry, he gave a disconcerting one-word answer: "Both!" He was not to be budged from this position. One can, I believe, extrapolate this one-word answer to explain a great deal of what happens throughout other areas of Brecht's life where his answer seems to have been almost invariably: "Both!"

After "answering" Ma and Bie in this way, Brecht then negotiated simultaneous contracts with both women. He agreed to marry Marianne ("Ma") because she was again pregnant with what Brecht referred to in his diary as "a little Brecht," but the marriage contract was to have several subsidiary clauses. Ma was to agree that she would remain faithful to Brecht only, while Brecht's sexual independence was to be guaranteed because, as he put it, "some things a wife has to accept as irrevocable."[2] Having established that any marriage contract must absolutely allow him to maintain as many other simultaneous liaisons as he wished, quite logically Brecht then set up a contract with Bie Banholzer. According to her own accounts, her contract specified that after Brecht had married Ma, as soon as the "little Brecht" was born and given Brecht's name, he would then divorce Ma and marry Bie.[3] Brecht further recommended that Bie should begin to order her trousseau in anticipation of this blessed tertiary event. When Bie took her "contract" to a lawyer for an assessment of its legal merits, the lawyer declared that it offended all public morality, had no valid legal precedent, and would never hold up in court. Years later, after never marrying Bie but finally divorcing Ma, Brecht was simultaneously involved (with a view to marriage and not counting other minor affairs) with Marieluise Fleisser, Elisabeth Hauptmann, Helene Weigel, and Carola Neher. The traffic in mistresses was sufficiently brisk and Brecht's requirement for dress and undress of "his" women so strict that a Berlin tailor gave a discount on the custom-cut merino wool coats that they were required to wear.[4] In the midst of all this, quite suddenly Brecht and Weigel entered a formal (i.e., state-sanctioned) marriage contract in Berlin. But again there were loopholes in the contract for Brecht. As he observed to Carola Neher in April 1929 (on the day of his marriage to Weigel) and as he presented Neher with a handsome bouquet (surely it was not the recycled wedding bouquet of Weigel?), "It [the marriage] couldn't be avoided, but it doesn't mean a thing."[5] It meant enough to Fleisser that it would have an indelible effect on her life, and it meant enough to Elisabeth Hauptmann that she attempted suicide.

But Brecht's personal *Abkommen* did not concern only the regulation of sexual relations. Hermann Kesten, in his wonderfully lively memoir, *Lauter Literaten,* reported:

> About 1935 in Paris Brecht called me up as he urgently needed to speak with me. Could I go to his place? He didn't feel well. He lived in a hotel on the Boulevard St. Germain, between the monuments to Danton and Diderot.
>
> As my wife and I entered Brecht's room he was saying goodbye to the philosopher Ernst Bloch, the film director Slatan Dudow, and one or two women coworkers. We had hardly exchanged a few words

about health, Hitler, and the weather before he put down his cigar and declared to me in a friendly but threatening way: "We are going to make a contract" [Wir schliessen ein Abkommen].

I smiled.

Brecht remained serious: "A contract that we will become friends."

"But," I said and laughed, "we get along fine together."

"I hear," he said, not being led astray, "that quite regularly in all the literary salons and in the Paris cafés you make jokes about me and criticize my work. That has to stop."

"Yes, I do make jokes in cafés," I said, "but I hardly ever enter literary salons."

"Our contract," stipulated Brecht, "shall provide that everywhere you go, you speak well of me and of my work, and I'll do the same for you. I have contracts like this with Lion Feuchtwanger, Arnold Zweig, and Alfred Döblin."

"I am glad about that," I said, and unfortunately I had to laugh. "Your offer amuses me and does me honor. Why shouldn't we praise each other's work? But up to now I have managed to hang on to my literary friends without such contracts, and my friendships have even survived my jokes. From what I know of myself, I wouldn't be able to enter such a pact with a friend. Suddenly I would have an urge to make a joke. How would we be able to joke about our enemies, if we couldn't from time to time joke about our friends?"

"I hear it from all sides that you laugh at me," Brecht declared, not being led astray, "that cannot continue without consequences. When it is necessary, I'll climb over dead bodies to get my way. In Hessen there was a young director who opposed me. He ended up committing suicide.''

I stood up. ''On this point I can set your mind at rest, dear Brecht. On neither my father's nor my mother's side have there been suicides in my family.''

''You are the literary advisor to the Allert de Lange Press,'' said Brecht, ''where we are both authors. I must go to Mr. de Lange and say to him: It's either you or me.''

''Why not?'' I said. ''Landshoff [former owner of the Kiepenheuer Press in Berlin] will be glad to choose one or the other of us. So I don't see problems for either of us there.''

Brecht escorted my wife and me to the lift in the Hotel.[6]

Given the fact that Brecht paid such strict attention to regulating personal relations on a contractual basis (and usually a very one-sided contractual basis at that), it should not surprise us that he was just as concerned with his own interest in his multiple business contracts. In December 1921 he noted in his diary that he was juggling potential business arrangements with Reinhardt, Warschauer, Oswald Films, and Terra Films, while also considering his options in draft contracts he had obtained from both Reiss and Kiepenheuer Verlag. By 23 December he had signed up with Reiss for 750 marks a month, he had collected another 1000 marks from his father, he had signed on with ''The Untamed Stage'' to sing his mesmeric ballads for 500 marks in a six-day engagement, and he was still in hot pursuit of various other contracts. His love life was not abating for a moment by 7 January 1922 when he renegotiated the Reiss contract. His diary entry for that day gives the current status of his love arrangements and then continues:

> First of all dealing with publishers. Reiss offered 750 Marks, Kiepenheuer 800. Both want stage rights too. I've already signed up with Reiss, but took the contract back in order to show it to Kasack [of Kiepenheuer]. I also had to talk to Dreimasken. It seemed a good idea to ask them for 1000 a month for one year. I also pushed Kiepenheuer up to 1000. On top of that, I got Kiepenheuer to leave Dreimasken the stage rights for my next plays. Dreimasken waivered, offered 500. I hadn't brought *Garga* with me, as I didn't want to let them have it. But stuck out for the 1000. Finally they agreed after I had talked them into a stupor.[7]

These arrangements reward close examination. As contract negotiator, Brecht had moved within two weeks from one rather comprehensive contract for his work that yielded 750 marks a month to two fragmented contracts worth 1000 apiece and had kept one of his hottest properties, *Garga,* off the negotiating table entirely, so that he could negotiate for it separately. By skillfully playing off one publisher against another, he had obtained multiple contracts, all highly favorable to him and all subject to renegotiation at his discretion, while holding the other signatory implacably to every provision in his own favor. In effect, just as he had proposed to marry Bie and Ma, while keeping all other liaisons open for himself, he had now "divorced" Reiss and "married" both Kiepenheuer and Dreimasken and had contractually established his right to innumerable other liaisons. Thereby Brecht could now collect multiple salaries as a writer, also sign on later for a stipend as a dramaturg with Reinhardt, reserve the right to be a guest director at other theaters, keep the rights to all plays written with others, and invoke an escape clause if any censorship was attempted on his deliberately scatological and sacrilegious writings. To ensure that all these business enterprises were kept in good order and that he could produce on schedule, he later managed to add a little rider to the Kiepenheuer agreement, a rider that put Elisabeth Hauptmann on the Kiepenheuer payroll, even though she reported literally 24-hours-a-day exclusively to Bertolt Brecht. Later, when more favorable terms and greater freedom of expression were offered by Propylaen Verlag (a subsidiary of Ullstein), Brecht would cheerfully switch publishers while retaining the rights to works "written with others." As most of his work then was written at least *with* others, if not at times *by* others, in 1929 he could boast to the economist Fritz Sternberg that his was a rare case in which "Ullstein was exploited by an author" rather than vice versa.[8]

This is the person with whom Kurt Weill would deal in 1927. Although the artistic collaboration between Weill and Brecht started with enormous appreciation of each other's work, as they began to complete joint projects, enormous difficulties over contractual arrangements gradually developed. At the outset of their collaboration, Brecht was so inordinately skilled in contractual negotiations and Weill so relatively unskilled that it was quite predictable that their joint contracts would prove a lifelong nightmare for Weill and Lenya and a lifelong bonanza for Brecht and his heirs.

Weill's initial contract with Universal Edition, dated 22 April 1924, is stupefyingly straightforward in comparison with Brecht's deliberately entangled contractual relationships during the same period.[9] Weill simply agreed to give Universal Edition the rights to his work for eight years.

Basically the contract was U.E.'s standard one, with substantial portions unmodified on the printed form it used for all its young composers. The royalty arrangement was also standard. Weill even accepted the clause in the contract that allowed Universal Edition to reduce his royalties if he failed to live up to any of the other terms of the contract. Weill's signing of this contract in April 1924 actually required no contractual expertise whatsoever. He reserved no special rights for himself. As with other artists of the same period, by signing his *Hauptvertrag* he relinquished both film and stage rights to the publisher. While the general contract made no mention of ownership of Weill's autograph manuscripts, in the specific agreements for individual compositions he ceded this property to the publisher too. Since Brecht usually reserved all kinds of rights for himself in contracts from this very same period (1924), when Brecht and Weill began to sign contracts jointly in 1927, two radically different styles came into genuine conflict.

If we look closely at Brecht's career in the years prior to his first meeting with Weill, it is worth noting that Brecht was successful not so much by reason of production of his plays but almost, startlingly enough, in spite of the production of his plays. There is virtually no production of one of his plays before he meets Weill that was an actual box office success. The Leipzig production of *Baal* in 1923, the one performance of *Baal* in Berlin during 1926, and the short-lived 1924 production of *Eduard II* in Munich are typical. Each of these productions led to a wild outcry and mixed opinion at the premiere, and each was canceled after only a few performances.[10] But each production increased Brecht's fame through extensive and intensive critical reviews. As Brecht's friend Arnolt Bronnen was to observe with some puzzlement: his own plays had *succeeded* in theaters but he had been *defeated*, while Brecht's plays had *failed* but Brecht had *won*. From 1924 to 1927, and only then with a great deal of help from Elisabeth Hauptmann, Brecht actually completed only one play, *Mann ist Mann,* as most of his work as a playwright during this period remained unfinished. But despite a string of what many people might regard as failures, Brecht managed to project an image of extraordinary success, arrogance, and confidence. He was a one-man wave of the future. Short stories, poems, and advertising slogans published under his name kept him in the public eye, and his bitter attacks on Thomas Mann ensured him of notoriety, if not fame. The failure of one of his works at the box office was a measure, said Brecht and his supporters, of the inadequacy of the public rather than the inadequacy of Brecht. Failure, therefore, dialectically was, in fact, success.

Apparently Kurt Weill was drawn to the playwright by the radio production (reviewed by Weill in *Der Deutsche Rundfunk*) of the one completed play, *Mann ist Mann,* and some of the poems in Brecht's deliberately provocative and scatological collection, *Die Hauspostille,* particularly the group of poems on that mythological place or state-of-being called Mahagonny. Although the *Hauspostille* volume bore only Brecht's name on the cover, at least two, and perhaps more, of the five Mahagonny poems were almost certainly written by Brecht's "secretary," Elisabeth Hauptmann.[11] But this *is* and *is not* a side issue here. When Weill met with Brecht in 1927 and began collaboration on the Mahagonny materials, there is no evidence that Weill thought that anyone but brash Bert Brecht had written the Mahagonny poems and *Mann ist Mann.*

When the joint work on the Mahagonny materials was well advanced, storm clouds began to gather about the actual staging of the *Songspiel* in Baden-Baden (as was usual with Brecht's work as a director in this period).[12] Everything was being manipulated to create Brecht's usual theatrical scandal. Although the boxing-ring set was accepted and used, Brecht's wish to have Lenya appear nude in the production was turned down by both Weill and the horrified management of the festival. But sure enough, the production was shocking enough to the gathering of musical elite that by the end of the performance the audience was on its feet as some booed and whistled while others cheered and clapped. Knowing full well what the reaction would be, Brecht had provided the cast with whistles and placards so that he and the performers could respond to the audience's response. So far, it looked like just another of Brecht's openings, but after the performance in the hotel bar it became apparent to Lenya that something else had happened. When she entered the bar, Otto Klemperer slapped her on the back and asked (quoting Hauptmann's pidgin English of the "Benares Song"), "Is here no telephone?" The whole bar-crowd began to sing the *Mahagonny* songs. Whether Brecht and Weill recognized it or not, the combination of Weill's music, Hauptmann's English lyrics, and Lenya's singing had placed Brecht and Weill in the considerable danger of becoming a popular success. Even though the Baden-Baden *Mahagonny Songspiel* had been a one-shot affair before a specialized audience, Lenya knew instinctively that it had been a real "hit." Almost by accident, it would seem, Brecht and Weill had created with "their" *Songs* something that could have enormous popular appeal. It would be a first for both.

In 1928, Hauptmann, whose knowledge of English enabled her to teach the language, was preparing for Brecht, whose English was virtually nonexistent at that time, a translation/adaptation of John Gay's eighteenth-century

Beggar's Opera, which had been successfully revived in London.[13] Brecht was devoting himself mainly to something different, a play that he never finished called *Joe Fleischhacker.* Indeed, when Ernst Josef Aufricht approached Brecht in the spring of 1928 to ask if he had a play suitable for the opening of Aufricht's company at the Theater am Schiffbauerdamm, Brecht tried to sell him on *Joe Fleischhacker.* Only when Aufricht had rejected *Fleischhacker* and got up to leave did Brecht refer to a "secondary work," then called *Gesindel.* As Brecht described this work, Aufricht knew at once that this adaptation of John Gay smelled of theater. The very next day Hauptmann's fragmentary text was accepted by Aufricht.[14] He even provisionally acquiesced to the alarmingly avant-garde and, as far as he knew, totally inappropriate composer Kurt Weill as a necessary, if unwelcome, part of the deal.

No sooner had agreement been reached with Aufricht than the whole array of questions concerning publication, film rights, music rights, etc. had to be addressed. Weill, who had been receiving a meager monthly stipend from Universal Edition under the terms of his original, all-inclusive contract of 1924 and who was obliged to give Universal all his new works, merely added the adaptation of Gay to his list of compositions with Universal under the standard provision which entrusted the publisher with virtually all rights to the piece. Meanwhile, Brecht was hard at work lining up a contract on *his* usual terms. In the spring of 1928, with large sections of the music and the libretto not yet written, Brecht and Weill went in to sign a contract with Felix Bloch Erben in Berlin. How Brecht persuaded Weill and Hauptmann to agree to the original terms is still a matter for further investigation, but the original *Dreigroschenoper* contract specified a division of royalties as follows: Brecht 62½ %

(net), Weill 25% (net), Hauptmann 12½% (net), with no provision for Klammer (K.L. Ammer), the Austrian translator of Villon whose published versions of several poems would be patched into the text. Only after the critic Alfred Kerr spotted and publicized the unacknowledged use of the Villon verses was the contract slightly modified with Klammer then awarded 2½% of the total (subtracted from Brecht's 62½% share). In extreme contrast to these terms, Weill had been awarded the traditional two-thirds of all royalties as composer of his two one-act operas with librettos by Georg Kaiser, who was the most famous Expressionist playwright at the time. The contract with Felix Bloch Erben, with its radically unequal division of royalties, was to remain in force until the late forties, when Brecht (ignoring Weill's rights) unilaterally canceled the contract and signed a new agreement with Suhrkamp that maintained the old percentages without even telling Weill directly that he had done so.

But in the spring of 1928 the contract being negotiated was not, as far as anyone could then have suspected, for a worldwide success worth literally millions of marks in royalties over the years, but a contract for a half-finished and probably unsuccessful mishmash by the then unknown Elisabeth Hauptmann, by a certain Bertolt Brecht, who had never had a popular stage success, and by Kurt Weill, a composer with an alarming reputation as a far-from-popular modernist. For betting people in Berlin in the spring and summer of 1928, it was a poor gamble as to whether or not the work would open at all, never mind become one of the greatest successes in German theatrical history.

Behind the scenes during these months, Brecht was still working on contracts. The contract with Felix Bloch Erben needed to be reconciled with Weill's agreement with

Universal Edition. On the plus side for Weill, because Brecht insisted on retaining his film rights, Weill, in essence, was in a legally defensible position to do the same. But on the negative side, Brecht now apparently started to ask for a larger share of royalties for himself under Weill's contract with Universal for "print rights" of the music. In a contract revision dated 15 November 1929 (i.e., after the show had opened and was clearly a smash hit and a major moneymaker), Weill allowed Brecht's share of the print royalties from Universal to be increased from 2% to 3% of net income. (In light of the huge income derived from the *Die Dreigroschenoper,* it is worth noting that Brecht established during this same period two other income-producing contracts with Felix Bloch Erben, one for *Happy End* and one for three as yet unwritten plays.) Early the next year, in a note dated 26 May 1930, Weill agreed to give up yet an additional 2% of his own royalty to Brecht, so that Brecht would now get 5% of income from publications of music issued by Universal Edition. Weill's percentage was reduced to 13%, but it should be noted that income from sales of the piano-vocal score and individual songs through Universal was only a fraction of the income derived from license fees for performance rights and sales of the book version of the complete *Dreigroschenoper* collected by Felix Bloch Erben, the latter of which Weill did not share in at all. While Brecht nibbled away at Weill's portion of the income from Universal, no compensatory modification of the Bloch contract was forthcoming. The net result of all this was that, although both Weill and Brecht were earning well from *Die Dreigroschenoper,* Brecht was earning at a vastly greater percentage-rate than Weill. But it does not appear that this was as yet a source of irritation for either Kurt Weill or Lotte Lenya. Both continued to work with Brecht, and Weill completed the music for *Der Lindberghflug* and *Das Berliner*

Requiem, both broadcast in 1929. However, in that same tumultuous year in Berlin the Weill/Brecht relationship was to be shaken severely by the events surrounding the unhappy ending of their work on *Happy End.*

Aufricht and others have described the *Happy End* project as an attempt to repeat in 1929 the extraordinary success of the previous year's *Dreigroschenoper.* The standard interpretation of the non-success of *Happy End* is that Brecht had moved sufficiently to the left in 1929 (following the shooting of workers by the police on 1 May 1929—events he witnessed)[15] so that he wanted nothing more to do with a piece planned by Aufricht as a commercial venture. This may well be true, but it is possible that personal/contractual events in Brecht's life may have had as much to do with the non-completion of *Happy End* as political events in Germany. If we are willing to accept the significant role of Elisabeth Hauptmann in the creation of *Mahagonny* and *Die Dreigroschenoper,* then let us look more closely at *Happy End,* a work prepared in the middle third of 1929. Why was the last act of the play never properly completed? Is it worth noting that on 10 April 1929 Brecht broke the agreements that Carola Neher, Elisabeth Hauptmann, and Marieluise Fleisser all thought they had with him when he suddenly married Helene Weigel? Hauptmann's reaction to the marriage was an attempted suicide. May we ask how enthusiastic was she in the summer of 1929 to return to work with Brecht? I think it highly probable that she (rather than Brecht) was the linchpin of the *Happy End* production and that she was the one who could not bring herself to complete it in those desperately unhappy months following Brecht's unexpected marriage.

By the time the curtain came down on *Happy End* in September 1929 after only three performances, it was abundantly clear to Lenya, Weill, and Aufricht that Bert

Brecht's and his new wife's behavior had ensured the failure of the project. Aufricht reckoned his losses at 130,000 marks and, as he wrote, "At my theater, we had to take a breather from Brecht."[16] For Felix Bloch Erben, the failure of *Happy End* was a very serious blow because, in anticipation of other successful plays and songs from Brecht's "collective," they had signed their two new contracts for large sums of money for "Brecht" to produce what they thought would be a string of moneymakers.

Despite the failure of *Happy End,* two more years elapsed before an open break between Weill and Brecht could be discerned publicly. Meanwhile, the opera *Aufstieg und Fall der Stadt Mahagonny* had been produced during March 1930 in Leipzig (and later in other opera houses) with only minimal involvement by Brecht. That year Weill also completed the music for *Der Jasager,* 80% of whose libretto Elisabeth Hauptmann claimed, in a personal interview with me, to have written.[17] Speedily, as we know, *Der Jasager* was complemented by a *Neinsager,* and Brecht's subsequent revisions of his original text (a customary practice throughout his life) were effected with no consideration for the music and without consultation with Weill. Brecht, it was clear, was going his own way and did not seem overly concerned as to whether Weill went with him or not. This becomes very clear with the lawsuit that swirled around the film version of *Die Dreigroschenoper* in the summer of 1930.

As far as I have been able to reconstruct events, Brecht's reworking of the stage material for the Nero film production was also accomplished in sovereign disregard for Weill's music. Weill seems to have joined the *Dreigroschenoper* lawsuit largely to ensure that his music be used in the film without interpolation of music by other composers. When Brecht's part of the lawsuit was settled in December 1930, the settlement document not only specified a payment of 16,000 marks, but, most importantly, the film rights for the work reverted to Brecht after only two years.[18] Not only is the two year provision extraordinary in film contracts, but the settlement document gives *Brecht* (not Weill and Brecht) the right to make a new film version. It is extremely doubtful that either Nero or Brecht had any legal right whatsoever to settle "their" case on these terms, but nevertheless settle they did. From now on, as one looks at the tangled history of the *Dreigroschenoper* contract through the exile years and into the postwar years, Brecht tends almost always to treat the work as something that he could unilaterally alter, sell, or reassign with little if any prior consultation with either of his collaborators, Weill or Hauptmann.

But before we follow these tangled threads through the post-1933 years, let us look briefly at the one time where the Brecht and Weill interests publicly diverged. In December 1931 Aufricht, despite the fiasco of *Happy End*, decided to mount an expensive commercial production of the full-length *Mahagonny* at the Theater am Kurfurstendamm. As Aufricht, Willett, and others have noticed before, Brecht's behavior at the *Mahagonny* rehearsals was such that, in essence, Aufricht bought him off by agreeing to finance a simultaneous production of *Die Mutter*. Aufricht hoped that Brecht would be so involved in rehearsals of *Mother* that he would keep his nose out of *Mahagonny*. Before Brecht went down to the cellar to rehearse *Mother*, public fights between Weill and Brecht had become commonplace, and lawyers representing both parties shouted at one another during the chaotic rehearsals. Brecht knocked a camera out of the hands of a press photographer who wanted to photograph him with Weill. And Brecht, who was already a legend in German theatrical circles for his temper tantrums, shouted that he would throw

Weill, "this phony Richard Strauss," down the stairs.[19] The Weill/Brecht collaboration looked to be very much at an end.

With both artists being driven into exile by events in Germany in early 1933, the earning power of each was drastically curtailed, since much of their respective incomes had been derived from the German market. They both needed to look around at once for alternative sources of income outside Germany. When Weill immediately landed a contract for a ballet in Paris, he both shrewdly and magnanimously shared the commission with Brecht—after Cocteau had refused the offer; as a result, Weill held the contractual cards, as well as the artistic control, of *Die Sieben Todsuenden*. After two years in Paris and London, Weill crossed the Atlantic in September 1935, not to return again to Europe—and then for only a brief visit—until after the war. Brecht, however, stayed in Europe until 1941, and during this time he basically, as far as can now be determined, acted very much on his own in determining what happened to European contracts for *Die Dreigroschenoper* and other works written jointly with Weill and/or Hauptmann.

According to Brecht's correspondence, the owner of Felix Bloch Erben, Fritz Wreede, had been having second thoughts about Brecht's contracts with the firm even before Brecht went into exile. Wreede had met with him in Munich during the summer of 1932 to propose changes in their agreements. In Wreede's view, Brecht had not properly fulfilled his contractual obligations.[20] The significant point here, as far as Brecht's relationship with Weill and the *Dreigroschenoper* contract is concerned, is that Weill was almost certainly unaware that Brecht was contesting his other contracts with Felix Bloch Erben and that this was having an effect on their joint *Dreigroschenoper* contract. According to

172

Wreede, Felix Bloch Erben had committed to pay Brecht under a general contract (separate from the *Happy End* and *Dreigroschenoper* contracts) an advance of 1000 gold marks per month for seven years for the rights to several plays that Brecht was supposed to write and assign to the firm. A dispute arose because Brecht did not, in Wreede's view, deliver on time any plays that could be used by the firm to recover these advances of 1000 gold marks per month. When Brecht left Berlin, the controversy was still unresolved. It boiled down to this: did Felix Bloch Erben owe Brecht another three and a half years of payments of 1000 gold marks per month, or was Brecht obligated to repay the three and a half years of advance he had already received? Each claimed essentially that the *other* party owed 42,000 gold marks. Neither party was willing to budge from his respective position, and Wreede wrote to ask how Brecht planned to repay the firm.[21] Brecht, in turn, demanded to know why he was not continuing to receive his monthly advance for the remainder of the contractual period. If Wreede was correct in his interpretation of the situation, then one can understand why he wanted to use the money collected from theaters for performances of *Die Dreigroschenoper* as *his* only feasible source of recovery for the huge sum of money owed to him by Bert Brecht. But Brecht argued in his numerous letters to Wreede that he had, in fact, observed the terms of his contracts with Felix Bloch Erben, that his "pension" (he called his monthly sum *"eine Rente"*) should be continued, *and* that he should also continue to get his royalties from *Die Dreigroschenoper* in full.[22]

If one looks in detail at the surviving records of Brecht's dealings with Felix Bloch Erben in the thirties, one sees that the situation was not clear-cut. However, it can now be shown that Brecht did, in fact, collect *some* money for *Die*

Dreigroschenoper during the exile years and that this money was paid to him with the knowledge and cooperation of Felix Bloch Erben. I have managed to obtain a copy of a handwritten document in French, dated 16 May 1938 and signed by Brecht, acknowledging receipt from Dr. Alexandre Banyai of 4,300 francs for performances of *L'Opera de Quat'sous* in France. In a letter dated 21 May 1938 from Dr. Banyai in Paris to Felix Bloch Erben in Berlin, we learn that Banyai received a total of 9,300 francs as royalties for the play, that he had sent 5,000 francs to Felix Bloch Erben in Berlin, and that he had remitted 4,300 francs to Brecht (through Brecht's attorney, Martin Domke) with the express understanding that Brecht was to share this money with Weill.[23] However, there is no extant evidence to suggest that Brecht did forward Weill a share of the royalties. Indeed, in a letter to Brecht dated 9 February 1939, Weill says explicitly that he has not seen one cent from the Paris production (or any other production) of *The Threepenny Opera*.[24] If he was correct here, and I am reasonably sure that he was, then Weill was not only failing to receive any payments from Felix Bloch Erben, but he was also being deprived of his share of royalties that Brecht collected on behalf of both creators.

It is, of course, quite possible that Weill might have allowed Brecht to keep all royalties collected in Europe if he had been informed of their existence and had been asked to donate them to the cause of Brecht's emigration from Europe. But as far as I know, Brecht never mentioned the money to Weill and never asked to be allowed to keep it. (In response to Elisabeth Hauptmann's plea in 1941 for funds to assist Brecht in coming to the United States, Weill sent a contribution of one hundred dollars.) For all Weill knew, Brecht too had received no income in Europe for the works under contract to Felix Bloch Erben, and Weill was certainly unaware that at least some money for Brecht had, in fact, been authorized by Felix Bloch Erben and paid as late as 1938! It appears that, until his death in 1950, Weill assumed that his own collaborative works with Brecht were earning him absolutely nothing in Europe, and his outrage at this was directed solely at Felix Bloch Erben rather than also at Brecht.

When Brecht and Weill did meet briefly on the American side of the Atlantic in 1935, Weill observed Brecht as he attempted to impose his iron will (by insisting absolutely on his own "rights") on the Theatre Union's production of *Mother* in New York. Here again Brecht was thrown out of the theater. Here again he wanted his own way regardless of what anyone else wanted. It is highly unlikely that Brecht's deliberately obnoxious behavior, behavior so reminiscent of the *Mahagonny* production in Berlin during December 1931, now prompted any nostalgia for their partnership from Weill, who was already trying to establish himself in the American theater. Brecht again returned to Europe, and by the time he emigrated to America in mid-1941, Kurt Weill had achieved fame with *Lady in the Dark*. During a trip to Hollywood in September-October 1942, Weill reported to Lenya on his first meeting with Brecht since 1935:

Then I met Brecht. He was just as dirty and unshaved as ever, but somehow much nicer and rather pathetic. He wants badly to work with me and the way he talks about it sounds very reasonable—but you know how long that lasts. Anyhow, I will try to see him once more before I leave. . . . If I don't go in the army I think I will do a show with Brecht *for you*. He has enough money now for two years and could come to New York.[25] (1 October 1942)

But behind the scenes in California Brecht almost immediately again attempted to treat work he had done earlier with Weill as exclusively his own. Early in 1942 he tried to set up a California production of *The Threepenny Opera* in English with an all-Black theatrical company. Weill had not been consulted in Brecht's preliminary negotiations with the producer, Clarence Muse. But when Weill first learned of the plans in a telegram on 5 March 1942, he responded immediately that he could reply only after discussing the matter with his agent and publisher. Meanwhile, Brecht and the producer enlisted both Paul Robeson and T.W. Adorno as intermediaries to convince Weill of the value of the project.

Although insulted and privately outraged by Brecht's characteristic disregard for his rights, Weill maintained a public silence about the situation. In private, however, he was very explicit about his reaction; in a letter to Lenya, dated 8 April 1942, Weill wrote:

> I am sick and tired of this whole affair and I wrote him [Muse] I would be willing to make a contract for a production *in California only,* but that I won't allow it to be shown outside of Cal. unless I have seen and passed it. . . . If they don't accept this, to hell with them! But at least I have shown my good will. Muse writes me that Brecht had told him last summer he had written to me and I didn't answer. The good old swinish Brecht method. Well, I wrote Wiesengrund [Adorno] a letter which he won't forget for some time. I wrote him: It is a shame that a man of your intelligence should be so misinformed. Then I explained [to] him that the American theatre isn't as bad as he thinks and in the end I said: "maybe the main difference between the

German and American theatre is the fact that there
exist certain rules of 'fair play' in the American
theatre. Three cheers for the American Theatre!''

Lenya replied by return mail:

The whole Brecht schit [sic] is just too funny for words.
"Could you come to Hollywood?". Good God! Sounds
like in the good old days when he tried to keep your
name off the program. . . . You know what they will
do, if you would give in. Cut the music to pieces and
make the whole thing cheap and ridiculous. And this
stupid Brecht, this chinese-augsburg *Hinterwaldler* [hick]
philosopher. It's too much already, that letter from
him, soil our mailbox.

In an undated letter from the same period, Lenya cautioned
Weill about renewing any relationship with Brecht:

I am very much against it, to send him money. I belief
[sic] to a certain extent, what he writes about the
procedure of that 3 penny opera project but I dont [sic]
trust him at all. I never believe, that he ever can change
his character, which is a selfish one and always will be. I
am sure he went through a lot of unpleasant things, but
not so unpleasant, that it would change him. I know
Darling how easely [sic] you forget things but I do
remember everything he ever did to you. And that was
plenty. Of course, he wants to collaborate with you
again. Nothing better could happen to him. But I am
convinced after a few days, you would be disgusted with
him, I just could write it down for you what would
happen. . . . I always believed in dicency [sic] and a
certain fairness. And Brecht hasn't got much of it. . . .
"DIE SIEBEN WINTER UND DIE GROSSEN
KALTEN" [sic] und die ganzen Gemeinheiten
tauchen for [sic] mir auf. *Nein, nein.*

Given Lenya's and Weill's distrust for "the business deals of Herr Bertolt Brecht," it is not surprising that Brecht's efforts to recruit Weill for the Schweik and Setzuan projects came to naught. The loss of what these works might have been with Weill's collaboration is directly, if only partially, attributable to Brecht's previous betrayals of their contractual relationship. But the squabbles were far from finished. All through the Hitler years Kurt Weill had believed that Felix Bloch Erben had paid neither author any royalties. For Weill, simply to carry on with the contract after 1945 as though there had never been a Third Reich was impossible; whatever differences Weill and Brecht had, they were in agreement that it was necessary to take the *Dreigroschenoper* contract away from Felix Bloch Erben. But once Brecht got back to Europe, he dealt with the property there just as he had dealt with it in California and in Europe before the war: unilaterally he began to talk of a new version of the text, to arrange for productions, to switch the contract to a new publisher, and to do all this without prior consultation with Weill.

On 2 September 1948, Universal Edition wrote an anguished letter to Brecht and a letter of inquiry to Weill. What, they asked, was going on with *Die Dreigroschenoper?* In a letter to Brecht dated 2 September 1948, Alfred Schlee of Universal Edition wrote that he had read a newspaper article announcing that Brecht had written a new version of the opera. If this were true, continued Schlee, could they have the new text at once to forward to Weill in case he wished to write any necessary new music. And finally, who held the contract now? Was it still with Felix Bloch Erben? Later that month, with no word from Brecht directly, a letter dated 9 September 1948 reached Weill in New York from an old friend during the Berlin days, Jakob Geis, now with Bavaria

Film in Munich and representing, so he said, Bertolt
Brecht.[26] The letter proposed breaking the Felix Bloch Erben
contract but did not give any specifics for a new contract with
a different publisher. At precisely the time of Geis's letter,
Weill's friend and attorney Maurice Speiser died, so Weill
was without legal counsel. Nevertheless, he wrote back
promptly on 28 October 1948 to say he agreed that the
contract must be taken away from Felix Bloch Erben. The
letter ended as follows: "Before I do anything definite,
however, I would like to know what we will do with *Die
Dreigroschenoper* if we do take it away from Bloch Erben."
"Can you write to me," he continued, "what Brecht has in
mind, or, can you ask him to write to me directly?"

Still having heard nothing from either Geis or Brecht
(Brecht had written a letter dated 6 December 1948 that must
have crossed Weill's in the mail), Weill wrote to Schlee at
Universal on 11 December 1948 asking for advice on how to
stop unauthorized productions such as one he had heard
about in Munich, where his music had reportedly been
altered. Replying to Brecht's 6 December 1948 letter, Weill
pointed out in a letter dated 20 December 1948 that he
remained very concerned about alterations being made in
either the text or the music of *Die Dreigroschenoper* and that he
wanted to see the altered text. By 17 January 1949 Weill had
received the alterations; he wrote to Brecht that he "honestly
could not understand what you have in mind with these
alterations." On 28 January Brecht wrote again to explain
his point of view and to ask that Weill refrain from making
further objections to performances of *Die Dreigroschenoper*.
Geis, said Brecht, would handle the royalties in Germany for
Weill. Weill replied on 14 February saying he did not want to
do anything until he had seen a very specific proposal for a
new contract. On 16 March 1949, a Mr. Hartmann of

Universal wrote plaintively to Weill in New York: "Most unpleasant things are happening with *Die Dreigroschenoper.*" "Brecht," reported Hartmann, "is supposed to have said in Zurich that he alone has a right to enter contracts in foreign countries."

By May various European agents were involved in the fray. On 18 May, a certain M. Kantorowitz wrote to Universal from Zurich declaring, among other things, that "Bert Brecht has written a completely new text, and this will not be entrusted to any publisher, but will be handled by the author himself." Universal, in a letter signed by a Mr. Wieser and dated 16 May 1949, replied at once to Kantorowitz and sent a copy of the relevant correspondence to Weill. In part, Wieser stated: "Since the new text by Brecht is to be used, we cannot agree to such a performance before we obtain the consent of Mr. Weill." In the midst of all this, on 7 January 1949, Felix Bloch Erben wrote to Weill saying that he should understand that, in view of what Brecht was doing, "we cannot be held responsible for Mr. Brecht's violation of your interests." In a telegram Weill ordered that the Munich production be stopped. Hartmann at Universal wrote at once to Felix Bloch Erben that no performances should be authorized until Weill could see the so-called "new version," and he, of course, wanted to see a new contract also.

No new contract arrived, and Weill still did not know what was happening to his music. Hard at work on *Lost in the Stars,* he wrote a firm but polite and friendly letter dated 5 August 1949 to Universal forbidding any use of his *Threepenny* music until such time as he could get some direct word from Bert Brecht on all these vexing matters. In November Universal wrote back to tell Weill that they thought that the *Dreigroschenoper* stage rights had been transferred from Bloch to Suhrkamp. Meanwhile, a letter from Brecht himself had finally reached Weill indicating that Brecht wanted to take the play away from Bloch and give it to Suhrkamp. Brecht did not mention anything about the situation concerning his other contracts with Felix Bloch Erben which had clouded the legality of any attempt to withdraw *Die Dreigroschenoper* from the firm. (Brecht himself was well aware of these complications: Jakob Geis had delineated them in a letter dated 25 May 1949, and Brecht's attorney, Dr. Wolf Schwarz, had said as much in a report sent from Zurich on 7 March 1949. Schwarz and Geis recommended that, because Brecht's prospects for a court-ordered solution were in real doubt, he should try to work things out directly with the firm on "a friendly basis.")[27] Weill, in his reply to Brecht's letter and without knowledge of Brecht's other contractual problems with Felix Bloch Erben, said that he wanted a draft contract *before* anything was signed with Brecht's friend Peter Suhrkamp. No reply to this request seems to have come from either Brecht or Suhrkamp—only a letter from Brecht dated 17 July 1949 saying that he had now terminated the Felix Bloch Erben contract and switched it over to Suhrkamp Verlag. How this could be done on his signature alone when both Weill and Brecht had signed the original contract remains a mystery to this day. In a letter dated 11 July 1949, Felix Bloch Erben expressed concern about Weill's rights and said that Ruth Berlau had claimed to have spoken on Weill's behalf saying that he was in agreement with these changes. How Ruth Berlau, a longtime lover of Brecht, would be representing Weill at the time is also not explained. In a letter dated 15 July 1949, Felix Bloch Erben simply confirmed to Weill that they had turned over everything concerning *Die Dreigroschenoper* to Brecht!

Weill's request to Brecht for news of the royalties from the 1949 performance in Munich also went unanswered. Finally, exasperated by the way he was being treated by Brecht, Weill wrote to Universal on 7 February 1950: "Unfortunately I have heard neither from Brecht nor from Suhrkamp in this matter, and all my letters to Brecht remain unanswered. Therefore, I have turned over this entire matter to my lawyers, especially since Bloch Erben—without having any authorization from me—submitted the entire royalty accounting for *Die Dreigroschenoper* in Germany to Brecht." Just as Weill was putting the matter in the hands of his lawyers, finally something did come, but it was an apologetic letter from Elisabeth Hauptmann, not Brecht. Hauptmann's letter mentioned Brecht's "antipathy to writing," repeated the terms of the second Felix Bloch Erben contract (the one including the 2½% for Klammer), and coolly stated that Brecht had given all his plays to Suhrkamp.[28] Hauptmann did not specify what percentage Weill was to get from the Suhrkamp contract but did complain that Brecht objected to the amount Weill was getting from the Universal contract. That, as far as I have been able to determine, is where matters stood for Weill at the time of his untimely death on 3 April 1950.

But the letters and the lawyers and the arguments about contracts went on and on and on. When Brecht himself died on 14 August 1956, he left behind a tangle of contracts and a large group of widows. But one contract prevailed. Helene Weigel, on the very day of Brecht's death, had obtained from him a little signed note in English which gave her *all* the rights to collect royalties for his work.[29] Her will literally and figuratively prevailed, and she became heir to all royalties. A little later, Peter Suhrkamp, knowing of Elisabeth Hauptmann's contribution to Brecht's plays and poems, insisted on her being given a portion of this income. After a decade of protests from Lenya and her attorneys to Brecht's heirs, Suhrkamp, and Universal Edition, Peter Suhrkamp, fully aware that the unilateral *Dreigroschenoper* contract with Brecht should not be allowed to stand, used his good offices to change the contractual terms so that Weill's estate would receive 35% and Brecht's estate (including Klammer and Hauptmann) 65% of book and stage rights in certain territories and that film rights be split 50/50 in Germany.

Some of the major *Threepenny Opera* battles ended there, but other battles would drag on for decades more, to be taken up by the heirs of the heirs. But that is too long a story to be told here, and not all the battles are over yet. What seems clear in all this is that when Brecht wrote in May 1929 that he had a "grundsatzliche Laxheit in Fragen geistigen Eigentums,"[30] he meant that he had a basic laxity with regard to the intellectual property *of others*, but not to his own—not to "The Business Deals of Herr Bertolt Brecht." In these deals he permitted himself, as far as I have been able to determine, no laxity whatsoever.

Notes

1. Brecht himself is very frank about this (and in this particular area he is reasonably accurate) in his somewhat fictionalized *Diaries 1920-22,* trans. John Willett (London, 1979). Other good sources for the early period are the memoirs of Bie Banholzer and the fine anthology of interviews with people who knew the young Brecht, *Brecht in Augsburg,* a collection assembled by Werner Frisch and K.W. Obermeier (Berlin, 1975).

2. Klaus Völker, *Bertolt Brecht* (Berlin/Vienna, 1979), p. 85.

3. Paula Banholzer, *Meine Zeit mit Bertolt Brecht* (Munich, 1981), pp. 87-88.

4. For this particular point, see Völker's biography and Marieluise Fleisser's long short-story, "Avantgarde."

5. Völker, p. 129.

6. Hermann Kesten, *Lauter Literaten* (Munich, 1963), pp. 439-440.

7. Brecht, *Diaries,* p. 157.

8. Fritz Sternberg, *Der Dichter und die Ratio* (Gottingen, 1963), p. 20.

9. I am deeply indebted to the Kurt Weill Foundation for Music and the Weill/Lenya Archive at the Yale Music Library, the Brecht Archive, and Felix Bloch Erben for providing me with the correspondence and relevant contracts, which provide the basis for this paper. All material relevant to Weill is quoted by permission of the Kurt Weill Foundation for Music.

10. See Sternberg's account of Brecht's "success," pp. 20-21.

11. In the preface to his English-language edition of *Rise and Fall of the City of Mahagonny* (London, 1979), John Willett states flatly: "Elisabeth Hauptmann had studied English, and she wrote him the two English-language Mahagonny Songs, which have ever since figured among his poems." See also my essay, "Whodunit: Brecht's Adaptation of Molière's *Don Juan,*" in *Comparative Literature Studies* XI:2 (1974), pp. 159-172. Eric Bentley told me that, when he worked with Elisabeth Hauptmann in New York during the exile years, she, to Bentley's astonishment, would write "Brecht texts" without even showing them to Brecht.

12. A good composite account of these events is provided by Ronald Sanders, *The Days Grow Short: The Life and Music of Kurt Weill* (New York, 1980), pp. 91-92. Also see pp. 414-15, where Sanders provides details on the various sources for his description of the performance of the *Songspiel* in Baden-Baden. More information is included in my forthcoming *Brecht the Director: Chaos, According to Plan* (Cambridge, 1986).

13. See John Willett and Ralph Manheim, eds., *Brecht: Collected Plays,* Volume 2, pp. X, 106. "Nothing of his first script has come down to us, and there is no real evidence that Brecht himself had as yet taken any hand in it. The process of

'adaptation' credited to him by the original programme probably only started once the play itself and the principle of a collaboration with Weill had been accepted [by Aufricht]."

14. Ernst Josef Aufricht, *Erzähle, damit du dein Recht erweist* (Frankfurt, 1966), pp. 63-65.

15. See Sternberg, pp. 24-27.

16. Aufricht, p. 101.

17. Personal interview with Hauptmann conducted in her Berlin apartment, 9 November 1970.

18. Document supplied by the Kurt Weill Foundation.

19. The incident is described in Aufricht, p. 126.

20. Wreede's views are set forth at great length in a series of letters to Brecht, commencing on 27 February 1933 (the historic date of the Reichstag fire) and petering out inconclusively, in the late thirties. The correspondence can be seen either at the Brecht Archive in East Berlin or at Harvard University's Houghton Library (BBA 783).

21. In a letter dated 16 June 1933, Fritz Wreede is extremely blunt with Brecht. It is clear that he felt he had been deliberately tricked by Brecht, and in his anger he wrote to the playwright: "Reden wir doch ganz offen miteinander, lieber Herr Brecht, Sie haben sich auf unsere Kosten ein sehr luxurioses Eigenleben gestattet" (BBA 783/49).

22. Although in all his letters to Wreede Brecht refers to his money from the firm as an earned "Rente" or pension and denies that it was an "advance" and hence repayable, when tax authorities had sought to collect income tax from Brecht during the period before he left Berlin, he refused to pay. He argued that he had earned no income; all he had received, so he said to them, were advances or loans from publishers. Because Wreede never saw Brecht's reply to the tax authorities and the tax authorities never saw Brecht's correspondence with Wreede, neither party knew that the other was being told something diametrically opposite.

23. This document is one of the very few relevant to Brecht that has survived in the files of Felix Bloch Erben. The original was kindly made available to me by the present officers of the firm

in Berlin. I have deposited a copy of the document in both the Weill-Lenya Research Center and the Brecht Archive.

24. A carbon copy of Weill's original letter is in the Weill-Lenya Research Center. Copies of all Brecht-Weill correspondence have been deposited at the Brecht Archive.

25. The letter is in the Weill-Lenya Research Center.

26. All the materials cited in this section of my paper are in the Weill-Lenya Research Center.

27. A copy of the letter from Dr. Schwarz to Brecht turns up rather mysteriously in the Weill-Lenya Research Center, but I have found no copy of the letter in the files of the Brecht Archive as yet.

28. According to Dr. Köhler of Felix Bloch Erben in a conversation with me on 15 October 1984 in Berlin, Brecht managed to cancel the *Dreigroschenoper* contract with Felix Bloch Erben with the following stratagem: "When Brecht returned to Berlin after the war, he came in to see Frau Wreede, who was then the head of Felix Bloch Erben. He demanded to know why his royalties had been given to the Nazis rather than to him. [According to Dr. Köhler, all royalties due to Jewish authors in the Nazi period had been paid directly to those authors by the foreign theaters themselves to avoid the Nazi bookkeeper who had been imposed on the Berlin firm. Once again according to Dr. Köhler, something went wrong with a *Threepenny* production in Denmark, and the royalties were not given to the authors but sent to Berlin and placed in a Nazi-controlled account.] Brecht began to shout at Frau Wreede and said that they were all a bunch of old Nazis at Felix Bloch Erben. Insulted by this, Frau Wreede asked an assistant to bring her Brecht's general contract with the firm and the *Dreigroschenoper* contract. She threw the contracts at Brecht and said: 'There is the door, young man!' " In light of the fact that no evidence has turned up so far to confirm the view of Dr. Köhler that royalties were regularly paid directly by foreign theaters to Weill, Brecht, and Hauptmann (with the one exception of the 1938 Paris payment of 4,300 francs to Brecht), it is difficult to know how

accurate his account of the encounter between Brecht and Frau Wreede may be. Dr. Köhler was not with the firm at that time; his account is not a first hand one. It is possible that Frau Wreede, who now is a nursing home resident in Munich, will be able to verify this encounter.

29. BBA 655/59. This note has never been published by Brecht's heirs.

30. Brecht originally made the comment in an article published in the *Berliner Börsen-Courier,* 5 June 1929.

[A version of this paper was read at the Kurt Weill conference at Yale in 1983, and is appearing simultaneously in a longer more fully documented version and titled "Most Unpleasant Things with *The Threepenny Opera:* Weill, Brecht, and Money" in *A New Orpheus: Essays on Kurt Weill,* Kim H. Kowalke, ed., Yale University Press, 1986.]

EXITS FROM
NO EXIT [1]

BY RUBY COHN

Entrances precede exits, and the first entrance into a play is necessarily its writing. Jean-Paul Sartre has informally charted that process for *No Exit*. He opens with a generalization: "When one writes a play, there are always accidental causes and deep concerns."[2] Sartre's deep concerns have provoked reams of criticism—not least by Eric Bentley—but my essay will focus on the accidental. Sartre continues:

The accidental cause when I wrote *No Exit* in 1943 and the beginning of 1944 [during the Nazi occupation of Paris] was the fact that I had three friends for whom I wanted to write a play, without giving any one of them a larger part than the others. In other words, I wanted them to be together on the stage all the time. Because I said to myself: "If one of them leaves the stage, he'll think that the other two have better parts in his absence." So I wanted to keep them together, and I said to myself: "How can one put three characters together without an exit, and keep them there on stage to the end of the play, as though eternally." That's when the idea came to me to put them in Hell and make each one of them the torturer of the other two. That's the accidental cause.

Sartre's memory is not quite accurate. He wrote the play not for three, but for two friends—both women—at the instigation of the husband of one of them.[3] In 1943 Marc Barbezat, a manufacturer of pharmaceuticals and a publisher of a luxurious magazine *L'Arbalète,* offered to finance a theater tour of the unoccupied zone of France. His wife Olga had acted in Sartre's *Flies.* Another friend, Wanda Kosakiewicz, was the sister of the Electra in that production, and she also wanted to act. Seeking to place the two actresses in a setting "without an exit," Sartre first planned to confine his heroines to a cellar during an air raid, but he soon shifted them to Hell.

Despite the author's later uncertainty as to the date of composition, Sartre scholars assign *No Exit* to fall, 1943. Disregarding critical disapproval of Dullin's production of his *Flies* in June, 1943, Sartre returned enthusiastically to playwriting, and in a period of two weeks at his customary table at Café Flore, he penned the drama he then entitled *Les Autres* (other people). Both actresses were delighted with the script about "three characters together without an exit." For the fourth character, the infernal Valet, Sartre summoned one of his ex-students, René-Jacques Chauffard, who had played small parts for Charles Dullin. Still needed was Garcin, the apex of the infernal triangle. Sartre thought of Sylvain Itkine, a daring actor/director who had remained in occupied Paris, even though he was Jewish.[4]

Itkine was the first to exit from *No Exit,* but I have been unable to ascertain the circumstances. It was unlike Sartre simply to replace an old friend with a newer one. The newer one had introduced himself—Albert Camus—to Sartre at the premiere of *The Flies*. By fall, 1943, Camus, who had played with theater in his native Algiers, was often in Sartre's company. So immediately trusting was the friendship that Camus recruited both Sartre and Beauvoir for Resistance activities in the Combat group. Camus worked for Gallimard publisher during the day and for the Combat group at night; although still weakened by tuberculosis, Camus accepted the key role of Garcin and also agreed to direct *No Exit*.[5]

With cast decided, play rehearsals began in Simone de Beauvoir's home, the round room of Hotel de La Louisiane at 60 Rue de Seine, only a few short blocks from the café where the play was composed. Since *No Exit* seemed a safe drama in its fantastic post-death setting, the cast expected no harassment from the Occupiers, but they neglected accidental causes. While Olga Barbezat was paying a casual visit to Resistance friends, their apartment was raided, and everyone on the premises was arrested. Olga Barbezat was in jail by April, 1944, when *Les Autres* was published in *L'Arbalète* #8 (along with texts by Genet and Mouloudji). So demoralizing was her exit from *No Exit* that the cast abandoned rehearsals. How could they know that she would be released in time to attend the performance of *No Exit* by another cast?

Within the claustrophobic setting, Sartre's characters act through speech; on the stage, three sinners lacerate one another with words, while a delayed exposition unveils their separate pasts. We gradually learn that the Brazilian journalist Garcin has abused his wife and fled from his country in time of war; the Lesbian postal clerk Inez has seduced her cousin's wife and goaded her to suicide and murder; the beautiful society matron Estelle has drowned her

191

illegitimate baby, driving its father to suicide. If their lives were violent, however, their deaths were maudlin: Inez was asphyxiated when her lover turned on the gas; Estelle succumbed to pneumonia; more striking was Garcin's execution for desertion.

Eric Bentley early recognized the stuff of melodrama within the Second Empire salon: "Adultery, infanticide, Lesbianism, a traffic accident, double suicide in bed, refusal to fight for France, death before a firing squad."[6] Aside from the understandable errors (One of the bedded deaths is not suicide, and the deserter is not French.) Bentley discerned the familiar structure beneath Sartre's "philosophic melodrama": "A man is . . . placed in the center; two women are peripheral. A neat, old-fashioned Parisian pattern."[7] Moreover, the man melodramatically pleads for physical tortures— "Je veux souffrir pour de bon"—instead of the mental anguish of not knowing whether he is a coward.

No Exit thrives on its stifling atmosphere. It accentuates spare properties and relentless lighting. What other play rises to the climax of a door opening—without entrance or exit? The characters finally choose their own damnation.

As early as 1945, Eric Bentley concluded his resonant *Playwright as Thinker* on Sartre and Brecht as "rival revolutionaries" of a new theater. Although philosophic farce rather than philosophic melodrama became the prevalent Paris avant-garde genre, *No Exit* formed dramas as different as Genet's *Maids* (1947) and Beckett's *Play* (1963).

Widely performed today both in Paris and abroad (even in Stuart Gilbert's careless English translation), the original production of *No Exit* was a minor miracle. After the arrest of Olga Barbezat, Sartre did not even submit the play to Paris theater directors. However, at the beginning of 1944 a businessman Annet Badel acquired the Vieux-Colombier

Theater, which had the most distinguished reputation in Paris. As the manufacturer Marc Barbezat indulged in avant-garde publication, the businessman Annet Badel decided to indulge in avant-garde theater. He too was married to an actress—Gaby Sylvia, who had some experience in ingenue leads. When Badel was introduced to Sartre, he asked for a play, and Sartre resurrected *No Exit.* Cannily planning a double bill—Sartre's shocker and a frothy farce—Badel chose a professional director with impeccable avant-garde credentials, Raymond Rouleau, who had worked with Dullin and Artaud.

Camus made a graceful exit before Rouleau's expertise, and the new director chose a new cast. Predictably, he selected actors he knew well, rather than celebrities—Michel Vitold as Garcin and Tanya Balachova as Inez. (Rouleau and Balachova were divorced in 1940, but that was no obstacle to their professional cooperation.) Unpredictably, he cast Gaby Sylvia as Estelle, much to the displeasure of Badel, who preferred his wife as an ingenue.[8] The only one of the original cast *not* to exit from *No Exit* was Chauffard who retained his role as Valet. During rehearsals it was uncertain whether the play would open at all, since Occupation authorities first approved it for production, then withdrew permission, then approved it again—all without explanation.[9]

The director Rouleau imposed a proscenium on the open stage of the Vieux-Colombier.[10] The designer Douy rendered a Second Empire drawing-room with bilious green walls. The single door was at stage left, and upstage center on a mantel was a false bronze sculpture of a nude woman sitting astride a nude man. Behind it was a mirror carefully angled not to reflect the actors. High ceilings dwarfed the infernal inmates, and an ostentatious chandelier hung low, all bulbs lit. The three sofas were uncomfortable as well as mismatched—yellow, dark green, and maroon in clashing styles.

Although subsidized theaters could indulge in lavish sets and costumes even during the Occupation, designer Douy had limited resources. Chauffard/Valet wore the white apron and striped jacket habitual in French hotels; he smoked a pipe and gave sulky service. Sylvia/Estelle, blonde hair piled high on her lovely head, was fitted snugly into a sleeveless white evening gown. Balachova/Inez, hair hidden under a turban, wore a nondescript short black dress. Vitold/Garcin in dark suit, dark shirt, and hat far back on his head, loosened his tie in the heat of the dialogue; he resembled a Humphrey Bogart of the avant-garde.

The exact date of the opening is uncertain. The Gallimard edition of *Huis clos* says May, 1944. In her autobiography Simone de Beauvoir mentions June 10, 1944. The Sartre scholar Michel Rybalka graciously informed me: "The official date is May 27, 1944, but the first accounts in the press are dated June 3, 1944. It is quite possible that the play had a first showing on May 27, and then, because of a holiday or for some other reason, the second showing was in June." It is also possible that the Allied invasion of Normandy on June 6, 1944, made for general confusion in the capital.

Instead of wooing the good will of Parisians, the Nazis escalated their cruelties, and Vichy escalated its collaboration. André Castelot, a powerful collaborationist reviewer, demanded that *No Exit* be censored "not only because of its mediocrity, but because of its evil ugliness, and disgusting garbage."[11] But the most powerful Paris reviewer, Alain Laubréaux, objected: "The play censors itself because it is so boring."[12] Other collaborationist reviews used adjectives like "scandalous," "rotten," "venereal," "lugubriously unhealthy." But the drama was also admired. The playwright Henri Lenormand praised the "nervous interdependence" of the infernal trio, and he described a performance where enthusiastic young spectators threw their cigarette rations to the stage.[13] Sartre himself was delighted with the first production of No Exit: "At the first performance in 1944 I had a very rare pleasure, very rare for a dramatist. The characters were incarnated in such a way by the three actors and also by Chauffard, the Valet of hell, who has invariably acted him ever since, that I can no longer imagine my own creations otherwise than as Vitold, Gaby Sylvia, Tania Balachova, and Chauffard."[14] Conceived for the feminine members of one cast, No Exit was indelibly incarnated by others. After playing in No Exit Vitold acted and directed several Sartre plays. Balachova acted, directed, and taught acting in the Paris avant-garde. Sylvia acted and directed in France and Japan. Although Chauffard played small roles in other Sartre plays, he also enjoyed a career in Paris avant-garde theater, often as the protagonist. The original production of No Exit played at the Vieux-Colombier (with interruptions) until July, 1945, and it has been frequently revived. It has also been filmed (twice), televised, recorded, and subjected to the indignity of a sequel, La Porte ouverte (the open door).[15]

In 1944 the most favorable review of No Exit was surprising—that of French fascist Robert Brasillach, in the penultimate issue of his Chronique de Paris. His eulogy concludes:

> Everything blends to make of this rigorous single act the most frightful confession of an age lacking faith. . . . I don't presume to offer a final judgment on the play.

Jean-Paul Sartre is certainly at the opposite pole from what I love and still believe. His play may be the symbol of a lucid and rotten art that was the unsuccessful result of the last war, but I don't think I'm risking much when I say that, by its dark cold structure, by its rigor, by its demonstrative *purity* opposed to its fundamental impurity, it is a masterpiece.[16]

And in his very last issue, Brasillach predicts: "*No Exit* will remain as a bizarre monument of an agonizing world when the future will undoubtedly seek evidence of the most lucid negation." He was not far off the mark.

As Allied armies fought their way south in July and August, 1944, the Nazis tightened their control on the French capital. Hitler ordered the destruction of Paris, and he was disobeyed only because the German commander thought him insane.[17] But Jews continued to be deported, hostages to be murdered, captured Resistance fighters to be methodically tortured. Theaters remained more or less open, playing sporadically under the stringent rationing. At the Vieux-Colombier laughter greeted the Valet's line: "We have all the electricity we want."

On August 3, 1944, Sylvain Itkine vanished from a Paris street, never to see the city again. On August 17, Robert Brasillach returned to the capital after a brief vacation and attended *No Exit* for a second time.[18] Sartre's play was his exit from theater.

Paris was liberated on August 25, 1944. Unlike fellow-collaborators, Brasillach did not flee from France, but he did go into hiding. When he learned that his mother had been arrested, however, he surrendered on September 14. *No Exit* reopened the Vieux-Colombier on September 20, and its 100th performance was celebrated on September 30. To jubilant Parisians *No Exit* was emblematic both of French culture and French resistance to fascism. Sartre and Vitold had been heard on Resistance radio; the Badels had hidden arms for Resistance fighters; Rouleau had been a stretcher-bearer in the Resistance. The Vieux-Colombier was seen as the cornerstone not only of avant-garde theater but of French civilized life.

Robert Brasillach went on trial early in 1945, and, unlike most collaborators, he was condemned to death. Led by François Mauriac, 59 French intellectuals—among them Jean Anouilh, Marcel Aymé, Jean-Louis Barrault, Paul Claudel, Jean Cocteau, Colette, Paul Valéry—petitioned General De Gaulle to commute the sentence. Except for Camus, Sartre's circle was not inclined to ask for mercy, recalling that Brasillach had not asked mercy for Jews or Resistants. De Gaulle denied the plea. Like Sartre's Garcin, Brasillach faced a firing squad—on February 6, 1945. Unlike Garcin, Brasillach died bravely—according to the eyewitness account of his attorney. No eyewitness reports how Sylvain Itkine died—under Nazi torture.[19]

Notes

1. This article has been adapted from the author's forthcoming book *From DESIRE to GODOT: A Decade of Paris Pocket Theater,* to be published by the University of California Press.

2. Quoted in Michel Contat and Michel Rybalka, eds. *Sartre: un théâtre de situations* (Paris: Gallimard, 1973) 237-8. Unless otherwise noted, all translations are mine.

3. Simone de Beauvoir, *La Force de l'age* (Paris: Gallimard, 1973) 568, 582.

4. Contat and Rybalka 240.

5. Beauvoir *passim* and Herbert R. Lottman, *Albert Camus: A Biography* (London: Picador, 1981).

6. *The Playwright as Thinker* (New York: Meridian, 1955) 197. (The book was originally published in 1946.)

7. *ibid,* 198.

8. Guy Dupré, *Histoire de rire et de pleurer* (Paris: Fayard, 1969).

9. H.C., "Au Vieux-Colombier. . . " *Libération* (September 8, 1944).

10. My description conflates reviews in *R. Supp.* 1600 of the Fonds Rondel of the Bibliothèque de l'Arsenal.

11. *La Gerbe* (June 8, 1944).

12. *Je suis partout* (June 9, 1944).

13. *Panorama* (June 22, 1944).

14. Contat and Rybalka 239-240.

15. Michel Contat and Michel Rybalka, *Les Ecrits de Sartre* (Paris: Gallimard, 1970) 99.

16. Robert Brasillach, *Oeuvres complètes* Vol. XII (Paris: Club de l'Honnête Homme, 1963-1966) 712-714; 719.

17. Larry Collins and Dominique Lapierre *Is Paris Burning?* (New York: Simon and Schuster, 1965) 284.

18. William R. Tucker, *The Fascist Ego* (Berkeley: University of California Press, 1975).

19. Information on Itkine comes from a conversation with his friend, the late Roger Blin.

THE DYNAMICS OF PETER SHAFFER'S DRAMA[1]

BY BERNARD BECKERMAN

At the conclusion of a devastating review of *Equus*, John Simon gives grudging credit to the play's "spectacular theatricality."[2] In the magazine *Commentary*, at almost the same time in 1975, Jack Richardson describes *Equus* as a combination of brilliant production and banality. "As a critic of the theater," Richardson reluctantly confesses, "I have to say that the presentation of this nonsense has a galling merit to it."[3] To explain the play's theatrical power and its popularity on two continents, Simon approvingly quotes Robert Brustein's diagnosis. The appeal of *Equus* is another confirmation of "the idiocy of Broadway."[4]

Few critics are so extreme in their deprecation of the play. Yet even among people who are more tempered in their criticism, a similar distinction occurs between the play proper and its theatrical impression. John Weightman in *Encounter* describes the climactic ride of boy and horse at the end of Act I as "an exciting piece of theatre," but he

199

deplores the lack of full understanding that the drama achieves.[5] Academic critics, though generally more positive about the play than journalists, also tend to admire what they regard as superficial theatricality more than the substantive action. One writer claims that "those elements which rivet the audience so intensely are elements of [stage] *direction*."[6] Another claims that "*Equus* is a schizophrenic play, because its theatrical fireworks cannot mask its muddled logic and tired philosophy."[7] Only rarely have any of the critics insisted on the wholeness of Mr. Shaffer's conception in *Equus*, and even then have not always demonstrated how the parts cohere.

Even when strongly impressed by the performance, they may be uncertain about its implications or the quote unquote meaning of it all. It is on this last point that most controversy converges. What is the play about? Does it expose the futility of psychiatry? Or does it praise irrational acts, however brutal, so long as they are passionate? Is it a religious play, and does it depict the failure of professionalized rationalism? Depending on how we interpret the psychiatrist's failed marriage or the patient's fixation on horses, we may see the play as a covert appeal to homosexuality, as John Simon does, or as a return to mythic tragedy, as Russell Vandenbroucke argues.[8] Yet, no matter how much critics and playgoers may disagree about the ultimate meaning of *Equus* or the validity of that meaning, most concur in their admiration of the play's stage magnetism.

Divorcing the play's production features from its dramatic movement, however, is a mistake. Shaffer's theatricality does not merely inhabit the more obvious elements such as the anthropomorphized horses. It goes beyond the equine noises and the stage direction for which John Dexter was

200

responsible. Shaffer, I believe, theatricalizes every facet of *Equus.* He creates stage not literary images. How effective he is cannot and should not be judged by his ability as a psychiatrist or a philosopher or a theologian, but solely by his accomplishments as a playwright. To judge these accomplishments, however, we have to have a better sense of his stagecraft than has yet appeared in print.

Before I make any claims, allow me to make some disclaimers. I am less concerned with evaluating *Equus* than I am with describing its structure. But to describe its structure, I need to make some remarks about dramatic organization in general. I shall confine my comments about Shaffer's plays to *Equus* for the most part although I think that my observations apply in large measure to his other plays as well.

Robert Asahina begins his piece on *Amadeus* in *The Hudson Review* by remarking that "there are two kinds of people . . . those who divide the world into two kinds of people, and those who don't. Peter Shaffer certainly belongs to the first kind. . . . [Over the years] the basic plot [of his plays]—a struggle between two opposing but mutually dependent males—remains the same."9 This observation is true enough—it is also true in a way that its author did not intend. The struggle between two opposing but mutually dependent human beings is the stuff of most drama. But the confrontation is seldom so sustained or so stark as Shaffer makes it. For every struggle between an Antigone and a Creon, there are more oblique encounters. Perhaps, as in *Prometheus Bound,* one opponent, in this case the god Zeus, appears on stage only through representatives. Or as in *Macbeth,* the prime contention inhabits the single body of the hero.

But even more crucial to the shaping of drama than its overall duality is the tendency of plays to be a sequence of scenes between two characters. This is a subject I have discussed elsewhere,[10] but is especially pertinent here. The Greeks recognized this natural tendency in drama, and so limited the number of actors who could appear on stage at any one time. Ever since then, western drama has both followed their lead and endeavored to break the confines of binary form.

It is no coincidence that naturalistic plays multiply characters on stage. Through increase of numbers they seek to create an illusion of reality. But they do so at the cost of dramatic concentration, and few playwrights have learned to pay the cost advantageously. Playwriting involves a peculiar tension. To maintain concentration, playwrights tend to limit themselves to two figures in a scene at one time. To achieve perspective, variety, and verisimilitude, they tend to expand the number of figures that they weave into the action. The more skillful they are, the better able they are to utilize the fundamental duet as the foundation of drama while, at the same time, transcend its confines by enlarging the field without diffusing the audience's attention.

Shakespeare, as we might expect, was eminently effective in doing this. Along with his fellow Elizabethans, he employed a variety of techniques for expanding the duet. Most common—and of immediate relevance to my discussion of *Equus*—is the scene-within-the-scene technique. He would present a duet between two characters, let us say, Iago and Cassio, while a third, Othello in this instance, watches unobserved, commenting on what he sees (IV. i). This type of arrangement—most commonly known as an observation scene—was exceedingly popular in the Renaissance. In *Equus*, Peter Shaffer uses variations of this technique in subtle and novel ways.

One last comment on the binary arrangement remains to be added. While the duet is the most frequent way of organizing action, it has variants that may not be immediately recognized. For example, Dysart the psychiatrist in *Equus* and Salieri the court composer in *Amadeus* repeatedly address the audience directly. We usually speak of these addresses as monologues or soliloquies, and that is accurate enough. Yet direct address to the audience is actually another kind of duality. In treating the audience as a homogeneous group, the character makes assumptions about them. In effect, he characterizes them. For Dysart the audience supplies a neutral sympathetic ear. For Salieri, on the other hand, the spectators are Ghosts of the Future, the last witnesses of his dying fame. He conceives them as active sensibilities with whom he can engage in continuous exchange. His monologues are, in effect, special kinds of dialogue. Despite their apparent single-sidedness, they are only variants of the primal model of action—the scene between two people. That scene may narrow to an exchange between actor and audience in which the audience is both a passive actor and an active observer. Or it may expand to two actors who are observed by an on stage character, the whole being watched by the audience. *Equus* includes variants of all these examples.

To make the binary model work, playwrights select terms of contrast that are peculiarly resonant when set against one another: the sprightly, romantic Nora against the stolid, conventional Torvald in *A Doll House*, the arrogant, unknowing Oedipus against the blind, all-knowing Tiresias, the passionate Phèdre against the priggish Hippolyte. Likewise, particularly since *Royal Hunt of the Sun*, Shaffer juxtaposes men of sharply contrasting temperaments. At first, he pits the foul, ruthless, unbelieving Pizarro against the god-like Atahualpa. Later, in *Equus* and *Amadeus,* he tunes the differences more precisely. In Dysart and Alan, Salieri and Mozart, he places man against child, social power against isolated vulnerability, normality against abnormality, rationality against irrationality and, in the latter pair, mediocrity against genius.

Because the striking production features of *Equus*—the horses, the stage, the lights, the sounds—have received ample attention, I shall say little about them. They seem to suffuse the entire play. But that is because they strike audiences as fresh and unusual. In actuality, however, although they provide a fascinating background to the action and dominate the climaxes of the acts, the spectacular elements take stage only intermittently.

More pervasive throughout the play is the use of an audience within an audience. Looking at the circle of spectators from outside in, we first have the actual audience. A part of that audience—the small part that sits on stage in "tiers of seats [arranged] in the fashion of a dissecting theater"—is both actor for the rest of the playgoers as well as audience for the play. Next, all the actors, when not performing, sit on benches upstage. Thus they too are both actors for the audience and audience for the actors who are then playing. Even on stage, in the midst of many scenes, a character may become a spectator of an event then being narrated. Indeed, throughout the play we are continually made aware that events are unfolding within successive rings of scrutiny.

Within those rings, the most usual scene is a duet. The principal running duet is that between the psychiatrist Dysart and his patient, Alan Strang. But there are other duets: between Dysart and the magistrate Hester Salomon,

Dysart and Alan's mother or father, Dysart and the stable owner. As the play proceeds, the duets vary. When Alan's father Frank lectures him on the stupidity of television, the mother Dora associates herself with Alan, thereby sustaining the effect of a duet (I. 6). Almost immediately afterward occurs a segment in which Dysart tells Hester about a session he has had with Alan. At times Dysart plays the scene with Alan, other times he speaks to Hester who, as it were, is observing the scene. Thus, in an essentially Elizabethan manner, the play expands its structure by placing a duet within a frame of narration, observation, or comment.

In the course of the action, this kind of scene within a scene becomes increasingly resonant. At one point in Act II, Alan tells Dysart the story of going to a pornographic movie with Jill and meeting his father there. Scene 9 shows Alan, Frank, and Jill in the street immediately after, waiting for a bus. While Alan is describing the experience to Dysart, Jill acts it out: she tries to persuade Frank that Alan went to the movie only because of her. During the first third of the scene, Alan speaks to Dysart. Both of them can be said to be looking at Jill and Frank. In the second third of the scene, Frank insists that Alan take the bus home with him. Alan refuses. For this segment of action, Alan plays directly to Frank while Dysart alone is "watching" it. As the conflict comes to a climax in the third part, Alan resumes speaking to Dysart, yet he keeps looking at his father, thus appearing to be watching himself as he relives a crucial exchange of glances with his father. This double moment makes Alan's act of being an audience intensely active and peculiarly painful. Through it all, the actors on the bench and the audience in the house share Dysart's observational stance.

This modulation from acting to observing to acting recurs repeatedly in *Equus*. It places duets within frames of observation or even, at times, sets a duet of observers around a duet of doers. The effect is to theatricalize every moment of the play. Theatricalize, in this sense, does not refer to what most critics mean by the word, that is, to make spectacular. Rather, it refers to the fact that almost every action in the play is also a performance for other characters, actors, or spectators.

At the heart of what is being observed, as I've said, is the duet. In *Equus* the core duet, of course, occurs between Dysart and Alan. It usually takes the form of question, resistance and, finally, answer. There are about two dozen sessions between the man and boy. In their first meeting every speech Dysart addresses to Alan ends in a question: "Is this your full name? Alan Strang? . . . Your father's a printer. What sort of things does he print? . . . Now that's a good song. . . . Can I hear that one again?" (I. 3). This mode of discourse, although it does not continue in so unrelenting an interrogatory manner throughout the play, remains the principal means of communication between Dysart and Alan and produces the effect, so often noted, of a detective story. One of the few scenes in which Dysart doesn't ask questions—Act I, scene 17—ends with Dysart despising himself for the way he spoke to Alan. Only in one scene (II. 6) is there a reversal, when Alan briefly turns inquisitor and Dysart replies. Ultimately, the recurrent pattern of question, resistance, and answer, by throwing emphasis on the story emerging, brings Dysart and Alan together only on an informational level. The true impact of the information is not felt between them but in Dysart's periodic monologues.

This is apparent in Dysart's scenes with Hester. They have five altogether. In the first (I. 2) Hester persuades Dysart to take Alan's case. Subsequently, she hears periodic reports of Dysart's progress and in their third meeting has to urge him to continue treatment. Except for this bit of action, the core of their last three meetings are monologues by Dysart. Hester is merely a member of the audience. These monologues can just as well be delivered to us. Indeed, the last encounter in the last scene of the play shows Dysart shifting from Hester to us with hardly a transition. In short, Dysart uses Hester as he uses the audience: as a listener to his own self-examination. The result is that neither in the duets with Alan and Hester nor in the direct addresses to the audience is there a dialectical process at work. There are never two sides to a complex question, sides vested in two opposing figures. Instead, the uncovering of Alan's story is balanced by a persistent effort on Dysart's part to define himself.

Yet even the action of self-definition is not a matter of self-discovery. From the very beginning of the play, Dysart has reached the full apogee of uncertainty. As he himself states it: "In a way, [my problems have] nothing to do with this boy [Alan]. The doubts have been there for years. . . . It's only the extremity of this case that's made them active." In the process of narrating Alan's story, Dysart articulates and expresses his condition, a condition that is already fixed from the opening lines. And the fact that it is so fixed contributes, in my opinion, to the critics' perception of a disparity between the action and the theatricality of the play.

Dysart's monologues themselves—there are six substantial ones in the text—reinforce the impress of fixation. Whether he is telling Hester his dream of sacrificing children (I. 5) or describing a typical evening at home, Dysart fashions his recital as a story. Even as he reports his growing horror of killing the children of his dream, he avoids all expressions of internal distress. Indeed, the climax of the monologue is not stated subjectively—but descriptively. Dysart describes becoming nauseous at slitting the young bodies. The mask he is wearing starts to slip. Then, he observes: "The priests [who assist him] both turn and look at [the mask]—it slips some more—they see the green sweat running down my face—their gold pop eyes suddenly fill with blood—they tear the knife out of my hand . . . and I wake up." Through it all, Dysart is the observer of his own story, his own life.

Ultimately, the closed form of Dysart's monologues serves to emblemize his character. He is less a complex human being than a nexus of contemporary states of mind and behavioral habits. His fascination with primitive Greece dramatizes a romantic longing for purified existence. His alienation from his wife represents a congenital revolt against domesticity. In the course of the play we learn nothing much about the source of or motivation for these attitudes. They merely exist, as fixedly as do the relations between Alan and his parents or Dysart and Hester.

The play is thus as abstract as its chief character. Without fully being ceremonial, it shows the inevitable procession of outworn mental habits. Dysart tries to unravel a mystery. But his probing only solidifies the way he thinks. His monologues celebrate—if that is the word—his negativity. His tragedy is his theatricality: he is the observer, but not the actor, of his own life.

Notes [M.B.]

1. This is the first printing of an essay Dr. Beckerman read at the 1983 MLA convention in New York. Peter Shaffer was in the audience.

2. John Simon, "Hippodrama at the Psychodrome," *Hudson Review*, 28 (Spring 1975), pp. 97-106.

3. Jack Richardson, rev. of *Equus, Commentary*, 59 (February 1975), pp. 76-78.

4. From a letter Brustein wrote to Simon.

5. John Weightman, rev. of *Equus, Encounter*, 44 (March 1975), pp. 44-46.

6. Hélène Baldwin, "*Equus:* Theatre of Cruelty or Theatre of Sensationalism?" in *West Virginia University Philological Papers*, 25 (1979), pp. 118-127.

7. B.B. Withram, "Anger in *Equus,*" *Modern Drama*, 22 (March 1979), pp. 61-66.

8. Russell Vandenbroucke, "*Equus:* Modern Myth in the Making," *Drama & Theatre*, 12 (Spring 1975), pp. 129-133.

9. Robert Asahina, rev. of *Amadeus, Hudson Review*, 34 (Summer 1981), pp. 263-268.

10. See Dr. Beckerman's "Shakespeare's Dramaturgy and Binary Form," *Theatre Journal*, 33 (March 1981), pp. 5-17.

SAM SHEPARD: ICONOGRAPHER OF THE DEPTHS

BY ARTHUR GANZ

When Eric Bentley published *The Playwright as Thinker* in 1946, he accomplished much more than can be summarized here, but one of his notable achievements was almost single-handedly to make the study of the modern drama intellectually respectable (and thus, incidentally, to make certain careers attractive, perhaps even possible). Another was to proclaim that the popular commercial theatre, as a source of dramatic art, was dead. It was certainly moribund and, except for an occasional spasmodic twitch, has remained so. Bentley argued that the drama, which is to say the drama of intellectual and artistic significance, would best be created and served by Little Theatres and by People's Theatres subsidized by the government. Looking back from our standpoint in the political climate of the mid-eighties, we may smile at the latter notion, Bentley more mordantly no doubt than anyone else. But he was right about the Little Theatres, except that they were not to be on campuses, as he then thought, but—in their origin at least—in the church basements, store fronts, and coffee houses of lower New York.

In 1946, however, Bentley could hardly have anticipated the drug-sex-art-politics "scene" of the East Village, out of which twenty years later a new drama, or perhaps more precisely a new dramatist, was to emerge. For the theatrical ferment of that time and place seems now to have found its most viable form in the work of one figure: a restless, ill-read young nightclub waiter and would-be rock and roll drummer, as he was then, originally called Samuel Shepard Rogers, who rebelled (in that environment one could not do much else) against a family name passed on through generations and became Sam Shepard. Whether he is the Great American Playwright who will compensate us for the limitations of O'Neill and his successors is not the point here. (Literary history, after all, has its own way of sorting out such matters.) The questions are rather what sort of playwright Shepard is, and how we may come to grips with the nature of his dramatic concerns and with the technique that embodies them.

Defining Shepard's preoccupations, however, is not a simple task. The question of rebellion, for one, goes far beyond the matter of choosing a name. Shepard after all began his career in the sixties, an intensely anarchic age when it seemed possible to change the course of political events in America, to change society, even to change the natures of its members. If the first of these was, to a very limited extent, achieved in the withdrawal from Vietnam, the subsequent triumph of conservatism dashed the millenarian hopes of the age; as for the other two, they have, not surprisingly, been more difficult to manage. It will be important, however, to acknowledge that the relationship of some of Shepard's more overtly political plays to the climate of events from which they stemmed is ambiguous. (Indeed, the radicalism of the age often derived from a frustrated effort to realize traditional values; one remembers that a favorite author on campuses was the conservative, sentimental Tolkien.) In his overtly political work, Shepard's stance is always both critical and nostalgic, his denunciation of the American present rarely separable from some affectionate reminiscence of its past.

Moreover, even these political plays, important if small in number, prove to be concerned with the personal, psychological, and moral obsessions that dominate most of Shepard's work. For those extraordinary dramatic fantasies that he has constructed out of such pop artifacts as cowboys, movie monsters, and creatures from outer space conceal beneath their theatrical surface a profound private concern with psychic forces lurking in the depths of the self and the travails of coping with them. Predictably such concerns spill over into the plays dealing with the traditional subject of the demands the world makes on the artist. Yet the significance of Shepard's drama, whose range of themes is here merely suggested, cannot be addressed without close attention to the most characteristic verbal mode of his theatrical art.

Among the ironies of Shepard's career (e.g. that a writer obsessed with the myths of American popular culture should himself become that most "mythic" of American figures, a movie star) is the fact that this playwright of evidently very circumscribed culture—we know little except that he had read *Godot* before beginning to write and has spoken of his admiration for Brecht—should be among the most eloquent of dramatists. Not since the plays of Bernard Shaw were accused of presenting characters who merely made speeches on behalf of the author (and were, in effect, defended by Granville-Barker on the grounds that these works were

"Italian opera") have we had such theatrical loquacity. At any moment a Shepard character may burst forth into a big speech, a monologue almost Elizabethan in its linguistic fecundity. (One is reminded of Pinter's verbal antics, but it will be more profitable to return to this comparison later.) Indeed, in certain plays a character may do nothing but verbalize. *Cowboys #2*—a rewritten version of Shepard's first play, *Cowboys*—is made up almost completely of the rambling fantasies of the two main characters, who remain essentially actionless. *Killer's Head,* subtitled *a monologue,* consists entirely of one long speech, the pathetic discourse of a convicted criminal, as he sits strapped into an electric chair in the moments before execution and his mind turns to what he seems to have loved most, horses and trucks (means of a more beneficent escape than the one he is about to experience). And finally there are the late, neo-Beckettian experiments done with Joseph Chaikin, *Tongues* and *Savage/Love,* that are almost purely verbal in nature.

Where such grand rhetorical gestures are parts of larger works, however, they are at their most intriguing and suggestive. For in that fuller context these logorrheic outbursts reveal more clearly than any other device the themes, indeed the obsessions that dominate the Shepard world. Not least, they illuminate the poetic style of what may be the most lyrical of postwar playwrights.

Shepard's lyricism has thus far in his career not encompassed dramatic verse, beyond some of the texts for songs in those plays that use them, but it has always involved a striking sense of the evocative possibilities of visual, as well as verbal, imagery. In *Chicago,* for example, a play dating from 1965, when Shepard was only twenty-two, the central character, Stu, spends the entire play, until its final moments when he comes down front and addresses the audience directly, seated in a bathtub in the center of an otherwise empty stage, splashing water and only occasionally making coherent contact with the other characters. There is no sense here of a "real" bathroom with toilet and sink, to say nothing of walls, omitted, but rather of the striking visualization of a state of psychic retreat into an enclosed and protected, even womblike (seated posture with inevitably raised knees, presence of imagined fluid) environment. It is fitting that this image should be one of the first of Shepard's career, for fantasies of retreat and escape are among the central motifs of Shepardian drama.

Yet only when such fantasies become verbal do we fully understand the motives that inspire them and the direction in which the fantasist is fleeing. Stu's initial speech, a rambling monologue full of childlike rhymes and rhythms projecting a sense of isolation and loss (". . . This is it. It's the day that ya' say is okay. Anyway. Anyhow. You know by now. That yer dog is dead and ya' don't care anyhow. . . . [3]") is interrupted when his wife or girlfriend, the ironically named Joy, calls from offstage words suggestive of traditional American domestic values: "Biscuits are ready!" (4). Even though he eats one, Stu rejects them and what they represent: "Biscuits were invented to trick people into believing that they're really eating food! . . . They're just dough. . . . Biscuits are shit" (6). But Stu rejects more than Joy's homey virtues and practicalities (she is about to leave for a job she has just gotten). There is a further, more overtly sinister fantasy that comes near the middle of the play.

In strikingly handled images Shepard deals with the violence that lurks beneath the sexual impulse and that is equally part of its repression. Pretending that the bathtub is a boat, Stu and Joy envision fish swimming beneath them, which Stu insists are barracudas "with long teeth and pink

215

tongues" who are "lookin' for a nice young virgin." "They want you," he tells Joy, "for their very own" (11). This intense mixture of possessiveness and hostility, projected through the barracudas, is counterbalanced in a soliloquy by Stu following shortly after, in which he warns the barracudas that people will come out fishing for them: "Out in the deep part. And they'll break out their thermos bottles full of coffee and split pea soup. And they'll drink and whisper about you. About how big you are and how striped you are and how nice it would be to have your head cut off and mounted over the fireplace" (13). For the bourgeois inhabitants of the surface the sexual savagery that lurks in the depths has to be dealt with through an amputation; the long teeth and pink tongue can only be contemplated as part of a trophy. But the stultifying of instinctual life, of this violence in the depths, is itself a kind of murder, as suggested by the drowning of a fisherman's bait, with its "little spasm and wriggle on the hook." Contemplating the intolerable dilemma, Stu concludes his speech to the fish: "You're down there moving slowly around this worm, taking your time. And they're up there drinking split pea soup and grinning. . . . You're both hung up." It is as if Shepard, even here at this early stage of his work, were looking ahead to the rival brothers of *True West* (1980), the writer and the brute, locked in their eternal struggle.

The sense of being enclosed in a horror from which one cannot escape marks Stu's next oration (14-16), a series of speeches about a railroad trip. Although the ostensible occasion is Joy's departure for her new job, the trip becomes the inevitable generalized metaphor for the journey through life. Beginning with a reminiscence of a comfortable dining car with a pitcher of ice water and "silver cup full of toothpicks" on each table (it is suggestive of an unexpected nostalgia that such a detail in the work of a writer not yet in his middle forties should be so dated; one thinks of Dickens living in the age of the steam locomotive and writing of the stagecoaches of his youth), the speech becomes an evocation of claustrophobic entrapment as the passengers sleep on while through the night a fat man keeps breaking wind: "One fart after another. . . . The car stinks more and more. The smell gets into the seats and the pillows and the rug. Everyone's smelling it at the same time. They sleep more and more" (16).

Although the travelers of Stu's vision awake in the morning, it is clear that in reality this journey leads only to death, for its central motifs—of confinement and repellent physicality—recur at the climax of the play, a gigantic monologue, one of Shepard's most extraordinary creations, that runs, aside from interruptions, for four pages of text (19-25). Stu begins the monologue in a voice he sometimes adopts, that of a "little old lady," who suggests Shepard's ambiguous feelings by being at once a parodistic image of old-fashioned values and a grudgingly admired embodiment of them, but he soon shifts to his own voice. At first there is a sense of sexual fulfillment and release as he envisions sailors "drinkin' gin and singin' sea songs" arriving on a shore "horny for the young virgins that walk the beaches in their two-piece flimsy things." But the sexual utopia evoked as "everybody's screwing on the beach" becomes associated with images of corrupting lassitude and grotesque obsession: "And all those boats just sitting out there with their sails down and their nets hanging and rotting in the sun. Years go by and they're still screwing. Old sailors with bald heads and old virgins with gray hair." A generation passes and the sexual paradise has become an ultimate vision of animalistic horror: "Males and females up and down the beach. No clothes any more. A mound of greasy bodies rolling in sperm and sand sticking to their backs and sand in their hair. Hair growing all over. Down to their feet. Pubic hair without bows or ribbons. . . . Hair on their toes. Fires! Fires at night. . . . They lie there fucking by the fire and picking each other's nose. They lick each other's arms and growl and purr and fart all they want to. They roll around farting and spitting and licking up and down. Long tongues and wet legs.''

As the speech develops, Shepard turns its focus from the general delineation of Yahoo-like bestiality to the claustrophobic self-loathing it evokes, and to the ultimate act of revulsion. The creatures stop fornicating and take a year to build a house ''with one room and a fire pit in the middle'' (suggesting still, perhaps, the traditional fires of lust). There they make ''big huge heavy rugs. . . . Years of making rugs until the whole house is covered. The walls are covered and the ceiling and the floor. The windows are blocked up and they sit.'' Even this retreat into the protective darkness of the inner being is not enough for the creatures to escape from themselves. They begin to giggle, then to thrash about: ''They bump into each other because it's dark. They can't see so they hit and claw each other with their nails. They have long nails.'' (These anticipate the nails of the grotesque Howard Hughes figure in *Seduced,* who also engages in a Shepardian flight from the world.) From this fury of self-loathing—''They kick and scream and the sweat is rolling off them''—there is only one escape, the ultimate flight into death. They come out of the house and walk silently through the woods: ''They don't even breathe. They just walk in a line. Down to the beach. They walk across the beach and right into the water. One behind the other. They just keep walking until you can't see them anymore.''

218

Having brought this vision of unbridled eroticism to a climax in this suicidal fantasy, Shepard expands it to include Stu—and through him the audience—and evokes a mode of desperate escape: "You can't move your head. Your head stays straight and your eyes are wide open. You can't blink your eyes." But fear of this condition and the suicidal impulse that has brought him to it makes Stu envision himself panting and running toward the lights of a town, a community of living persons. Although "the lights go out" in this place of rescue before Stu can imagine reaching it, he nevertheless ends the play with a desperate effort at self-assurance. Jumping out of his bathtub retreat and coming downstage to the other characters, friends of Joy's wearing their dark glasses (behind which they hide from the terror of reality) and numbly dangling their fishing poles into the audience (where the barracudas of violence swim), Stu assures his hearers that all is well because he is breathing: "The air. What a fine bunch of air I'm taking in. . . . Ladies and gentlemen, the air is fine! All this neat air gathered before us! It's too much! . . . All you do is breathe. Easy. One, two. One, two. In. Out. Out, in. I learned this in the fourth grade. . . . Ladies and gentlemen, it's fantastic!" In a final image of hysterical conformity Stu joins the other characters in unison breathing while Joy backs across the stage pulling a wagon loaded with luggage for her mindless, endless journey to business success.

At this climactic moment, one may hear resonating somewhere at the back of one's mind a sadly bitter voice—one probably not heard by Shepard, but curiously appropriate nonetheless—that of Tennyson's Ulysses contemplating the emptiness of his futile existence in Ithaca: "As though to breathe were life!" Stu's leap from the sheltering bathtub into spiritual conformity hardly seems to resemble Ulysses' heroic voyage "beyond the utmost bound of human thought," but both are quintessentially romantic journeys in which a hero of higher sensibilities leaves a place of retreat to undergo a fatal voyage. The gulfs that will wash Ulysses and the sailors down are no less lethal than the sea into which the bestial creatures of Stu's fantasies make their somnambulistic march. And if Ulysses' intellectual voyage is an attempt to leave behind the commonplace life which Stu finally accepts, both these movements—involving as they do a kind of obliteration of the self—are very dubious modes of achieved escape. The contrast between the high romantic tone of a poet who takes his mythic figures from classical antiquity, and the contemporary idiom of Shepard, who draws his from the pop culture of our time, need not blind us to a central similarity between these writers. Both are mournful visionaries, dubious about their age and inclined to excursions, of a rather dangerous nature, away from it. Stu, curled in his bathtub complaining that Joy's biscuits do not offer him the sustenance he desires, is assuredly not one of the Laureate's "mild-eyed melancholy Lotus-eaters," but Shepard, who knew the drug scene of the East Village, has created, in his own idiom, a work that has certain surprising associations with at least one facet of the Tennysonian vision.

That such echoes constitute a significant aspect of Shepard's work is demonstrated by the recurrence of this escape motif in a place where one would not necessarily look for it, in Shepard's more overtly political plays of the sixties. Of these works, the two most attractive are *The Unseen Hand* and *Forensic and the Navigators,* both fantastic Shepardian variations on pop-culture stereotypes, the first being a sci-fi thriller with "western" characters and the second a "caper" melodrama with radical overtones. In *Forensic* two revolutionaries, Forensic and Emmet, are planning, with the assistance of an alluring girl named Oolan (played originally by Shepard's wife, O-Lan), to assault and free prisoners from a desert fortress maintained by the authorities. On the arrival of two exterminators, evidently government agents assigned to gas the radicals, Oolan pretends to faint; the First Exterminator, thinking himself alone with her, kisses her, strokes her hair, and offers her a characteristically Shepardian verbal creation, a vision of escape and refuge that Stu, curled in his bathtub, would quite understand:

> Oh my darling. You mustn't worry now. We'll get you out. I'll get you far away to a safe place where we can be quiet and you won't even know. . . . It was a tree house but now it's a fort. It's very strong and beautiful. You can trust it to keep you safe and sound. It's colored just like the trees. Orange and yellow and green and blue. And it makes sounds like birds and dogs and wild boar. . . . I'll never leave for a second. You can count on me. . . . If you could wake up in my arms and act like I was supposed to be here. . . . If you could wake up like that then we could go away from here now. Right this very minute. We would leave and live in the trees. (62)

But when this sought-after place of refuge is actually found, it is not this distant romantic dreamworld, but the revolutionary hideout itself, a place dedicated to games, childish gratification, and especially to words. As the play opens, we realize that Forensic and Emmet, the supposed insurrectionists, are costumed for a game of cowboys and Indians in which each can play either role: Forensic wears "a brown cowboy hat . . . and moccasins," Emmet "a green Cherokee head band . . . and cowboy boots" (53). Not only are they dressed for childish games, but, as the play opens, Emmet is typing a letter to his mother rather than the revolutionary manifesto we might expect. Even Oolan, so alluring to the First Exterminator, is for them more a maternal figure, a provider of nourishment than of sexuality. When she offers them a pancake, the dubiousness of Emmet's claims to emancipated values is grotesquely apparent in his peevish rejection: "How many times I gotta tell you I don't eat that buckwheat Aunt Jemima middle-class bullshit. I want Rice Krispies and nothing else" (56). And later, in a suggestively maternal action, Oolan presses her hands on the cereal while Emmet pours milk over them so that she can make out of the Rice Krispies an infantile mush, which Emmet ravenously consumes. Although Emmet protests against Oolan's being traded for information, he does nothing to prevent its happening, and Forensic views her sexuality only as bait for the Exterminator, offering her with a Shepardian flourish: "Big Bopper," Forensic exclaims enthusiastically, "you are on the brink of having for your very own the hottest little discotheque mama ever to come on the set" (67).

Above all, what we find here in place of adult sexuality and adult action is words. (When Emmet is typing at the rise of curtain, Forensic has "a note pad and pen" before him.) Of the four male characters, three are at one time or another addressed as Forensic, as one who merely talks. In his examination of the First Exterminator (which in its manic incoherence seems to owe a good deal to the examination of Stanley by Goldberg and McCann in Pinter's *The Birthday Party*), Forensic appears as much interested in expression as information: "Make yourself clear. . . . Wouldn't that be a better way to put it?" (71). This concern returns intensified at the climax of the interrogation when the First Exterminator tells of the existence in the fortress of vacuum pumps (as part of his identification with Forensic the verbalizer, he insists on revealing more than he is asked) that can be cut off at the throttle. At this point Forensic's supposed intellectual and political concerns are swept aside in a wild outburst that combines savagely emotive—that is to say, infantile—hostility with an incongruous insistence on verbal pedantry, suggesting a nature so disturbed that the manipulation of words is its only way of attempting the ordering of the world; the murdering that Forensic dreams of can only take place in the area of language:

AT THE THROTTLE! WHAT DOES THAT MEAN, AT THE THROTTLE? DON'T YOU MEAN AT THE THROAT? CUT IT OFF AT THE THROAT! DON'T YOU MEAN THAT? ANSWER YES OR NO! (73-74)

And, receiving a reply in the affirmative, Forensic addresses the Exterminator by his own name: "THEN HOW DO WE GET TO THE THROAT, FORENSIC!" (74), and thus, in this exchange of roles, suggests that it is his own throat that he must contrive to reach, that it is the fortress of his self that he must attack.

It is this theme of lurking violence—and, not surprisingly, its counterpart, the retreat from such violence—that dominates the extended oration by the Second Exterminator at the end of the play. Like the First Exterminator (now hiding under the table with Oolan, who seems to have accepted him as her lover), the Second Exterminator (who had left to telephone for instructions and, evidently, reinforcements) becomes attracted by the hideout: "A place like this could get a man dreaming about settling down. Finding some roots. A kind of headquarters. A place to come back to" (77). This view complements his sense of the outer world and his recognition, evident in his first words on returning, that Forensic and Emmet have lived in their inner

one: "Boy, is it ever weird out there. Have you guys ever
been out there?" (75). Although the Second Exterminator
sees his colleague as a kind of *doppelgänger* ("We must have
decided the very same thing at the very same time" [76]), he
is taunted by the First ("You don't have to stay" [80]) when
he warns of approaching danger. Then the Second
Exterminator launches his concluding speech, an extended
verbal fantasy in which he imagines himself protesting to a
new team of exterminators that the hideout is a perfectly
innocent place—"We don't even play the phonograph after
eleven o'clock" (80)—and inviting them to investigate as
much as they wish: "Sure, search wherever you like. You
won't find a thing. . . . Sure, tear up the bed, tear off the
sheets, rip out the drawers, tear off our clothes. You won't
find a thing" (80). But suddenly the fantasy of innocence
turns to a recognition of guilt: "Guns? Guns? You think we
have guns? Not on your life. Where would we hide guns?
Under the floor! You hit the nail right on the old head. Guns
under the floor. Under the table. Guns all over the place. See
for yourselves. Every turn you make there's another gun.
Automatics, elephant guns, Marlin four hundreds" (80-81).
Rather than reveal to the forces of the world what potential
for violence lies "under the floor," that is to say in the depths
of the self, the Second Exterminator resolves to break contact
with outer reality and join his fellow verbalists in their
hideout, whatever the dangers of this withdrawal. "I'm not
going out there ever again," he says in the final words of the
play. "I'm staying right here" (81).

The revolutionary politics of *Forensic* are thus transmuted
into an impulse toward personal withdrawal by the end of the
play; in *The Unseen Hand* these elements recur, but in new
guises. The place of retreat here is not a revolutionary
hideout but the remains of a battered old Chevrolet

convertible dumped beside a California highway near Azusa
("'Everything from "A" to "Z" in the USA' " [6],
Shepard is at pains to have the characters tell us more than
once). The central figure of the play, a hundred-and-
twenty-year-old outlaw named Blue Morphan, who is the
inhabitant of the car, finds the modern world too sinister,
even though in his youth when he had been "a free agent,"
he used to "bring in a few bushwackers just for the dinero"
(5), as he explains in the long, rambling soliloquy that opens
the play. But in the age in which the old gunslinger is
marooned, a dark technology has replaced individualism:
"They got nerve gas right now that can kill a man in 30
seconds. . . . That ain't all. They got rabbit fever, parrot
fever and other stuff stored up. Used to be man would have
hisself a misunderstanding, and go out and settle it with a six
gun. Now it's all silent, secret" (5). The hissing alliteration
at the end of this passage, evoking a sinister modernity,
contrasts with the affectionate parody of cowboy talk to
suggest that a certain nostalgia, even conservatism, lurks
beneath the surface of Shepard's inventive theatrical
imagination and iconoclastic stance.

In fact, something near to political despair appears in
Blue's capsule history of the 60's in America that he presents
to his brother Cisco (called up from the dead, as part of the
play's fantasy), the repetitive phrases suggesting the ubiquity
of acts that lead to nothing of significance:

> Things change over night now. One day there's a
> President, the next day he gets shot, the next day the
> guy what shot him gets shot. . . . Next day they outlaw
> guns and replace em with nerve gas. Stuff can turn a
> full grown man into a blithering fool. Then they change
> the government from Capitalism to Socialism because
> the government's afraid of a full blown insurrection.

Then they have a revolution anyhow and things stay
just like they was. (22-23)

A more decisive political stance, however, appears to be
taken toward the middle of the play when the Morphan
brothers (Blue and Cisco have been joined by a third,
Sycamore) and their friend "Willie (The Space Freak)"—a
creature who, in the science fiction aspect of the play, has
come from another dimension to ask the Morphans for
assistance in freeing his people from the oppressors who hold
them in thrall—confront their enemy, the Kid. An
apparently pathetic creature, he is a cheerleader for an Azusa
high school who, having been abused and whipped by a gang
from a rival high school, spends most of his time on stage with
his pants down around his ankles, refraining from pulling
them up because his legs sting too much. Shepard uses the
Kid to project two opposing political viewpoints, both of
which become ridiculous by their association with him.
When he is caught eavesdropping on Willie's explanation of
how the Morphan brothers can help liberate his people (the
Kid supposes they are planning to take over Azusa), he
claims to be an expert on guerrilla fighting who can help
them. "I learned it in school." This improbable claim is
followed by a long lecture, suggesting that he has committed
to memory some revolutionary textbook that he can rattle off
at a moment's notice, thus: ". . . Guerrilla warfare is a war
of the masses, a war of the people. The guerrilla band is an
armed nucleus, the fighting vanguard of the people. It draws
its great force from the mass of the people themselves. . . "
(38).

A moment later, however, when the Kid seizes a gun and
threatens to turn them in as subversives ("'commie faggot"
had been his blanket term of abuse earlier), he espouses a
mindlessly sentimental American chauvinism projected

through a long speech in which expressions of violent hatred for outsiders surround a single immense sentence cataloguing the paraphernalia of small-town America:

> Shut up! Shut up! I'll kill you all! I'll kill you! This is my home! Don't make fun of my home. I was born and raised here and I'll die here! I love it. That's something you can't understand! I love Azusa! I love the foothills and the drive-in movies and the bowling alleys and the football games and the drag races . . . and the Junior Chamber of Commerce and the Key Club and the Letterman's Club and the Kiwanis and the Safeway Shopping Center and the freeway and the pool hall and the Bank of America and the Post Office and the Presbyterian church and the Laundromat and the liquor store and the miniature golf course . . . and my Mom, I love my Mom most of all. And you creeps aren't going to take that away from me because I'll kill you first. I'll kill every one of you if it's the last thing I do. (42)

But this mixture of aggression, immaturity, and mindless conventionality into which, in the Shepardian vision, modern America has degenerated has no power over Willie, who nullifies its force by enunciating a rival speech in "*a strange ancient language*" that leaves the Kid rigid and helpless. On the page it is clear that Willie's speech is simply the Kid's speech set up backwards, starting from the last word of the final sentence: "Od i gniht tsal eht sti fi uoy fo eno yreve llik lli. . . . " is more than an infantile word game; it releases Willie from the control of "the unseen hand" that has kept him and his people in the power of their oppressors: "It was all in my brain the whole time. In my mind. The ancient language of the Nogo. . . . They have no control. We can do what we want! We're free to do what we want" (45). It

227

would seem at this point that Shepard's "message" is that freedom depends on the precise reversal of current American values and that it can be achieved as soon as this fact is recognized. Fortunately, this simplistic, even meaningless notion is obscured on stage, where Willie's speech is merely gibberish, and the audience can sense only that he has triumphed over the Kid through the exertion of some inner force. (The triumph itself is evoked with whimsical imaginativeness as a flood of luminous ping-pong balls descends on the stage and bounces around the dancing characters.)

For a moment Shepard's hortatory awkwardness seems to continue as Willie, departing to help his people build their world, counsels his friends: "This is your world. Do what you want with it." But this facile injunction is countered by Cisco's "But we're strangers too. We're lost, Willie" (45). Confronted by the complexity of the modern world, these embodiments of America's mythic past can think only that they might "hide in the drainage ditch" (47) or "blend right in" by getting a job that would lead to a pension, a car, and "one a' them lawnmowers ya' sit on like a tractor" (47-48). Finally Blue and Cisco simply depart without knowing where they are to go or what they are to do, leaving Sycamore, the most nearly intellectual of the Morphan brothers, to assume Blue's original persona of an ancient, garrulous old drifter talking to a driver who has just stopped and offered him a lift. As he slowly climbs into the wreck of the old Chevrolet, this fantasy takes hold of his mind, and in the big speech that ends the play—the precise counterbalance to Blue's that opened it—he offers a vision of the cars hurtling by on the neighboring highway at "eighty, ninety, a hundred mile an hour" as a symbol of America's retreat from the knowledge of itself. "Don't even see the landscape. Just a blur. Just a blue blur. . . . Don't even see the country. Not to speak of. Most folks is too scared, I guess. That's what it mounts up to. A certain terrorism in the air. A night terror" (49). But this terror of the night of the soul is not Shepard's final recognition. Hoisting himself into the back seat of the old wreck, Sycamore explains that he has "a hankerin' to take stock of things. . . . Gotta make plans. Figure out yer moves. Make sure they're yer own moves and not someone else's. That's the great thing about this country, ya' know. The fact that you can make yer own moves in yer own time without some guy behind the scenes pullin' the switches on ya'. May be a far cry from bein' free, but it sure comes closer than most anything I've seen" (49-50). A few lines further on, however, at the end of his speech, the old outlaw seems to contradict even this moderate, engaged optimism as he asks for "a little peace and quiet" for himself: "Just let 'em go by. Let the world alone. It'll take care of itself. Just let it be."

This desire to retreat from the world derives, inevitably, from a sense that the effort to deal with it more effectively would be futile, that one will never be "free," that there are no "moves" to be made, whether in one's "own time" or not. Ultimately, Shepard offers us not the political activist's sense that there is some obscure conspiracy to frustrate all right-minded people but the artist's and moralist's sense that the "guy behind the scenes pullin' the switches on ya' " is always oneself. It is this monstrous self who finally appears on stage at the end of *Back Bog Beast Bait* and from whom the hero of *Suicide in B^b* flees through his various identities. But in no play is the confrontation of the aspiring self and its corrupted aspect expressed with more striking verbal and theatrical force than the one in which Shepard deals most powerfully with his own circumstance—that of the artist in the world, more specifically of the writer in Hollywood—*Angel City*.

And just as *The Unseen Hand* is a parodistic rewriting of the "creature-from-outer-space" adventure movie, so *Angel City* is a grotesque, brilliantly theatrical reworking of an ultimately familiar sort of drama, that of the innocent artist entrapped by the fleshpots of Hollywood (Clifford Odets's *The Big Knife* is a classic example). Coincidentally, as *The Unseen Hand* begins and ends with lengthy speeches by different but closely related characters, so *Angel City* begins and ends, or at any rate draws to an end, by presenting the elaborate discourses of linked figures (one a demonic film producer, the other his assistant), each presented for his evaluation to the central figure, a writer brought in to create "something which will open entirely new fads in sadomasochism" (71) and thus make a shaky film successful. The writer, Rabbit Brown, whose name evokes a natural, even timorous creature (and perhaps the magic success he is to pull out of a hat), has come to Hollywood by means that suggest an allegiance to older and nobler values: "I rode the buckboard down. I got a team a' horses. Stopped off at all the missions. . . . To pray" (65-66). But if his prayers are that he be allowed to turn away from the impulses of his own self, as Shepard characters so often wish to, they are not answered. "I'm ravenous for power" he tells us later, in a venerable theatrical gesture, an aside, "but I have to conceal it" (69). Meanwhile he is greeted by a bizarre vision of Hollywood, created out of a sequence of horrifying images: ". . . the city teems with living things. Things crawl across upholstered seats. Deals are made in remote glove compartments. And we exist, here, walled in. A booming industry. Self-sufficient. Grossing fifty million in just two

weeks. Our own private police. Our own private food. . . .
Outside, the smog strikes clean to the heart. Babies' eyes
bleed from it. . . . Dogs go paralyzed. Used-car lots melt
away into the black macadam'' (64).

Although Rabbit dismisses this mass of images as
"Terrible. Old time. . . . Worse than Jack Webb I'd say,"
it has the familiar Shepardian nightmare quality. Rabbit's
negative judgment serves not to discount its meaning but to
characterize it as an artistic effusion, and thus make it viable
as part of the play. Left alone to await the coming of his
antagonist, the producer Wheeler (the maker of deals),
Rabbit has a considerable soliloquy in which he evokes the
lure that has drawn him away from the life of an
"underground" artist/musician/communer-with-nature and
brought him to the city whose angels are the malign powers
of the cinematic world. Standing in a largely empty but
highly symbolic stage space—a rectangle of illuminated neon
tubing to evoke a movie screen and a high-backed swivel
chair to hint at the producer's domain—the writer suggests
how much the hypnotic power to control common life has
drawn him away from his past and come to dominate his
desires:

> I've connived in the deepest cracks of the underground.
> Rubbed knuckles with the nastiest poets. Done the
> "Rocky Mountain Back Step" in places where they've
> outlawed bubble gum. But that's neither here nor
> there. . . . The point is I've smelled something down
> here. Something sending its sweet claws way up North.
> Interrupting my campfires. Making me daydream at
> night. Causing me to wonder at the life of a recluse.
> The vision of a celluloid tape with a series of moving
> images telling a story to millions. Millions anywhere.
> Millions seen and unseen. Millions seeing the same

story without ever knowing each other. Without ever having to be together. Effecting [*sic*] their actions. Replacing their books. Replacing their families. Replacing religion, politics, art, conversation. Replacing their minds. (68-69)

The speech offers a striking evocation of the artist as social enemy, concealed in the "deepest cracks," maintaining his identity as the opponent of conventional verities, rubbing not shoulders but the attacking "knuckles" with the "nastiest" of poets, who is most hostile to the commonplace, and who asserts natural vitality by doing the "Rocky Mountain Back Step" even in places where puritanical restraints have banished something as innocent as bubble gum. Curiously, however, it is this bohemian exile who, at the speech's hortatory climax, becomes the advocate of the familiar values of "books . . . religion, politics, art, conversation," even of that most sacred of bourgeois institutions, family life. Shepard's critical stance, like that of so many romantic artists, derives less from a rejection of common social aims than from the sensitive observer's constant and tormented awareness that they are unlikely to be realized, given the pervasive need for self-aggrandizement, which in the artist takes the form of self-expression achieved in "telling a story to millions."

To convey this sense of social and personal corruption Shepard turns back to a pattern he had used with notable success a few years earlier. *Angel City*, which dates from 1976, echoes the essential structure, as well as the linguistic originality and macabre fantasy, of *Tooth of Crime*, from 1972. In both plays a figure of entrenched authority, albeit of criminal force, is overthrown and replaced by a younger or, apparently, more innocent rival. Although in both these works the erotic element in this Freudian fantasy has been largely sublimated (the women in these plays—indeed in most of Shepard's—are incidental figures), they nevertheless derive part of their power from the psychological resonance always present when the overthrow of a father figure and his replacement by a son/rival is dramatized with the force and originality found here.

The sexual theme that does indeed become a subsidiary aspect of the confrontation at the end of *Angel City* is not the struggle between father and son for the love of the mother but the endless love/hate relationship between male and female that Shepard was to dramatize at greater length in *Fool for Love.* Here it becomes part of the film scenario that Wheeler finally presents to Rabbit for his evaluation. As Wheeler tells the story in a long narration near the conclusion of the play, it is pantomimed by the producer's assistants, Lanx and Miss Scoons, who appear at first in robes resembling those of samurai warriors and, when they are dropped, in grotesquely American costumes of crash helmets and the heavy paddings worn by football players. The film that Wheeler describes is a vast futuristic epic in which the conflict between two armies is finally concentrated in the personal duel between their generals:

> On and on they fought into the night until slowly the armies began to thin out and wander away into the desert. Finally the generals were left all alone. Their sounds were lonely and distant like two wild bucks on an empty prairie. . . . They were battling into another time. They were crossing continents as they fought. They were passing history by. . . . As far as they knew they were the only living things. . . . Finally, after days of constant combat, one of the generals revealed himself as a woman. . . . In that moment, the opposing general was caught off guard, and the female plunged

her weapon home. . . . At last the generals saw their situation. They were one being with two opposing parts. (107-108)

The sexual connections here, with male and female roles interchanged, is made clear by the thrust of the victorious general's phallic weapon into the body of the other and their final impassioned embrace.

Although Rabbit, now beginning to assume the dominant role in his verbal combat with Wheeler, dismisses this scenario, as an example of "hanky-panky love stories, romantically depicting the end of the world," the effect (as with Rabbit's denunciation of the opening depiction of Los Angeles) is to account for the speech's bizarre theatricality rather than to dismiss its content. The speech prefigures the interchange of personae that is central to the final battle between Rabbit and his antagonist. Wheeler, whose persona in the first act had been that of a slightly effete business-man, has in the second act assumed an appropriately cinematic image, that of a wolf-man/Dracula-like creature with green skin, fangs, and long fingernails; as he denounces Wheeler's scenario, Rabbit appears himself to have descended even further into the same presence, having now developed the same green skin, fangs, and nails, with the addition of "*a long, thick mane of black hair*" (108). Like the generals of the scenario, they have become "one being with two opposing parts." Now Rabbit assumes the identity of his opponent, becoming the ruthless movie tycoon despite Wheeler's desperate protests: "WAIT A MINUTE! I'M NOT YOU, GODDAMIT! I'M ME!" (109). But Wheeler is pushed helplessly into the role of his opponent, the humble provincial script writer, as Rabbit tells him to "go back to making campfires" (109). And when Wheeler attempts to defend himself by opening the "dangerous bundle" Rabbit has brought, the one representing "The West," the " 'Looks-Within' place" (101), it merely oozes a *"green liquid, the color of their faces,"* confirming their ultimate identity. Rabbit has achieved the corruption he desired; the combat has been an embrace after all. The City of Angels has confirmed itself as the city of demons, or at any rate of cinematic monsters.

The pervasiveness of this combat/embrace relationship in Shepard is suggested not only by its recurrence in the sexual battle of *Fool for Love,* already noted, but in the merging of the antithetical father and son figures of Shepard's later "family" plays, *Buried Child* (Vince assuming his grandfather's position at the end of the play) and *Curse of the Starving Class* (Wesley actually dressing in his father's dingy cast-off clothes). In the latter play occurs one of the most remarkable verbal symbolizings of this conflict between related yet hostile elements that takes so many forms in Shepardian drama. Again it is a narrative, the father's story of the eagle, suggestive of freedom and aspiration, sweeping down over the farm where lambs were being castrated to seize upon the discarded testes ("those fresh little remnants of manlihood" [183]), then becoming entangled with a tomcat—something feline, slinking, intrusive, violent (perhaps sexuality itself)—and finally soaring up and then crashing down to destroy both itself and the creature with which it was locked in an inextricably savage embrace: "They fight like crazy in the middle of the sky. . . . /And the eagle's being torn apart in midair. The eagle's trying to free himself from the cat, and the cat won't let go. . . . /Both of them come down. Like one whole thing" (200).

From the first, Shepard has been concerned with such conflicts within the self, the "one whole thing" that has so many disparate elements. In his exploration of the violent encounters among those elements and of the effort to retreat from the most disturbing of those inner forces Shepard's work suggests that of Harold Pinter more than of any other contemporary playwright. Beyond the obvious similarity in the plot materials of two important plays, *The Homecoming* and *Buried Child* (an offspring's return to a family's psychic turmoil), lies something much deeper and more pervasive. Each writer is centrally preoccupied with the simultaneous attraction and repulsion from the passional aspects of the self—violence, sexuality, the desire for power—that are most alluring and most frightening. Kent's wild leap through the backstage wall of the set at the end of Shepard's *La Turista* has a very different theatrical feel from Stanley's or Davies's retreat into protective lassitude in Pinter's *The Birthday Party* and *The Caretaker,* but the impulse to escape by any available means from the dangers within, as well as from the demands of the world without, motivates all three. It would not have been hard for Shepard to mention his acquaintance with Beckett or his admiration for Brecht (as a playwright rather than a political force). Whatever the influence of these figures may have been in suggesting the symbolic possibilities of a nearly empty stage or a fragmentary narrative structure, it did not go to the moral and psychological heart of Shepard's work. But the Pinterian influence—direct or indirect, conscious or unconscious, it could hardly have been escaped during Shepard's years in England—did. That connection is worth observing not because it determined Shepard's work (which in all probability would have been much as it is in any case), but because it lets us see more clearly by the light of comparison what Shepard's central concerns are.

Similarly, a consideration of Shepard and Pinter as writers of grand speeches can be helpful; even as it brings us back to the matter of verbalism, our point of origin here, it suggests that special quality of Shepard's linguistic method. Like Shepard, Pinter is an intensely verbal creator of a kind of poetic dialogue that swiftly passes beyond the confines of realistic expression. But as soon as we glance at some of the great speeches in Pinter, we realize that his characters inhabit a prosodic world very different from that of Shepard. The subtle parody of bourgeois sentiment in Goldberg's discourse *(The Birthday Party)*, the manic surreality of Mick's travelogues *(The Caretaker)*, even the poised brutality of Lenny's stories *(The Homecoming)* are all foreign to Shepard. We notice at once that the control of nuance, the sensitivity to rhythm and sound to be found here are not Shepard's to command. (This absence in a musician is curious indeed.) But in their place he offers a boundless fecundity of imagistic invention. He is above all a great iconographer of the grotesque. Although Shepard has, as any playwright must, a sense of dramatic movement and conflict, it is his remarkable sense of the pictorial that, as much as any quality, gives his work its special character. Sometimes his images are stage pictures, Tilden entering with the vast armful of carrots in *Buried Child,* for example. But often they are pictures evoked by the language itself, such as that of the immense ejaculative explosion at the end of *Icarus's Mother.* And often these pictures pile up in vast accumulations such as the images of sweating, fornicating bodies in Stu's vision of sexual horror at the climax of *Chicago.* These pictorial conglomerations may not always be composed with perfect control, but they are rarely less than memorable. Till now the American drama has not had a genuinely poetic writer. The stylistic infelicities of O'Neill and Miller are too evident to need rehearsing here. Even the fevered reshaping of Southern speech by Tennessee Williams too often teeters toward self-parody. But Sam Shepard offers us a pictorial drama of extraordinary theatrical and verbal force. However painful and partial the sense of life it projects—and it is singularly lacking in humor and charm and sensibility— Shepard's drama is one of, literally, visionary intensity; we are fortunate in having it.

WORKS CITED

Shepard, Sam. *Angel City. Fool for Love and Other Plays.* New York: Bantam, 1976, 1984.

————. *Chicago. Five Plays by Sam Shepard.* New York: Bobbs-Merrill, 1967.

————. *Forensic and the Navigators* and *The Unseen Hand* in *The Unseen Hand and Other Plays.* New York: Bobbs-Merrill, 1972.

III
ON ACTING

BUT DO FILM
ACTORS ACT?

BY ALBERT BERMEL

While playwrights have demonstrated for centuries the potentialities of the stage, the screen is as yet an only partly explored territory. We have still to learn what its possibilities are. I have acknowledged that they are different from those of the stage, especially in certain kinds of emphasis. But they may not be as different as many have supposed. Eric Bentley, *The Playwright as Thinker.*

Screen versus stage: Pictures versus talk; close-ups of lips, eyeballs, fingers, feet versus entire bodies; actual versus factitious scenery; natural versus exaggerated behavior; moving and angular perception versus still viewpoints; cutting versus scenic changes; typecast versus versatile acting; the objective and subjective lens versus the responsive, or sometimes heedless, audience. . . . Authorities on cinema have repeatedly confronted us with these and other distinctions in order to promote conceptual autonomy for film. They have also obscured the similarities between film and theatre.

Eric Bentley was replying to Allardyce Nicoll who, some ten years earlier, had argued that films call for realism of story and treatment, while the theatre requires fantasy and the incantatory force of poetic language. Since *The Playwright as Thinker* first appeared in the 1940s, technical sophistication in both arts has drawn them closer together, rather than separating them further, and occasionally it has let them overlap. In criticism, semioticians, with their definitions of terms on which one can hardly find two writers who agree—if, to start with, they accept one another's terminology—have taken over much of the more recondite film criticism, and are now invading the theatre and hoisting their signs and signifiers on its landscape. Yet there remains at least one divide between the two arts when they unravel a dramatic narrative: in the acting. The distinction is an apt one for discussion here, since Eric Bentley, like the few other outstanding critics of the drama, is an exceptional connoisseur of acting.

Let me begin by skirting the peripheries of acting. If the cinema has E.T., R2-D2, the Disney menagerie, and Bugs Bunny, the theatre has its puppets, from Punch and Judy to Bunraku. If the cinema has Lassie, the theatre has its performing circus seals, who have also been known to bark. The pig who performed so ably in *A Private Function* was in fact three little pigs, Betty One, Betty Two, and Betty Three, of whom Betty Three was the most adept at following instructions, according to one of the film's stars, Michael Palin. In a radio interview Palin nominated her for an Oscar; and if the theatre has produced no pig-actors of note and no donkeys as talented as Bresson's Balthazar, it has presented credible horses which were not present in *Rosmersholm* and Jean Anouilh's staging of *Becket.*

When we think of acting, we think first of performances by human beings. The differences between playing in films and in the theatre have come in for frequent comment by actors, directors, screenwriters, and other interested parties, much of it sharp-witted, some of it indignant, but almost all cursory. Otherwise admirable biographies and books that analyze the artistry of Lang, Renoir, Pasolini, Ford, Fellini, Godard, Hitchcock, Truffaut, Kurosawa, Bergman, Bresson, Griffith, Sternberg, and others allude to the relationships between directors and actors as colleagues and sometimes as adversaries, but the only sustained discussion I know of is fifty years old, Pudovkin's essay *Film Acting*, translated into English in 1937. From Pudovkin, I would guess, Nicoll deduced that films demand realism in the acting, as in the story and settings. And yet when Pudovkin, who pays tribute to Stanislavsky's System for training actors, writes of "typage" as a desirable form of acting, he comes near to asking for stylized performances not unlike the ones required by Brecht, in which the *gestus* helps actors reveal not only individual characters but also character-as-a-function-of-social-class.

Among its other virtues, *Film Acting* recommends that directors enlist actors as partners in film-making, instead of exploiting them as adjuncts or implements; they should be consulted and engaged at every stage of the film, from the script to the editing. In practice, as Pudovkin points out, the actors may be unwilling or unversed in the technicalities. (They may also be outvoted.) But while advocating this deeper participation by the actors, Pudovkin himself did not give it to them; he visualizes actors in the editing room as an ideal, rather than as a likely culmination of their efforts. Since then, seldom have actors taken part in the editing, which Pudovkin calls "the most important stage of work on the film"—and then only when they were marquee names who financed or directed their own films.

We usually distinguish film acting from theatre acting by citing the cutting up of film performances into tiny units. (As it happens, Chekhov anticipated something like this device in his later plays by intercutting separate conversations.) Fragmentation is one token of film actors' lack of control over their portrayals. But there are others:

• Framing, the artificial positioning or composition of actors or bits of actors: A photograph in Buñuel's autobiography, taken during the filming of *Belle de Jour,* shows the director lovingly using both hands to arrange an actor's mouth against Catherine Deneuve's bare shoulder—to kiss or bite it?

• Shooting a script out of sequence for reasons of money, convenience, or caprice, thereby jeopardizing the actors' chances of "building character" and an "organic" performance ("We'll take the first and last scenes in Death Valley, the battle in Yugoslavia, the banquet in Vienna, and fill in the rest between times on the back lot");

• Synchronization of sound: this includes dubbed dialogue, songs rendered by invisible mouths, voiceover narration between and during scenes, and—a gimmick that has become faddish, if not a fetish, in recent films—lines and voices floated in from the scene to come, before a fade, a dissolve, or a retreating long shot ("To hell with the transition—let the soundtrack make it for us").

Because of these inroads into the actors' initiative, film performers are no longer whole artists. The director, editor, composer, possibly the producer, and sundry technicians make their living at the actors' aesthetic expense. But the director alone makes many further inroads into their initiative during the shooting by various means, some coercive, some insidious, some considered "cinematic," and all defended in the sacred name of results. Three of these means deserve more elaboration: Directors' suggestions and manipulation, retakes, and the insistence on bland acting.

Directors' suggestions and manipulation. Pudovkin describes how he coaxed a desired smile out of the small boy in *The Story of a Simple Case*. Any director who has used amateur actors, most blatantly in fictionalized documentaries, such as Flaherty's, must have done something comparable, and so has every director who has worked with proud, obtuse, or incompetent professionals. Or, at times, with masterly professionals. During the filming of *Wild Strawberries*, Ingmar Bergman supposedly won the heart-piercing look of wonder from Victor Sjöström—in truth, a look of desperation, verging on disappointment—by requesting him to postpone his ritual five o'clock glass of Scotch. The story may be untrue but it is all too plausible. The classic example, related by Pudovkin again (in *On Film Technique*), and since retold in film textbooks, has him and Kuleshov in the palmy days of Russian montage experiments matching photographs of the actor Ivan Mosjukhin—"close-ups which were static and did not express any feeling at all—quiet close-ups"—with shots of a plate of soup, a dead woman, and a little girl, to demonstrate simulations of hunger, grief, and affection. "The public raved about the acting of the artist. . . . But in all three cases the face was exactly the same."

At the Academy Awards festivities, as the winners of statuettes for acting pay excessive tribute to their collaborators, they are not faking modesty but proclaiming truth. "Design-directors," as opposed to "acting-directors," often prefer actors who are (that favorite actors' word) vulnerable, and therefore pliable. They are "pros," as Hitchcock once said on television of Cary Grant and James Stewart. They are what King Vidor said of Robert Young: "a director's dream." Actors, in turn, often profess to like demanding directors. "He gave me so much . . . I really learned from him what screen acting was all about . . . I'll work with him again any time he asks. . . ." Again and again one comes upon these devout expressions of gratitude, or their like, and I never suspect their sincerity. Actors are the most generous people on earth, despite the disdain or offhandedness they must sometimes affect in public for protection. Actors give themselves, not *of* themselves, as do authors, directors, designers, and other film artisans. The characters they create should belong more to them than to anybody else. The actor played by Jeff Daniels in *The Purple Rose of Cairo* says of his independent-minded screen image, "He's my character." "Not the author's?" asks Mia Farrow. "No," Daniels replies. "I gave him flesh." He might have added, "And a soul."

Retakes. These cause some of the most serious depredations of the screen actor's initiative. A gifted stage actress who had just completed her first Hollywood assignment told me that she was asked to run along a beach toward the camera. This was not a critical scene in the film, "but we retook it twenty-three times," she said, "and in the final cut it lasted for about three seconds." When she saw the take selected by the director and editor, she did not remember whether it was number one, number sixteen, or what; but it was certainly not twenty-four and, more annoyingly, not number nineteen, which she recalled as the most convincing she had done, with the least forced smile, and the one most apt for that place in the film. She went on to speak of other takes that were shot twelve, twenty, thirty-four times. Perhaps the director was fastidious, indecisive, or spendthrift. More likely he was simply hewing to the tradition laid down by that major studio once known as Retake Valley. But like many actors before and since, this young woman could not hold herself responsible for a performance in a ninety-minute movie assembled out of something like fifteen thousand pieces of film. To her the synthesis amounted to an arbitrary and unrecognizable mishmash. By way of contrast, the late Jack MacGowran felt that forty takes for one little segment of *Dance of the Vampires* and sixty takes for another were "only a part of [Polanski's] overall perpetual seeking for perfection." Loyalty of this caliber can proceed only from a shared vision of perfection or from blind trust. According to Janet Maslin's review of a science-fiction exercise called *Enemy Mine,* the actor Dennis Quaid "did thirty retakes of a scene that required him to be drenched in ice water."

In the theatre a performer keeps rehearsing to fix, but not rigidify, an interpretation, to pack high-quality soil around its roots so that it can seem to grow spontaneously. In films retake may follow retake while considerations other than acting supervene. The lighting may improve, the background may look better in (or out of) focus, the dresses swirl with more abandon, the colors fall into harmony (or discords), and more striking cloud formations give richer texture to the sky, while the acting doesn't change, or gets worse, or turns mechanical.

Retakes, it is worth remembering, do not always occur in quick succession. During new or modified set-ups, the stars may retire to their tents or trailers and the supporting players to their poker game—and grow "cold." The sheer technicality of film-making comes between them and their art: the delays lessen their chances to approach what they

247

conceive to be the definitive interpretation. As they weary, they can become defiant, indifferent, or compliant, usually the latter, like Gilda Radner in the *Saturday Night Live* sketch in which John Belushi, caricaturing Sam Peckinpah, kept slapping her to the ground as he murmured, "I still don't quite see it. Again!"

Of Sternberg, John Baxter writes:

> In common with many directors who depend on believable expressions in close-ups to make a point, he pressured actors, forcing them to repeat scenes until exhaustion and frustration gave the desired reaction. Dietrich's scene on the spiral staircase in *The Blue Angel* took a day to shoot, Sternberg demanding continual retakes until she lost her temper, whereupon he expressed himself satisfied. In the same film her casual pose on stage with one leg upraised was arrived at only after much experiment, with more than a dozen possible attitudes tried and discarded.

I am not about to start picking holes in *The Blue Angel* at this late date. Still, I wonder how many of the engrossing performances Sternberg captured from the likes of Dietrich, Jannings, Cooper, Arnold, Lorre, McLaglen came about in spite of the actors. Does it matter? Well, yes, it does if the performances could have been even finer.

In the theatre despotic directors played havoc with actors' equanimity long before movies were a gleam in anybody's lens. Their successors still do. Some actors are easily intimidated and not their own most helpful appraisers. They succumb to casual hints; they find it hard to articulate their reasoning and to refute decisions they disagree with, particularly in the early stages of production. But I contend that good actors (and the rest are merely would-be actors) know what they are doing and "feel" when they are doing it right, whether they can justify themselves verbally or not. While they may make unreliable judges of the acting capabilities of others, they are, with few exceptions, resolutely *and soundly* self-critical.

It looks as if the retake tic will persist, both out of habit and as a directorial power-grab, as long as movies remain wastefully expensive and complicated. Indeed, takes are getting shorter all the time. Today's directors, especially American ones, seem embarrassed if they dwell on one subject for a full minute. Inspired more by commercials and videos than by Eisenstein's and Vertov's editing feats and the New Wave's jump cuts, they grind up their movies into more particles than ever and blunt further the actors' initiatives and resources. I wonder whether Pudovkin would still maintain that

> . . . the concept of the edited image is by no means an affirmation of the doctrine that the film actor is merely a type actor providing piecemeal material for mechanical composition into a pseudo-whole in the process of editing.

These days the average performance on film is no more acting as an integral art form than ground round is steak.

Bland acting. Natural (sometimes miscalled naturalistic) or realistic acting of the sort Nicoll advocated for the screen has hampered film-making since the introduction of sound. Admittedly, the content of run-of-the-mill pictures, the ones that used to have a "general release" and now enjoy "saturation distribution," dictates the under-acting or non-acting that is conspicuous in most of them. If they attempted anything bolder, they would sink into deeper ludicrousness. The close-up, Griffith's momentous discovery, must often stand for expressions of high emotion, when the face will be contorted to denote fear (circular mouth and eyes) or love (droopy lids, pursed lips) or hate (taut nostrils, mouth pulled into an extended hyphen). But much of the time the face in close-up expresses nothing, nothing at all. It hangs in space, a frozen asteroid, relying for its efficacy on music or silence, lighting and the darkened auditorium, the preceding moments, and some inevitable expectations. The audience ascribes a state of feeling to empty features. On such vacant lots lofty reputations have risen. But to coin an anti-Bauhaus and anti-minimalist slogan, less is less. I do not refer here to actors who get by only on their good looks or, now and then, succeed mightily because of them. They give us the pleasure of watching enviably winsome humanity, not necessarily beauty of acting.

The casual beliefs persist that natural acting means being oneself; that everybody is, potentially at least, an actor; and that everybody is therefore capable of acting before an audience or camera. The beliefs are mischievous because they derive from a partial truth. In such documentaries as James Blue's *The Olive Trees of Justice,* certain people do possess, without preliminary training, whatever it takes to act convincingly, as convincingly, anyway, as some trained professionals do, much as many untrained do-it-yourselfers have the skills of professional carpenters, house painters, and plumbers. But what do these talented novices prove? Only that they have not matched their abilities with their vocations or that they have overflowing abilities, more than their professions can encompass.

As a further complication, psychologists and sociologists tell us that we are all actors. In our daily routine we play roles, enact scenes. Therefore, acting is tantamount to natural behavior. Here we run into the longstanding confusion over the word "natural" (not to mention the even worse confusion over the word "is"). Applied to acting, does natural mean *an imitation of nature,* as observed, or *ordinary,* that is, *commonplace?* Does it mean understudied or unstudied? Bessie Berger in *Awake and Sing!* enjoys Wallace Beery: "He acts like life: very good." She speaks for uncounted spectators when she pronounces that good acting is like life. In films, as in plays, acting does often seem *like* life, and the resemblance constitutes one of its delights; but the most effective acting looks and sounds like life because it artfully transcends the ordinariness, the fleetingness of "being" and ceases its "becoming." A single performance may be evanescent, but it has been fixed for a while by selective art—relatively fixed in the theatre by deficient memory and defective rehearsals; absolutely fixed in the cinema by chemistry and moved into the museum of photography. Unlike life, it has protected itself against the ravages of time more securely than Pirandello's characters have done, for the latter are still subject to the vagaries of interpretation.

What of those occasions when the natural or lifelike ideal is a misplaced one? Films that pursue it while they tackle declamatory texts tend to tone down not only the grimaces but also the voices and, thence, the passions. In the BBC-PBS version of *King Lear* on television, for example, Robert Lindsay's recitation of Edmund's soliloquy, "Thou, Nature, art my goddess" (please notice the juxtaposition here of nature and art) through "Now, gods, stand up for bastards!", although dedicated to Nature, cried out to be cried out, not savagely muttered. It needed to issue, like Lear's later counter-rumblings at the heavens, from a vast theatrical void, a heath that is a hole in the world. But then, films with far humbler texts equally give the impression of shame and shrinking in the presence of some fervor.

If, as I am saying, bland means blank when it comes to acting, it is a matter for wonder that certain "natural" actors come across strikingly. They contrive mannerisms, deliveries of their lines and themselves which change little from film to film, and they cast their emotions in more or less the same facial mould during each silence; but we watch them, fascinated by the swirl of new stories around their unvarying personalities. Arkin, Bogart, Hepburn, Falk, Greenstreet, George C. Scott, Ronald Colman, Savalas, George Sanders, Mastroianni, Rosay, Matthau, Gabin, Nicholson, Belmondo, Loren—they each exert a power accumulated in part from previous films as their intricately carved masks, like those of Noh actors, catch unexpected gleams of light.

What I like about the films of the twenties and early thirties is that the long takes, often considered uncinematic, benefited actors who could spot an opportunity. They scorned the chilliness of the lens. They brought themselves clean through it and out beyond the screen's flatness and rectangular edges; and they relayed to us a mysterious intensification of what their characters were supposed to feel. Chaney, Baranovskaya, Garbo, Barrymore, Laughton, Michel Simon, Raimu, Jannings, Baur, and (supremely) Chaplin and Keaton made possible against all the odds, all the handicaps inherent in film-making, the money pressures and other prejudices, a continuation of their breed. And so we have Ullman, Mifune, Shimura, Brando, Sternhagen, Durning, Welles, Papas, Olivier, Tognazzi, Finney, Ashcroft, Magnani, Hoffman, and others whose names I will remember after this book has gone into print all of whom appear to experience emotions so complex that they are irresoluble. Occasionally with, usually without, one twitch.

Each one's "presence" or "magic" or "magnetism" or whatever other inadequate word we use to convey their amalgam of art and temperament compensates us in some measure for the cinema's habit of splintering performances. By no accident, these are all actors who came from the stage.

Since the force of any performance depends to an extent on each spectator, its gauging is colored by irrational likes and dislikes. Much as, in life, I take instantly to some people and am repelled (or repulsed) by others, so, in the playhouse or moviehouse, my determination of whether acting is good or bad draws upon personal reactions I may not be aware of, akin to the personality clash and its opposite. I enjoy watching some performers because they remind me, unconsciously perhaps, of a teacher or schoolmate or friend or agreeable acquaintance, of my parents or siblings, or myself. I may find them unsympathetic for the same reasons. Or for some other reason that has at least as much to do with my background as with their skills or want of them. Professional critics' assessment of actors in public, as well as amateurs' depreciation of them in private, owes more than is generally acknowledged to these subjective factors. Which may, like almost everything else, turn out to be a consequence of biochemistry.

Yet even allowing for what amounts to discrepancies in taste, a consensus has come to pass: certain performances on film stand out; they are memorable, and would survive without the aid of VCRs. The actors in question have enlarged their roles in such ways that these roles are identified, perhaps forever, with those names. If I had to find a single adjective to sum them up, it would be either Andrew Undershaft's *unashamed* or, better, *theatrical.*

Pudovkin warned that film should not revert to stage practices. Any move in that direction would be "reactionary." All the same, a specific uneasiness over the future

253

of acting in films pervades his stimulating and openhearted essay. Half a century later, when many hopes remain unfulfilled, one cannot help asking this: If film acting deliberately took on some of the expansiveness of its theatrical counterpart, would it turn stagy?

It might. The most compelling acting does not conceal traces of self-consciousness. If too much self-consciousness leaks into a performance, the actor's personality obtrudes and distracts us from the characterization, or else makes the latter look irritatingly complacent, mannered, and isolated. We describe this effect as being too "knowing," because the actor negates any dramatic irony there may be in the play by seeming aware of dangers and subsequent triumphs that the writer has purposely kept hidden from him.

However, a judicious salting of self-consciousness keeps acting from seeming needlessly naive. It also keeps it, as an imitation, from being slavishly natural by holding it at a slight aesthetic distance. The most satisfying performances, in theatre or on film, come from actors who have burrowed all the way into their roles, and then emerged from them—but only just. Perhaps Hazlitt had something like self-consciousness in mind when he remarked that "the height of [actors'] ambitions is to be *beside themselves.*" Laurence Olivier trades on self-conscious tricks more openly (I'm tempted to say: more bravely) than anyone else, especially in the theatre. When the *Othello* he starred in, staged by John Dexter and mixing Olivier's tempestuous Moor with Frank Finlay's small and guarded Iago, was transferred to film stock, the reviews and public found Olivier hammy and Finlay quietly appropriate. But the production had not been adapted for the screen, merely bundled onto it. Olivier has understood as well as most artists how big acting can exploit the cinema.

Most popular film directors evidently have not much more than a grudging respect for acting, and in some cases evince an open contempt for it. They are infatuated with its pictorial standbys: chop-and-splice, flying stunts and special effects, telescopic shots across shimmering terrain at noon, sunrise, or dusk, models and miniature catastrophes, torn bodies and fountains of blood—cruelty and motion. The dangers of staginess lie elsewhere than in the acting. Bold acting in place of the bland stuff would surely prove less numbing than successions of zooms, swoops, vertical and swish pans, irising in and out, slow motion (generally of murder sequences, car smashes, and athletic prowess), pixilation, blinking from one tight close-up to the next, computerized animation, and the rest of the showing-off which, for the spectator, resembles sharing a cell with a five-year-old who is taking a course in vocabulary enrichment.

The movies of Eric Rohmer, such isolated instances as *After the Rehearsal, The Return of Martin Guerre, The Draughtsman's Contract,* and up to a point, the home-grown *Lost in America* remind us that the arts of film, as they evolve, can thrive on the eloquent, all-out acting and the extensive scenes that sustain the best in theatre. Film remains one of theatre's legitimate offspring.

Once again Bentley was prophetic.

References

The Playwright as Thinker, Meridian Books edition, pp. 15-16.

Allardyce Nicoll's book is *Film and Theatre,* London, 1936.

V.I. Pudovkin's *Film Technique and Film Acting* combined two seminal essays in a "memorial edition," published in London, 1958, and reprinted in paperback, New York, 1970, Ivor Montagu, tr. and ed.

Buñuel's autobiography, written in association with Jean-Claude Carrière, and tr. by Abigail Israel, is *My Last Sigh*, New York, 1983.

King Vidor on Robert Young: from the Young entry in David Thomson's *A Biographical Dictionary of Film*, p. 624, New York, 1976.

Janet Maslin's review appeared in the N.Y. *Times*, 12/20/1985.

Jack MacGowran quotation from *The Cinema of Roman Polanski* by Ivan Butler, p. 182, New York, 1970.

John Baxter: *The Cinema of Josef von Sternberg*, p. 19, New York, 1971.

Hazlitt quotation from his *Examiner* piece of Jan. 5, 1817, reprinted in *Hazlitt on Theatre*, p. 133, New York, 1958. The italics are his.

EB ON ACTING

BY GORDON ROGOFF

Eric Bentley has never been swept away by the tidal waves of romantic slush so often reserved for actors and the art of acting. If somebody had slighted Uta Hagen's Joan (in Shaw's play) as a performance "pieced together," Bentley caught immediately that behind the pejorative remark was a popular respect for "something vague, sweeping, impressionistic," precisely what he was avoiding in his own performance appraisals. Instantly, he turned it around; "pieced together" could mean something else: the selection of "bits of reality . . . the way a peasant girl walks . . . to be rendered step by step." If you notice "her rubbing her shins when the chains are taken off," and if you think a little, then you might also observe—as Bentley does—that "this is not a Rosalind in tights." EB can do this not merely because of a reluctance to gush, but also because he respects plays as much as acting.

More: he knows plays as few critics ever bother to know them. Not just their pedigree or partial successes, but their reasons for being, their structured intelligence, all those specific assaults on a specific formal world. What follows, then, is that he obtains ideas from the plays about how they might be acted. "It is the others," he says, "not Joan . . . who grow poetical and chant a litany." Hagen's Joan, he is saying, is not the Joan of mooning enthusiasts, she "is a real girl . . . genuinely bewildered." Carrying on where Shaw left off, Bentley notices that when Hagen cleans the dust off Joan, she is rescuing Shaw from creaking Shakespeareans of the day. Shaw was addressing "himself to the problem of credibility and knew that the Shakespearean actors would be his arch-enemies." Just for good measure, he adds a suggestion still worth heeding today both for Shaw and Shakespeare: find "the fine Elizabethan woodwork" underneath "the wallpaper and the plaster."

On acting as on plays, Bentley's phrasing glides effortlessly between an austere regard for observable truth and an expansive concern for subliminal ebb and flow. To know text is to honor sub-text automatically. Bentley does this free of jargon, never the slave of theory at the expense of practical reality. In the last chapter of *In Search of Theater,* called *1900-1950,* his summation is breathtakingly plain and comprehensive. Here is the playwright's champion acknowledging that "the theater's principal instrument is the actor." If this seems scarcely revolutionary, it isn't meant to be; against the background of feuding academicians viewing Shakespeare only as poet, never as actor, or conceptual directors selling Bright Ideas rather than Live Performance, Bentley's casual claim for the actor's sovereignty still needs to be argued rather than defended. "The purpose of theater," he says as the chapter begins, "is to produce great performances." His ideal critical world would have long ago produced more direct descriptions of "Duse and Bernhardt, Irving and Moissi, Chaliapin and Mei Lan-fang, Louis Jouvet and Laurette Taylor." Lacking such an historical criticism, we can move with him through the century's movements, ranging from Wagner and Ibsen to Brecht and Barrault, noticing along the way that Stanislavsky's achievement—the theater's response to realism—could find itself mixed into such diverse figures as Copeau and Reinhardt. Like all great critics, Bentley finds links within links, getting his poetry from the facts.

For a time, Barrault was his hero, but never a conquering one. Who but Bentley at the time had more right to notice "an actor as thinker"? Were our directors today to read him on Barrault (but do they read?), how could they possibly refute his reference to "Barrault's sanity," an approach to drama as "an art in which the actor serves the author and in which *the other theater arts and artists serve the actor.*" (My italics because that emphasis screams for a hearing now more than ever.) Bentley's other heroes—Brecht and Shaw—always had advice for the players, either formally or (with Shaw) informally in the shape of letters. Surely Bentley was the first to make uneasy reconciliations with two artists—Brecht and Barrault—so different from one another. Brecht's committed view of life is contrasted with Barrault's less definite nature: on the one hand, distance, light, ironical comment; on the other, magniloquence, ceremony, magical illusion. Lucky enough to see Weigel's Mother Courage, he tells us what she looked like, standing outside the role, "cool, relaxed . . . with great precision of movement and intonation."

There it is, of course: who could be more precise in movement, more punctiliously aware of tone, than Barrault? Bentley, always ahead of everybody in his reading, found still another authority, now unhappily forgotten, for explaining his embrace of artists who might normally appear antagonists: Louis Jouvet, remarking after the Occupation that Artaud might not be the answer for everyone, said that "None of the theater's manifestations follows a straight line.

259

None of the gestures or rites of genuine theater comes from a 'tendency.' '' Bentley was tirelessly pulling all of them into his circle of research and discontent. Stanislavsky, Shaw, Ibsen, Brecht, Barrault, Artaud, Copeau, Dullin, Decroux would drop into his pages like the most natural companions, friends, at least, for a day. Hovering behind them in the mists of recent theatrical history were the cantankerous ghosts of Wagner and Craig. It's easy to forget that nobody—not Agate in England or even his beloved Stark Young in America—was interested in, let alone capable of, these remarkable duos, trios, and sextettes. EB was conducting a new opera all his own.

Young, however, had to be a daunting model for his younger disciples, especially when writing about actors and the art of acting. Sculpting actors' images with a molded, jewelled prose, Young meant to freeze their most ephemeral moments in an hourglass. He was—and shifting metaphors may be the only way to keep up with Young's mercurial descriptive imagination—like a delicately poised hunter of butterflies sweeping them into his net only to give them swift release after noting the way a stripe or color catches the sun. Bentley has always been steadier, less susceptible to the mix *and* the metaphor. But Young's example had to be inspiring. Young, for him, was "a critic in the fullest sense—one who *judges* by *standards* that are not imposed from without but prompted and checked by his own first-rate sensibility."

His jewels, pro and con, may not have glowed, like Young's, in the pervasive critical darkness surrounding him. (The daily newspapers rarely see and describe; they sell and explode.) Bentley could honor any performance with appreciative detail, but he didn't simply collapse in awe or anger. For him, context—stress on "text"—was just about everything. More than anyone, he saw the whole performance in the whole play, never patronizing the actor with dithering flattery. He couldn't be intimidated—and how refreshing this continues to be—by what Shakespeare called "bubble reputation." Brando, for example, may have been an amazing young actor, but for Bentley, he was destabilizing *Streetcar:*

> . . . Brando has muscular arms, but his eyes give them the lie.

Here he is on some of the others:

Katherine Cornell:

> . . . She can neither raise herself to the semblance of greatness nor lower herself to the semblance of baseness, and acting Cleopatra involves both.

On Maurice Evans:

> . . . The perpetual "poetic" singsong! The laborious explanatory manner. . . . Evans's Tanner is simply Evans got up to look as pretty as possible. And the whole play is transposed accordingly into a key of good-looking idiocy.

On Lee J. Cobb:

> . . . one of our finest actors. I do not mean we have no misgivings about him. His besetting temptation is sentimentality. When in doubt, he thumps the table, screams his head off, or wallows in a fit of weeping. Like most actors of his school, he sometimes seems to mistake the jitters for creative energy.

And on Viveca Lindfors he allows himself at the end a positively Youngian vocabulary:

> . . . Miss Lindfors' hands and arms perform large gestures; one watches them perhaps with surprise,

perhaps with incredulity, but hardly with pleasure. Passion, with her, is never convincing. She suddenly yells. She uses a sweeping movement of hand or arm. But we hear the yell and see the movement in isolation from the context. There is no connection, no cohesion, let alone liquefaction and flow.

If anything, however, he is even better when transported by those rare moments when performance slips with apparent inevitability into the textures of the play:

On Godfrey Tearle's Antony:

> . . . I had no idea that the many sides of this Shakespearean hero could all be enacted by a single artist. Dignity and indignity, courage and self-indulgence, astuteness and apathy, swift practicality and amorous abandonment—all these are equally well suggested.

On Ina Claire:

> . . . Such precise timing, such delicate underlining, such subtle modulation from phrase to phrase and word to word are almost unknown to our stage today. Our younger actresses, whose hands creep so nervously about in so many directions, might watch the fewer but righter paths travelled by Miss Claire's. Our light comedians, who so regularly practice the double take and other tricks of the eye and turning head, might profitably watch the quickness of muscle and attention by which Miss Claire avoids having her devices identified as tricks at all.

On John Gielgud as Clarence in the recording of *Richard III:*

> . . . a model of Shakespearean speaking. The assignment was a very hard one: to tell the story of a dream,

keeping all the values of the story itself, though the teller of it is a man distraught and near death. Perhaps none of our actors but Sir John could realize both sets of values so fully: he gives all the flamboyance of the narrative plus all the inwardness of the character. Here is a great actor who has much that Olivier has and much that Olivier has not, including warmth, richness, and grandeur of utterance.

Even allowing for the moderately cranky, corrective reminder that Gielgud has been acting for a half-century with an extraordinary, if flawed, competitor getting most of the glamorous notice, only Bentley would be so quick to place Gielgud's achievement within the framework of the story itself. Great acting for him is never technique or display alone; rather, it is a meeting of textual complexity with acting complexity, the latter in touch with realms where there are no subordinations: Gielgud, master of shape, nuance, rhythm, rubato and crescendo, all of these giving sway to momentary reality, the sudden call of inner voices, lifelike spontaneity sweeping all before it. Soberly, calmly, using a vocabulary and phrasing that keep transforming feeling into thought, EB tells us not merely what he knows, but what he adores. A rare, generous critical gift.

When he wants to be plain, he's plain, whether describing Laughton as "sublime" when reading Bottom in a living room, or viewing Martha Graham and Charlie Chaplin not only as performers, but as actors who just happen to be writing plays. Bentley is especially good—unique, in fact—in finding good or great acting where nobody is looking for it. Could anybody else so audaciously link Graham's "projection" with Mae West's? Yet why not? Such a show-stopping allusion keeps the imagination crackling with images supportive of one another. One might even say that

EB's greatest gift when dealing with acting is his continual release into discreet illuminations—quite simply, ideas and images fielded modestly for the first time.

Perhaps the best summation of his enveloping appreciative powers has been his lonely championship not of Brecht, Pirandello, or even Shaw, but of that solitary Neapolitan genius, Eduardo De Filippo. It is literally crazy that references to naturalism or any theatrical version of reality are usually subsumed under the Stanislavsky or Brecht headings, as if there haven't been others, sometimes equally graced, pursuing similar inspirations. Italian theater—what there is of it—has not in this century been the sum of its conceptual directors' decorative dreams, but the singular, unaggressive, maverick work of Eduardo—a "commedia" fugitive, living out of time yet rooted in specific place, a dialect comic totally (in Stark Young's famous phrase about Martha Graham) scraped back to the image.

"It is no slur on his playwriting," says Bentley,

> to say that he is first and foremost an actor, perhaps the finest actor in Italy today! . . . For five minutes or so he may be a complete letdown. This is not acting at all, we cry; above all, it is not Italian acting! Voice and body are so quiet. *Pianissimo.* No glamour, no effusion of brilliance. No attempt to lift the role off the ground by oratory and stylization, no attempt to thrust it at us by force of personality . . . a series of statements, vocal and corporeal . . . beautiful in themselves—beautiful in their clean economy, their precise rightness—and beautiful in relation to each other and to the whole: there are differentiations, sharp or shifting, between one speech and the next; there is a carefully gauged relationship between beginning, middle, and end.

But isn't this, however unintended, a description of Bentley himself as critic, not least on Bentley as critic of actors and acting? There he stands—a pensive observer, melancholy at times, wishing for something better from life, aware of his pedigree, yet never playing on it, more complete than his predecessors, an unswerving explorer, the best possible theatergoer teaching the rest of us because he's such an adventurous student. It is no slur on the playwriting that he has been doing in recent years to say that he is first and foremost an actor playing seriously and delightfully with the critical possibilities of theater.

How lucky we have been to know him, read him, follow him. He taught us tradition, enthusiasm without delirium, scholarship without pedantry, the love of plays coupled to the love of players. Special, he has not been isolated. Years ago, Henry James wrote of Coquelin in terms that reflect Bentley's lessons: "If . . . the American spectator . . . learns, or even shows an aptitude for learning, the lesson conveyed in his finest creations, the lesson that acting is an art, and that the application of an art is style, and that style is expression, and that expression is the salt of life, the gain will have been something more than the sensation of the moment—it will be a new wisdom."

Mining wisdom, new or old, in journalism's quarries is never completely satisfying: editors don't want meditative intelligence, or indeed, anything new, only whatever momentary fancy they can see as news. Meanwhile, somebody like EB sets standards because, luckily, he doesn't know how to do anything else. Writing of Eduardo again, he asks if "we understand what it means to live in a tradition—as against merely believing in tradition, professional traditionalism?" For Bentley, Eduardo stood "in direct contrast to that dissipation of energy by which talents elsewhere are frittered away.'' Those gifts—and once again he could be writing about the great EB himself—''took him across . . . the threshold of great theater . . . and it is thus that one of the most traditional artists of our time became one of the most original.''

IV

THEMES

THE COMING OF THE BARBARIANS

BY DANIEL GEROULD

Problem: where are the barbarians *of the twentieth century?*[1]
—Friedrich Nietzsche

During a trip to Saint Petersburg in the autumn of 1900, the symbolist poet, playwright and novelist Valerii Briusov noted laconically in his diary: "In the evening we saw the Siamese ballet. Not savage enough."[2] His disappointment was proportionate to the expectation, shared by many Russian intellectuals at the time, that barbarism would reinvigorate the arts, transform society and usher in the apocalypse. As the turn of the century approached, there was a presentiment that human history was drawing to an end, at least in the forms by which it had hitherto been known.[3] "A new year, a new century," Briusov recorded in his diary; "Since childhood I have dreamed of this twentieth century."[4] But where were the barbarians?

Fear and longing characterize the waiting for the barbarians—but above all, there is uncertainty: when would they come, and from where, and how to recognize them?

Because of its geographical position at the edge of Europe—or just beyond it—facing the Mongol hordes; and given its historical moment on the eve of revolution, Russia in the early 1900s was unusually sensitive to the barbarian menace (or was it a promise?), as France had been in the nineteenth century.

Prior to 1789 there was for Europeans little problem with barbarians; who they were and where they came from seemed clear enough. They were the "giants of the north" (in Gibbon's phrase) whose incursions against the decaying Roman Empire led eventually to the rise of the modern nation-states. But with the French Revolution, questions of the imminence and identity of contemporary barbarians became urgent. At times of revolution savages appear as if from nowhere, and the eyesight of barbarian-watchers grows sharper than ever before. The search intensifies with each new social upheaval—1789, 1848, 1871—causing increased apprehensions or anticipations.

Attempts to locate the barbarians, to ferret them out of their hiding places, transformed the hunt into one for internal or "vertical" barbarians[5] lurking within the city walls, at the bottom of the urban colossus sapping the foundations, more dangerous than their counterparts hammering at the gates. The socialist novelist Eugène Sue, author of *The Mysteries of Paris* and *The Wandering Jew,* gave the rallying cry—"The Barbarians are among us"—and the critic Saint-Marc Girardin, known for his *Course on Dramatic Literature,* amplified, explaining where they might be found: "The Barbarians who menace society are not in the Caucasus or in the steppes of Tartary, they are in the working class districts of our manufacturing towns."[6]

Whether viewed as signaling the end of civilization or as rejuvenating exhausted societies, the barbarian invasion from within and from without became a commonplace topos in nineteenth-century thought. The Goncourt brothers gave a classic statement of the regenerative value of savagery in the cyclical revolutions of civilization and barbarism:

> Every four or five hundred years savagery becomes necessary to revivify the world. The world would die of uninterrupted civilization. There was a time in Europe when, an old population of a pleasant land being reduced to a decent state of anaemia, there would come down from the North, on its back, a horde of six-foot barbarians to remanufacture its race. Now that there are no longer any savages in Europe, the workers will be doing this job in another fifty years. And the job will be called social revolution.[7]

In England, William Morris interpreted the fall of Rome as "a parable of the days to come; of the change in store for us hidden in the breast of the Barbarism of civilization—the Proletariat." Flaubert's barbarians in the historical novel *Salammbô* have a wild energy and freedom, but when during the Paris Commune the writer saw the urban working classes threatening the property of the bourgeoisie, he was horrified by their destructive power:

> What barbarism! What a disaster! I was hardly a progressive and a humanitarian in the past. Nevertheless, I had my illusions! And I did not believe that I would see the end of the world. But this is it. We are **witnessing the end of the Latin world.**[8]

As a consequence of the burning of Paris by the Communards, all Flaubert's fellow writers in the French literary establishment agreed that the people were wild beasts who should be caged or shot. After the mass executions and deportations used to crush the Commune, it was taken for granted that the masses were consumed by bloody thoughts of vengeance, as was the case with Etienne Lantier, leader of the mine strike that has been broken at the end of Zola's *Germinal:*

> If any class must be devoured, would not the people, still new and full of life, devour the middle class, exhausted by enjoyment? The new society would arise from new blood. And in this expectation of an invasion of barbarians, regenerating the old decayed nations, reappeared his absolute faith in an approaching revolution, the real one—that of the workers—the fire of which would inflame this century's end with the purple of the rising sun which he saw like blood on the sky.[9]

Such were the perceptions of vertical barbarians made entirely along class lines, and the lessons to be drawn for those who held an elite view of art and culture were simple: the status quo must be maintained, and the barbarians held down. "The essential thing," wrote Ernest Renan, "is less to produce enlightened masses than to produce great geniuses and a public capable of understanding them."[10]

The analogue of barbarians and proletariat—with its grim warnings of class warfare and impending revolution—which obsessed French men of letters at the *fin de siècle* appears not to have engendered any drama in Western Europe at this time. The reasons are many. The elitist authors haunted by antibarbarian presentiments disdained the stage of the period and wrote for it rarely, and then with condescension. Fear and anxiety about the subversion of culture from below could not have seemed a possible subject for a smug, conservative theatre whose boldest themes centered around questions of sexual morality, adultery, divorce, and keeping courtesans and fallen women in their place. The conventions of nineteenth-century drama were not suited to the exploration of large ideological issues, and historical plays were weighed down in local color and elaborate "scientific" reconstructions, ruling out any play of ideas or contemporary significance. And even if it had been dramaturgically feasible, portraying present-day savages on stage as a genuine menace to civilization was out of the question due to the strict censorship reinstituted in France after 1871, and to the prevailing mood of chauvinism in the theatre, with its glorification of patriotism, the French Army, and traditional values of law and order.[11]

Vertical barbarians remained a private obsession on the part of the intelligentsia, finding its way into the history of ideas, whereas romanticized Huns, Vandals and Ostrogoths appeared in the popular theatre in melodramatic adaptations of *Ben Hur* and *Quo Vadis,* in costume dramas like Sardou's *Theodora,* and on the operatic stage in works such as Verdi's *Attila.* These picturesque barbarians, bare-chested, wearing animal hides and horns, constituted no threat to present civilization, nor did they suggest any parallel to the urban proletariat.

In order to find the barbarians of the twentieth century on stage, we must return to Russia where we left Valerii Briusov at the turn of the century, waiting for something sufficiently savage. Within five years the Russo-Japanese War and the Revolution of 1905 had made the coming of the barbarians a reality, although who they were remained unclear. Briusov equated the event with the triumph of socialism, which he welcomed, and in 1904-5 he wrote essays, stories and poems in which revolution is celebrated as the unleashing of a destructive, rebarbarizing force that will cause humanity's regression to a primitive state of nature. In the science fiction tale *The Last Martyrs,* set in an unspecified time and place, the Brotherhood of the Temple—guardians of the crumbling world of culture—are assaulted by the barbarians without ancestors, who represent a spiritual void. "The Coming Huns" is a welcoming hymn by the poet to his destroyers who will burn all the books and drive the "custodians of mystery and faith" into the catacombs:

Upon us like a drunken horde
Rush from the dark tents of your camps—
Revive our withered bodies
With a flow of ardent blood.[12]

On December 3, four days before the Moscow uprising that was the culmination of the Revolution of 1905, Maxim Gorky read aloud his new play for the members of the Kommissarzhevskaya Theatre. At this moment of crisis and social upheaval, apocalypse and the end of a decaying empire appeared imminent, and Gorky gave the title *Barbarians* to his fourth drama, a seemingly Chekhovian study of a group of small-town characters whose inconsequential lives of eating, drinking, talking and lovemaking are disrupted by the arrival of more glamorous city dwellers (in this case, railway engineers). The central issue of the play—the identity of the barbarians—made the public uneasy. The critic Alexander Kugel wrote:

And note how extremely confusing the moral thesis of the play is. Who the barbarians are no one can tell. It would appear the visiting engineers are the barbarians. But it is possible the barbarians are the native inhabitants of the small backwater town. Nor can we tell what is meant by barbarism. It looks as though barbarism is the young, bright, upcoming, untapped force which is destined to turn everything upside down. On the other hand, it may be that barbarism is the destruction of the elemental traditional forms without replacing them by newer ones. . . . In *Barbarians* the question of what is truth and where it is to be found absolutely defies definition.[13]

We cannot imagine the author of *The Cherry Orchard* calling any of his plays *Barbarians*. Whereas Chekhov's more introspective characters confront the loneliness and anguish of not knowing who they are, Gorky's aggressive *dramatis personae* cannot tolerate for even a moment such uncertainty and must belong to a group that stands united against the "others." Only by distinguishing themselves from an antithetical self can these angry and confused people find an identity. So civilization defines itself in opposition to the barbarians.

The garden setting of Gorky's play suggests paradise; as the Chief of Police tells Bogayevskaya, "Your house is an Eden." But there are savages in the garden—and a Chief of Police. Interrogations take place and an arrest for embezzlement. Culture is a matter of appearances, civilization only skin deep. Beneath the surface of frustrated love entanglements, ugly crime and violence have reached the boiling point. In this sleepy provincial town that becomes a microcosm of Russia, we hear of and sometimes actually witness fraud and theft, husbands beating wives and children, wives poisoning husbands, parents selling daughters in marriage, abuse of authority, informing to the police, and driving one's nearest to despair and suicide.

Each side accuses the other of being "wild beasts"—the familiar animal analogy accompanying charges of barbarism. The engineer calls the town "Tierra del Fuego" and the local inhabitants "savages," while the Doctor says of

Tsyganov and his even more belligerent associate Cherkun, "You're both beasts of prey . . . you're vultures—"; and the Mayor exclaims, "These freethinkers here—they are barbarians—wreckers! They topple everything over—at their touch everything falls—."[14]

Chekhov's obsessive dreamers can sometimes withdraw into the unique self that exists in solitude and nurtures individuality. Gorky's hotheaded and noisy "savages" lack inwardness, have no inmost being. They exist in the public arena, by virtue of their positions as Chief of Police, Mayor, Revenue Collector, Timber Merchant, Engineer, Treasury Clerk. Crass and crude swindlers, cheaters, crooks, wife-beaters, they contend to assert authority. They are rapacious for money, position, influence, and even in matters of love and romance sentiment takes second place to wielding power over others.

When instability in the social structure unleashes hostile impulses, contacts among humans grow abrasive and partisanship replaces introspection. Joining forces to gain power, resist abuse and abuse others, Gorky's unreflective characters are a prey to mob psychology and demagogic myths, such as the "coming of the barbarians." Their haste to take sides finds full expression in Gorky's next play, *Enemies,* whose title further elucidates the perception of others as adversaries. Skrobotov, assistant district attorney and brother of the factory owner killed by a worker during labor disturbances, proclaims a counter-slogan to Marx's rallying cry in *The Communist Manifesto:*

> "Culture-loving people of the world, unite!" It's time we shouted this. The barbarian is coming to trample thousands of years of human effort under foot. He's on the march, driven by greed. . . . What can these

people bring with them? Nothing but destruction. And, mind you, in this country the destruction will be more terrifying than anywhere.[15]

In *Barbarians* the destruction has already begun, with the entry of the serpent-engineers into the garden. "This is nature in its elemental state," Tsyganov declares, to which Cherkun, the former peasant seeking revenge for past humiliations, replies, "I don't like pastorales." A proponent of blind might, whose red hair recalls Tacitus's Teutonic barbarian and Nietzsche's blond-beast, Cherkun defines the conflict as between a powerful machine and an old way of life: "We have to build new highways—railways. Iron is the force which will destroy this stupid, wooden life."

"When he writes plays," Alexander Blok wrote of Gorky, "he almost always loses his own point of view."[16] This frequent accusation of indecisive neutrality seems to miss the point, that the author of *Barbarians* and *Enemies* is writing the drama of those who too readily take sides; his own absence of a clear stand is itself a position, and a highly dramatic one. Gorky sets barbarians against barbarians, the pseudo-civilized of steel and fire against the under-civilized of village superstition. Anatoly Lunacharsky, future Soviet Commissar of Education, writing in 1906 about *Barbarians,* found the process dialectical: out of the battle between the wooden age of old rural Russia and the iron age of new industrial, capitalist Russia there will be born, in the form of the younger generation, the golden age of the future, which, according to Marxist mythology, in a reversal of classical precedent, comes last.[17]

The response of Briusov and the Russian Symbolists to the coming of the barbarians was ambivalent. On the one hand, they adopted the cult of the barbaric in an attempt to overcome the rational superstructure of Western civilization and return to an elemental state of pure essences captured by the geometric forms of primitive and archaic art. Primordial man from a utopian stone age was the object of nostalgic longing. On the other hand, when it came to the present and the uncouth rabble that would sweep away the crumbling *ancien régime,* the elegant and fastidious Symbolists were less enthusiastic. For example, they called Gorky's friend Leonid Andreyev (then an immensely popular novelist and playwright) a "barbarian" in a purely negative sense; in the eyes of the elite, he was a semieducated savage and his work vulgar and hysterical ranting, lacking in literary refinement.

Barbarians had been originally defined linguistically; they were those outlanders who could not speak Greek correctly but only emit strange sounds onomatopoetically represented as "bar-bar." Significantly, Briusov refused "to fall into ecstasies over" the Revolution of 1905, finding that its leaders for the most part "spoke poor Russian."[18] Evidently these were only half-literate pseudo-barbarians, not the real thing. The authentic menace was external and came from the East. The racial theme of the "yellow peril" (made immediate by the Russo-Japanese War and adopted from popular literature) appeared as a source of pleasurable dread, exploited in Vladimir Solovyov's poem "Pan-Mongolism" (1894), and in Andrei Bely's novel *The Silver Dove* (1909), where it served as a sinister cryptomotif.[19]

Whereas the Russians rendered histrionic and apocalyptic their visions of the coming onslaught against civilization, the Greek poet from Alexandria, Constantine Cavafy (twice removed from the center of Europe and thus a double outsider), in his poem "Waiting for the Barbarians," was the first to strike a modern, ironic tone, suggesting that the barbaric threat may be only a myth used to justify the status quo.

What are we waiting for, assembled in the forum?
The barbarians are due here today.

. . .

Why this sudden bewilderment, this confusion? . . .
Because night has fallen and the barbarians haven't come.
And some of our men just in from the border say there are no barbarians any longer.

. . .

Now what's going to happen to us without barbarians?
Those people were a kind of solution.[20]

With the destruction and chaos brought about by the Bolshevik Revolution of 1917, it appeared that the waiting was over and that the barbarians did in fact exist. The "Scythians"—under the leadership of Ivanov-Razumnik—were a circle of mystical revolutionaries, including the poets Blok and Bely, who believed in Russia's messianic destiny and welcomed the Revolution as a cataclysm of purifying power that would do away with the obsolete humanist civilization of Europe and usher in the "culture of eternity." From the *tabula rasa* left after the extinction of the decaying bourgeois world of materialistic values, a new spiritual life would arise.[21]

In his diary on January 11, 1918, Blok wrote of the European nations, France, Germany and England, hostile to the Soviet Union:

If you do not wash away the shame of your wartime patriotism with at least a "democratic peace," if you destroy our revolution, then you are no longer Aryans. And we shall open wide the gates to the East.

We looked at you with Aryan eyes, so long as you still had a face. But your animal muzzle we will run over with our squint-eyed, cunning, glancing look; like changelings we will change into Asiatics, and the East will flood over you.

Your skins will go for Chinese tambourines. He who has brought down such shame on his own head, who is so sunk in lies—is no longer Aryan. We're barbarians? All right then. We'll show you what barbarians really are. And our cruel reply, our terrible reply, will be the only answer worthy of man.[22]

Blok's poem of January 30, "The Scythians," expresses the same warning that Europe will be abandoned to the "fury of the Mongol horde" unless she supports Russia "in true fraternity."

We shall resort to Scythian craft and guile. . . .

We shall not stir, even though the frenzied Huns
    Plunder corpses of the slain in battle, drive
Their cattle into shrines, burn cities down,
    And roast their white-skinned fellow men alive.

                              . . . For the last time
O hear the summons of the barbarian lyre![23]

In the aftermath of revolution, Blok struck a belligerent pose and turned momentarily xenophobic and vindictive towards the West, threatening to let the savages loose. In neighboring Poland, newly independent after a century and a half of oppression by occupying powers (Russia, Prussia, Austria), a sense of precariousness afflicted poets and artists, giving rise to an apocalyptic mood. The spectacular last minute victory in a brief war with the Soviet Union (1920-21) could not dispel the ominous warnings for an over-civilized, decaying social structure that revealed little talent for governing itself.

Back from four years in the Tsarist army and a first hand view of the Russian Revolution, the Polish writer and painter Stanisław Ignacy Witkiewicz—known as Witkacy—adopted a distanced historical perspective with regard to the layers of cultural detritus that weighed upon his country, and cultivated a playful and ironic tone toward the barbarian threat from the East that soon might blow away the tottering relics of the past. In a series of plays dealing with the unleashing of vertical barbarians by demented dictators out to seize power and destroy the old order, Witkacy at the beginning of the 1920s forecast the "age of crazy ideologies and fanatical ideologists"[24] that would dominate the following two decades and bring on World War II.

In all these works the destruction of the *ancien régime* is perceived from the viewpoint of the class that is going under, but that lacks any belief in its own right to exist. The disintegration and dismemberment of such a society from within seem inevitable, even though the cost may be the demise of art and culture. In *The Water Hen* (1921), the decadent Alice, Duchess of Nevermore, delights in the annihilation of her former social class, and joins forces with the disreputable Tom Hoozy, who welcomes the cataclysm:

> Let's go out into the streets. I like the atmosphere of a revolution. There's nothing more agreeable than to swim in the black sea of a mob gone mad.[25]

In *The Anonymous Work* (1921), the unruly mob of "people in black pointed caps" led by the gravedigger Lopak create the "anonymous work"—revolution from below by spontaneous combustion—which has as its goal the total destruction of the existing civilization.[26] In *The Cuttlefish* (1922), a new breed of strongman, Hyrcan IV—self-fabricated ruler of the imaginary kingdom of Hyrcania—is contrasted with Pope Julius II, warrior, consolidator of papal power and patron of the arts, who exemplifies past Renaissance greatness when civilization could produce men uniting within themselves strength, political cunning and active love of beauty. Nowadays, without a name or heritage, the would-be dictator and superman is simply a modern barbarian interested in power for its own sake.

Alert at an early point to the rise of totalitarianism on either side of Poland, Witkacy foresaw the alliance of science, technology and barbarism, drawing upon ideas in Oswald Spengler's *Decline of the West* (1918-22) and anticipating those in Ortega y Gasset's *The Revolt of the Masses* (1930). *Janulka, Daughter of Fizdejko* (1924), set in a mythical Lithuania in what may be either the seventeenth or the twenty-third century, or a combination of both, portrays a postrevolutionary world of endless, meaningless change and deepening stagnation, where all that remains is the fabrication of artificial selves and kingdoms. Grotesque monsters, on wheeled platforms, chanting the shrill refrain "We're alive, we're warm, we're hungry," contain the secret of the future. As Gottfried Reichsgraf Von und Zu Berchtoldingen, Grand Master of the Neo-Teutonic Knights, explains:

> The new state composed of the greatest barbarians combined with the highest civilization is the principle of future reality. There can be no civilization without barbarians to serve as a contrast.[27]

In Witkacy's final surviving play, *The Shoemakers* (written from 1927 to 1933), the triumphant barbarians who take over at the last minute are no longer terrifyingly bizarre creatures, but chillingly ordinary technocrats in business suits, mouthing pragmatic, pseudocommunist platitudes. Witkacy's catastrophic novel *Insatiability* (1930) gives comically exaggerated treatment to the Eurocentric racist nightmare of the "yellow peril." When millions of Chinese Communists—the "mobile yellow wall" with its countless invisible feet marching in unison[28]—threaten to overrun Western Europe, having already conquered the pseudo-Bolshevik USSR, only Poland stands as a bulwark against the "fury of the Mongol horde," until its surprising and unheroic capitulation in the face of a more powerful reality.

Witkacy was one of Poland's leading catastrophists in the period between the wars, but in his works we find that elements of sarcasm and theatricalization have infiltrated the usually solemn *fin de siècle* themes. While partaking of the elite view of vertical barbarians as "herd" and "cattle," the Polish writer's humor, fantasy and flamboyance infect the prophecies of doom. His parodistic use of what were already clichés of cultural criticism, for their theatrical and coloristic values, shifts emphasis from the discursive content to the imaginative shape of the apocalyptical. In other words, Witkacy lets his catastrophic beliefs (which were by no means new but part of a European tradition) serve as material for his dramas, rather than making his dramas serve as vehicles for his apocalyptic ideas. Truly innovative and modern in sensibility was Witkacy's ironic theatricalization of the stereotypes of cultural catastrophism.

Hitler and Stalin gave new life to the stereotypes of apocalyptic thinking. By the late 1930s the rise of barbarism, the approaching end of Western civilization, and the new dark ages had become menacing realities for those with eyes to see, giving rise to eloquent jeremiads such as Leonard

Woolf's *Barbarians Within and Without:*

The barbarian is, therefore, not only at our gates; he is always within the walls of our civilization, inside our minds and our hearts. In times of storm and stress within any society, his appeal is very strong.[29]

The Spanish Civil War and Guernica, the Ethiopian Campaign, the triumph of the Nazis, the concentration camps and final solution, all made it impossible ever again simply to equate Europe with civilization and to see culture as threatened by barbarians. In fact, European culture itself seemed to be the source of the barbaric.

Following World War II, barbarians underwent reappraisal and rehabilitation. Comparative anthropology fostered cultural relativism and a new awareness of diversity, leading to admiration for primitive art, acceptance of other cultures as being equally as valid as one's own, and recognition that for each race or nation what is alien is perceived as barbarian. As Europe ceased to be the center of the universe, Europeans grew willing to turn back upon themselves the epithet barbarian, which now seemed too derogatory and ethnocentric to be used except "with mock facetiousness."[30] Thus trivialized as comic and harmless, barbarians entered the world of popular culture, appearing in comic strips, science fiction tales and adventure films. Taken unabashedly as stereotypes, the hairy Teuton or Gaul draped in animal hides acquired new life and new uses as clichés. From being bugaboos for Eurocentric philosophers and custodians of high culture in the 1920s and '30s, the barbarians have made new and subtler incursions into civilization, winning acceptance as amusing and non-threatening boors. They are among us everywhere—we are the barbarians. In accord with Marx's prescription for the evolution of world-historical forms, the final phase for barbarians appears to be comedy.

It is at this point, when the theme had become ripe for irreverent treatment, that two of Europe's sliest humorists and most incisive cultural critics, Friedrich Dürrenmatt and Sławomir Mrożek, took up the barbarians and, using the techniques of cartoon and cabaret, wrote allusive satires dealing with history, power and the state.

In Dürrenmatt's *Romulus the Great* (first written in 1948, performed in 1949, revised in 1956), the traditional distinction between civilized and barbarian is revealed to be a false one, as all the old clichés are paradoxically inverted or subversively undermined. It is not civilization that is threatened by the barbarians, but both that are menaced by history, absorbed by the mechanism of the state and forced to continue its futile cycle. "The Teutons are marching on Rome"[31] is a familiar warning cry robbed of its terror, since the barbarians are already copying Imperial civilization and assimilating its culture, setting up academies in the forests, ordering plaster casts of classical busts from art dealers, and collecting primitive art made by their forebears.

The last Roman emperor and the first Teutonic king resemble each other in their desire to escape the roles thrust upon them. Both chicken fanciers and men of peace, Romulus and Odoaker would like to escape from the relentless forward pressure of chronology and the "terror of history,"[32] into a timeless realm where duration is measured only by the diurnal cycle, mealtimes and the laying of eggs. Romulus has ceased to think and feel as a Roman, or to believe in the patriotism that demands "mounds of human sacrifices" of its citizens. Recognizing that "Our state has become a world empire, an institution engaged in murder,"[33] he is content to play the clown in order to be

Rome's judge and bring about its downfall as just punishment for its crimes. Overcome by guilt for suffering caused by Roman tyranny and violence, Romulus refuses to defend a spurious civilization, and instead hopes to take his place among its victims.

> Shall I touch your eyes that you may see this throne, this pyramid of blood in endless waterfalls, generating Rome's power? . . . The Teutons are coming; we have spilled the stranger's blood; we must now pay back with our own. . . . Do we still have the right to be more than victims?[34]

Civilization means empire and the power of the state to crush all those enemies whom it labels "barbarians." For Romulus, it is this subjugating force that is the greatest danger, whereas for his counterpart Odoaker, the barbarian chief turned cultured pacifist, civilization appears as a desirable restraint on the heroic Teutonic virtues (exemplified by his warlike nephew Theodoric) that will lead to "a second Rome . . . a Teutonic empire as transitory as Rome and as bloody."[35]

Theodoric, who will slay both Romulus and Odoaker, is destined to become known as "the Great" for repeating the fatal patterns of history. Romulus, who wanted to bring the Roman Empire to an end, and Odoaker, who hoped that the Teutonic Empire would not begin, both fail. The uneventful interlude of peace they have established does not last long and is forgotten by history, which glorifies conquest and leaders of superstates and follows its inevitable cyclical course.

Romulus and Odoaker, kindred spirits who meet as equals for a moment, do not fit the stereotypes created for them as "civilized" and "barbarian"—categories imposed from the outside. Neither looks as the other imagined. "Obviously our ideas about different races and peoples are quite wrong," observes the last Roman emperor, commenting about Odoaker; "there is nothing about him except his trousers that is barbarian."[36] Culture is perceived to be a matter of clothing. Caesar Ruff, the Romanized trouser manufacturer and capitalist who is ready to buy the barbarians off, explains the crucial importance of dress in the march of civilization:

> There is a profound inner connection between the fact that the Teutons wear trousers and that they are making such incredible progress. . . . Only a Rome that wears trousers will be equipped to meet the onslaught of the Germanic hordes.[37]

The Barbarian Chief Odoaker, "of ancient lineage," takes notes on a pad pulled from his leather briefcase, much like a twentieth-century bureaucrat, and his Teutonic troops —Dürrenmatt insists—are not operatic barbarians, but modern mass men, dressed in monotonous linen clothes and simple helmets. The "barbarians" are little more than a myth, an illusion civilization needs to sustain itself. Mocking the eschatological mode of thinking from the perspective of cultural relativism, Dürrenmatt has his Romans describe the apocalypse as simply a change of historical orders—the end of antiquity, but a continuation of life: "Even on this day when the world's coming to an end the sun still shines."[38] The metahistorical order of chickens and eggs endures.

Through playfulness, clowning, anachronism and allusion (directed against the audience, themselves descendants of the Teutons), Dürrenmatt turns the dialogue between civilization and barbarians into comic cultural history, with reference to the recent Nazi era, the present divided state of Europe, and the fear of Communist invasion and subversion.[39] As a general parable of man and the state, its applications are to the future, and its lessons open-ended.

The contemporary playwright who has most thoroughly pursued the dialectic of civilization and barbarians is Sławomir Mrożek. *The Tailor* (written in 1965, published in 1977) is a fable about the role of clothing in human society that takes one step further into the realm of pure theatricalization the axioms enunciated in *Romulus the Great*.[40] Mrożek plays with the common cultural heritage (both Polish and European) and its traditional images and clichés, showing the power of myths and abstractions to entrap, and using his skills as a cartoonist to give the stereotypes of popular thought the vivid outlines of a comic strip.

Whereas Dürrenmatt in his "Historical Comedy Without Historic Basis" retained actual events and characters that are treated with fictional freedom, the Polish playwright abandons historicity entirely, constructing instead a synthetic model situation that combines the costumes of disparate periods and nations: dark ages, Elizabethan, Louis XIV and contemporary. The different fabrics and textures become the theatrical medium for propositions about clothing and nakedness that constitute the drama's argument. In their appearance and dress, Mrożek's barbarians reveal the ludicrous incongruities of conflicting layers of culture; they have long red hair and beards, naked bodies covered with animal hides, bare legs, and tennis shoes on their feet. The tennis shoes may be read as a sign that the barbarians are already growing civilized (although only at the lowest level), or as a link to modern savages who roam the world in jeans and sneakers.

"What too are all Poets and moral teachers of Mankind, but a species of Metaphorical Tailor?" Carlyle asks in *Sartor Resartus*.[41] Mrożek's title character is such a metaphorical tailor, conducting a series of lessons centered around problems of essence and social identity.

Consider the following exchange at the beginning of *The Tailor,* where the king and the king-maker introduce the play's central metaphor: civilization as fashion and the manipulation of its disguises as power:

His Excellency: So, Master Tailor, you say that the Barbarians are getting close?

Tailor: They're here already, in the antechamber.

Excellency: I always supposed that we were separated from them by at least 100 years and several oceans.

Tailor: Time flies, and oceans don't help much any more.

Excellency: It's unwelcome news. What do they look like?

Tailor: Awful. They're almost naked.

Excellency: How are they behaving?

Tailor: They're keeping astonishingly quiet. They stare at the wallpaper, and sniff the armchairs suspiciously. One of them ate a bouquet of roses.

Excellency: With the thorns?

Tailor: No, first he cut the thorns off the stem with a penknife.

Excellency: So he's not a complete Barbarian after all.

Tailor: Of course not. His Excellency has an imprecise notion of what the Barbarians are like.

Excellency: Are you defending them, Master Tailor?

Tailor: No, not at all! Your Excellency well knows that *I* am civilization.

Excellency: Oh, no! *I* am civilization and civilization is all those things that I represent: science, art, humanism. . . .[42]

289

The Tailor, as the producer of the forms of culture, recognizes that the barbarian in his nakedness is an antithetical identity, menacing in his shapelessness and lack of differentiation. The barbarians "came simply to get decently dressed," the Tailor explains; "they'll be defeated, not by our strength, but by their own vanity."[43] The howling savages in the anteroom have quickly quieted down when given fashion magazines to read.

The systematic elimination of nature advances civilization, making human raw material malleable to the Tailor's creations. Thus the creator of clothes would like to extirpate the ruler's primitive sexuality—"that remnant of age-old barbarism, the essence of nakedness, the last bastion of nature"[44]—by having His Excellency castrated. Clothing, the Tailor realizes, hides the commonness of nudity and gives its meaninglessness comprehensible form capable of producing individuality and mystery,[45] as in the case of the courtesan Nana, whose body the Tailor covers entirely in order to create undiminishing desire in her admirers.

Having fallen in love with this masked whore of culture (whose lies are art), the barbarian chieftain Onucy gets his beard trimmed (and orders his followers to do the same) and becomes the next Excellency, as the cycle of history goes on with the absorption of a new wave of barbarians into the matrix of civilization that overlays with clothing the brutish instincts. In the process, Onucy feels that he has lost his identity:

> I wish I'd never left the forest. No sooner had I come out of the woods than your quadrille began. . . . Civilization. All it takes is to get mixed up with people, and everything's lost, you can't tell any more whether it's me or them or who's who.[46]

In a converse movement, renouncing the culture of his elders, Carlos, the young son of the courtesan, defects from the civilized camp to join the barbarians, seeking the truth to be himself in nakedness, not in the appearances fabricated by the Tailor. This "generational" barbarian, who hopes to create a social revolution and overthrow the rule of the Tailor, is quickly cast off by Onucy as an embarrassment to his civilizing aspirations, and condemned to be flayed alive, like Marsyas who was punished for challenging Apollo's perfect form.[47] The Tailor directs the flaying himself, intending to make an ideal costume out of the skin. The ideological rebellion of youth will be skinned and turned into a fashionable object of apparel—in other words, emasculated and coopted by civilization.

The return to nature proves to be only an illusion, and nakedness is powerless against the weight of costume and custom. Civilization can accommodate many clients and absorb the barbarians who overrun it. As Mommsen, Bury and other historians point out, the conquest of the Roman Empire by the savage hordes meant the Romanization of the barbarians rather than the barbarization of the Romans.[48] The engineer and custodian of civilization, the Tailor survives all changes of regime and returns the first Excellency to power, having eliminated rebellious youth and entangled the barbarians, who abandon their animal hides and bloodthirsty desires for pillage, rape and murder to take part in the quadrille. As Léopold Flam writes in *L'Homme et la Conscience tragique:*

> Clothes therefore make the man, clothes are his style. Undressed and naked, he loses his essence, he feels himself nothing, he is ill at ease, he has lost what constituted his essential being. Western civilization is a

291

civilization of clothes and essence, based on shame and embarrassment.[49]

In *Tango, or the Need for Harmony and Order* (written in 1964 just before *The Tailor*), Mrożek's family, whose three generations recapitulate the recent history of Europe, is obsessed with their vertical barbarian, Eddie, who is waiting within the gates—a Trojan horse ready to unleash brute force and seize power. Members of the civilized family admire the vitality of this primitive type, praise his naturalness and usefulness, find excuses for his boorishness, court his favor. They are apologists for barbarism, which they have welcomed into their home.

In *Tango,* as in *The Tailor,* clothes and the dance are principal images. After killing Arthur (the intellectual whose admiration for pure power showed the way) by a quick blow to the head with the handle of a revolver, Eddie puts on the coat belonging to his victim, which is too tight for him, and bursts the ṣeams of the cloth of culture. As Carlyle noted in ''The World in Clothes'':

> The first spiritual want of a barbarous man is Decoration, as indeed we still see among the barbarous classes in civilised countries.[50]

Dressed in borrowed clothes, the thug-come-to-power next appropriates one of civilization's dances. Eddie, from the underside of society but now in control, dances the tango with Great Uncle Eugene, doddering representative of European civilization who follows the ''lead'' of whatever brute force takes command. The choice of the tango as Eddie's dance (rather than the Viennese waltz) suggests the relativity of barbarism and its rapid assimilation by culture. Once a low and barbaric dance from Argentina, full of blatant Latin sensuality, the tango was adopted and refined by European high society. It has become ambivalently barbaric and civilized at the same time. In dancing *their* dance, the lumpen-proletarian Eddie is reclaiming what is his as well as violating what is theirs. But in following the intricate steps of the tango, is the barbarian Eddie asserting his primitive nature, or already submitting to civilizing structures? No matter how ill-fitting his jacket or grotesque his dancing style, Eddie has become one of the "tailored" and joined the quadrille.[51]

In a later play, *The Hunchback* (1975), the potential for widespread social violence has grown, as distinctions between civilization and barbarians blur. While two mismatched couples staying at a pastoral country inn (run by the title character) pass the time in Chekhovian flirtations, philosophizing about life and love, a subterranean feeling of menace and unease mounts. A storm is brewing, and there will soon be an explosion; the barbarians are near—at the gates, in the anteroom. But who are they? To the attractive philandering couples, the Hunchback-proprietor seems a barbarian. The fact that he is deformed and looks different means that he should be kept out of sight, or removed. Denying that he favors exterminating the unfit, Onek, the bourgeois husband, nonetheless upholds certain forms of social cohesion:

> Civilization is the creation of people who are normal, standardized; so it follows that the hunchback cannot be included in civilization. . . . I'm not a barbarian. I don't advocate a return to savage and bestial solutions.

The radical student who arrives at the inn keeps his distance and treats the smug bourgeois with contempt and sarcasm—isn't he too a barbarian, one of the new hordes of uncivilized youths? Toward the end of Act II of *The*

Hunchback there appears a Stranger, in a derby and dark suit, who seems to be a secret agent working for the powers that be. He warns:

> In the times which are coming upon us, the question of identity, ladies and gentlemen, becomes increasingly difficult to resolve satisfactorily. . . . We are being confronted by another world: a world of antithetical identity. . . . We find ourselves on top of a volcano. . . . The volcano is erupting, bubbling under our very feet. We are being poisoned by conspiracies, secret societies, plots.[52]

During a midnight picnic in the nearby mountains that turns into a major *Walpurgisnacht,* the tenuous bonds holding together the group unravel, and when the agent is mysteriously shot, the situation takes a turn for the worse. The trains have stopped running and the telephones no longer function. The couples break up, all the guests leave on foot, and the Hunchback decides to close his establishment. A sense of impending disaster engulfs the empty stage on which the lonely figure of the Hunchback remains. Will he survive the apocalypse?

Kazimierz Dejmek, who directed the first production of the play at the Teatr Nowy in Łódź in December 1975, later commented, as the situation in Poland was rapidly growing more confused and menacing, "What has happened here recently was hard to foresee although Mrożek had predicted it in *The Hunchback.* I thought, however, that he was exaggerating a good deal."[53] As the old order was breaking down, Soviet troops were waiting at the borders, while within the gates plans for the military takeover were already being planned in secret.

At the end of the 1970s in the works of several English authors from Britain and South Africa, barbarians appear as the tragic victims of empire, seen on their own home ground not as a threat to others but as subject to invasion and extermination by civilization. Unlike the witty and playful subversions of expected paradigms created by Dürrenmatt and Mrożek (writers from smaller countries which never had colonies), these indictments of imperialism are tinged with powerful feelings of guilt and indignation towards a shameful past and an intolerable present. Two plays—Howard Brenton's *Romans in Britain* and Barrie Keeffe's *Barbarians*—and a novel—J.M. Coetzee's *Waiting for the Barbarians*—can serve as a stark and violent epilogue to the dialogue of culture and nature.[54] The coming of civilization means murder and conquest.

Romans in Britain (written in 1979, presented at the National Theatre in October 1980) has as its three juxtaposed times of action 54 B.C. and 515 A.D. in England and 1980 in Ireland. Successive waves of domination reveal invading Romans overpowering native Celts, Saxons subduing Celts, and British crushing Irish. Always it is the bearers of civilization who violate the barbarians, as in the notorious scene in which a Roman soldier rapes a Druid priest. Although the word barbarian is not used, its counterpoise—civilization—is held up as a talisman against the scorned nakedness and squalor of the barbarians. But what truly sets off the conquerors from the conquered is the ability to speak a superior and civilized language, and the Romans are contemptuously surprised to hear the natives making efforts to speak their tongue:

> **Second Soldier:** A nig nog? Talking Latin? . . . This nig nog talks Latin![55]

At the end of Act I, in a striking conflation of historic periods, Caesar and the Roman Army advance in British Army uniforms and with the equipment of the late 1970s, to the sound of an approaching helicopter. A Slave who throws a stone at the troops is cut down by automatic-weapons fire. Caesar, spokesman and apologist for the violence that maintains social order, delivers a Churchillian peroration:

> That everyday life will begin again. That violence will be reduced to an acceptable level. That Civilisation may not sink, its great battle lost.[56]

Much as Dürrenmatt's Romulus, anguished over the crimes of empire, refuses to defend the state and seeks a sacrificial death, Brenton's Captain Chichester—a British secret agent who has infiltrated the IRA—gives himself away and deliberately provokes his own killing in revulsion at the archaeological layers of imperial brutality of which he is the final heir:

> I keep on seeing the dead. A field in Ireland, a field in England. And faces like wood. Charred wood, set in the ground. Staring at me. Because in my hand there's a Roman spear. A Saxon axe. A British Army machine gun. The weapons of Rome, invaders, Empire.[57]

Keeffe's *Barbarians* (1976-7) is a trilogy of short plays—*Killing Time, Abide with Me* and *In the City*—about three young vertical barbarians from the London slums, two white and one black. In their substandard language and in their destructive boredom, frustration, rage and violence, they are barbarians, excluded from the reigning culture. In the first play, they wait at the doors to the Lord Mayor's banquet, but are not invited inside; in the second play, they are at the gates of a soccer stadium but unable to storm their way in.

Dispossessed of any individual identity, they dress in the tribal costumes of a sporting or criminal subculture, and turn their violence against society or against themselves. Only the military will accept them, to fight an imperialistic war. In the final play, the young barbarian who has joined the army and is about to be sent off to Ireland to brutalize the Micks, suddenly turns on his former black companion, kicking him savagely in order to provoke his own arrest and keep from being sent to Belfast. His final words contain the barbarian threat:

> I'm a trained killer. Lock me up. To protect myself . . . and society from everything you've done to me. 'Cause, 'cause . . . otherwise I'll do it back. To you. Worse.[58]

The dialogue between civilization and barbarians, seen in the light of late colonialism, crumbling empire and urban rots and riots, and against the background of Vietnam, Northern Ireland and South Africa, finds its fullest expression in Coetzee's *Waiting for the Barbarians,* a complex fable that takes its title and theme from Cavafy's poem. In Coetzee, as in Cavafy, the elusive "barbarians at the gates" are a pretext for all of civilization's evils. History is a long record of the conquest, victimization and enslavement of "others"—all those inferior people who threaten and can be labeled "barbarian." Having lost the regenerative power ascribed to them in the past, the roving bands of barbarians can only hope to remain invisible and stay out of the reach of the civilization that would annihilate them.

The narrator of the novel—an aging, cultured magistrate at a distant frontier outpost—sees his little oasis, a potential earthly paradise, become a place of torture when security agents from the capital interrogate kidnapped nomads (old men and women) to counter the supposed threat of a barbarian invasion and to seize still more of the land that once belonged entirely to the natives. Suffering from such a bad conscience that he can no longer take the side of civilization in its persecutions and plunderings, the magistrate is branded as a barbarian-lover and is himself interrogated and tortured. His interests in the archaeological remains of past barbarian settlements convince him that their indecipherable script is nothing but an endless record of suffering and oppression.

Like Dürrenmatt's Romulus, the magistrate becomes the judge of the civilization of which he is the product and the pillar. He would like to escape out of history, which is no more than a river of blood and pyramid of skulls, into the eternal cycle of life in accord with nature, as it was in Eden or the lost golden age. Now the earth is layered with the bones and graves of those killed in the name of civilization—a perception of the victimization of barbarians similar to that of Brenton's Captain Chichester.

> What has made it impossible for us to live in time like fish in water, like birds in air, like children? It is the fault of Empire! Empire has created the time of history. Empire has located its existence not in the smooth recurrent spinning time of the cycle of the seasons but in the jagged time of rise and fall, of beginning and end, of catastrophe. Empire dooms itself to live in history and plot against history. One thought alone preoccupies the submerged end of Empire: how not to end, how not to die, how to prolong its era. By day it pursues its enemies. It is cunning and ruthless, it sends its bloodhounds everywhere. By night it feeds on images of disaster: the sack of cities, the rape of populations, pyramids of bones, acres of desolation.[59]

Briusov, Blok and their *fin de siècle* fellow catastrophists hoped that the irruption of barbarians into civilization would hasten the end of history and usher in the millennium. But for Coetzee's broken narrator, as our own turn of the century approaches, it is the "irruption of history into the static time of the oasis"[60] that has brought corruption into the garden, and he can only dream vainly of recapturing an earthly paradise. As the novel ends, the graying magistrate is the last of the "civilized" left at the imperial outpost of a crumbling civilization, waiting for the barbarians. "They—the barbarians! They lured us on and on, we could never catch them!"[61]

Notes

1. Friedrich Nietzsche, "Aus dem Nachlass der Achtziger-jahre," in *Werke in drei Banden,* ed. K. Schlechta (Munich, 1966), III, 690.

2. *The Diary of Valery Bryusov (1893-1905),* ed. and trans. with an introductory essay by Joan Delaney Grossman (Berkeley, 1980), p. 108.

3. Nicolas Berdyaev, *The Russian Idea* (Boston, 1962), p. 204.

4. Bryusov, p. 109.

5. José Ortega y Gasset, *The Revolt of the Masses* (New York, 1960), p. 82.

6. The quotations from Sue and Saint-Marc Girardin are cited in Paul Lidsky, *Les écrivains contre la Commune* (Paris, 1982), p. 24.

7. *The Goncourt Journals,* 1851-1870, ed. and trans. Lewis Galantiere (Garden City, New York, 1958), p. 24.

8. The quotations from Morris and Flaubert are cited in Patrick Brautlinger, *Bread and Circuses: Theories of Mass Culture as Social Decay* (Ithaca, 1983), pp. 150, 116.

9. Emile Zola, *Germinal,* trans. Havelock Ellis (Garden City, New York, 1961), p. 478.

10. Lidsky, *Les écrivains contre la Commune,* p. 31.

11. Maurice Descotes, *Histoire de la critique dramatique en France* (Paris, 1980), pp. 315-22.

12. Renato Poggioli, *"Qualis Artifex Pereo!* or Barbarism and Decadence,"* Harvard Library Bulletin,* 13 (1959), 143-46. "The Coming Huns," with an epigraph from Vyacheslav Ivanov ("Trample their Eden, Attila"), appeared in 1905; the unpublished essay "The Triumph of Socialism" was written in 1903; and the story "The Last Martyrs" dates from 1906.

13. Cited by Alexander Bakshy in the introduction to *Seven Plays of Maxim Gorky,* trans. Alexander Bakshy in collaboration with Paul S. Nathan (New Haven, 1945), p. 6.

14. Ibid, pp. 116, 84, 138, 111-12.

15. Ibid, pp. 172-3, 124, 85, 117, 138, 111-12.

16. Aleksandr Blok, "On Drama," *Russian Dramatic Theory from Pushkin to the Symbolists,* ed. and trans. Laurence Senelick (Austin, Texas, 1981), p. 115.

17. Anatoly Lunacharsky, *O Gor'kom* (Moscow, 1975), pp. 57-60.

18. Bryusov, *Diary,* p. 144.

19. In "Pan-Mongolism," divine retribution for her sins will overtake Russia, the third Rome, and she will fall like Byzantium, the second Rome. See S.L. Frank, "Introduction," *A Solovyov Anthology* (New York, 1950), p. 26. "Russians are dying out; the Europeans are dying out too; only Mongols and Negroes are breeding. . . . Russia is a Mongol country," he said. "We all have Mongolian blood in us, and it will not resist the invasion." Andrey Bely, *The Silver Dove,* trans. George Reavey (New York, 1974), pp. 307-308.

20. C.P. Cavafy, *Collected Poems,* trans. Edmund Keeley and Philip Sherrard, ed. George Savidis (Princeton, New Jersey, 1975), pp. 31-33.

21. D.S. Mirsky, *Contemporary Russian Literature, 1881-1925* (New York, 1926), pp. 222, 228-29, 242.

22. Aleksandr Blok, cited in Avril Pyman, *The Life of Aleksandr Blok,* II, *The Release of Harmony, 1908-1921* (Oxford, 1980), p. 292.

23. Alexander Blok, *Selected Poems,* trans. Alex Miller (Moscow, 1981), pp. 321-22.

24. Leonard Woolf, *Barbarians Within and Without* (New York, 1939), p. 18.

25. Stanisław Ignacy Witkiewicz, *The Madman and the Nun and Other Plays,* trans. and ed. Daniel C. Gerould and Christopher Durer (Seattle, 1968), p. 77. These sentiments are similar to those in Briusov's 1905 poem "To the Contented": "Beautiful the ocean of a people's wrath/Beating to pieces a tottering throne."

26. *Twentieth-Century Polish Avant-Garde Drama,* ed. and trans. Daniel Gerould (Ithaca, 1977), p. 147.

27. Stanisław Ignacy Witkiewicz, *Dramaty* (Warsaw, 1972), II, 340.

28. Stanisław Ignacy Witkiewicz, *Insatiability,* trans. with an introduction and commentary by Louis Iribarne (Urbana, Illinois, 1977), p. 52.

29. Woolf, p. 65.

30. Catherine H. and Ronald M. Berndt, *The Barbarians* (Baltimore, 1973), pp. 20-24.

31. Friedrich Dürrenmatt, *An Angel Comes to Babylon* and *Romulus the Great* (New York, 1978), p. 114. Translation of *Romulus* by Gerhard Nellhaus.

32. Joseph A. Federico, "Time, Play, and the Terror of History in Dramatic Works by Dürrenmatt," *Play Dürrenmatt,* ed. Moshe Lazar, *Interplay 3* (Malibu, 1983), pp. 20-23.

33. Dürrenmatt, *Romulus,* pp. 154, 144.

34. Ibid, pp. 154-55.

35. Ibid, p. 167.

36. Ibid, pp. 161-62.

37. Ibid, p. 117.

38. Ibid, p. 154.

39. Kenneth S. Whitton, *The Theatre of Friedrich Dürrenmatt* (London, 1980), pp. 53-54, 65.

40. After the Thaw in 1956, Dürrenmatt became one of the most widely performed Western playwrights in Poland because of his treatment of history and power. See Urs Jenney, *Dürrenmatt: A Study of his Plays* (London, 1978), p. 92; and Marta Fik, *Trzydzieści Pięć Sezonów* (Warsaw, 1981), pp. 147-48. *Romulus the Great* had its Polish premiere at the Dramatic Theatre, Warsaw, in 1959, with settings by Andrzej Sadowski that suggested "the world after an atomic explosion," where "columns degenerated biologically and grew white roots." Zenobiusz Strzelecki, *Współczesna Scenografia Polska/Contemporary Polish Stage Design* (Warsaw, 1984), p. 98. Of *Romulus* in this production, Jan Kott wrote: "It concerns not past but future history, is a kind of history-fiction." *Theatre Notebook, 1947-1967,* trans. Bolesław Taborski (Garden City, New York, 1968), p. 97.

41. Thomas Carlyle, *Sartor Resartus* (New York, 1969), III, xi, p. 231. For a discussion of Carlyle, Gombrowicz and Mrożek, see Anna Sobolewska, "Pracownie krawieckie ludzkości," *Teksty* 5(41), 1978, 49-64.

42. Sławomir Mrożek, *Krawiec,* in *Amor* (Cracow, 1979), pp. 6-7.

43. Ibid, p. 29.

44. Ibid, p. 11.

45. Anne Hollander, *Seeing through Clothes* (New York, 1980), p. 447.

46. Mrożek, p. 54.

47. For these ideas I am indebted to David Brodsky's unpublished article, "Gombrowicz and Mrożek," which contains an

excellent study of *The Tailor* in relation to Gombrowicz's *Operetta* (1966), a quite different exploration of the clothes/ civilization metaphor. The myth of Marsyas, which appears in Book VI of Ovid's *Metamorphoses*, is treated by Frazer in *The Golden Bough* as an example of "dying and reviving gods." Zbigniew Herbert has a poem "Apollo and Marsyas" (1961), and Oscar Wilde wrote to Lord Alfred Douglas in 1897, "I hear in much modern Art the cry of Marsyas."

48. Gilbert Highet, *The Classical Tradition* (Oxford, 1949), pp. 27, 566.

49. Léopold Flam, "Les Vêtements de l'Homme," *L'Homme et la Conscience tragique* (Bruxelles, 1964), p. 140.

50. Carlyle, p. 30.

51. Sławomir Mrożek, *Tango,* trans. Ralph Manheim and Teresa Dzieduszycka (New York, 1968), p. 107. On the tango, see Lewis A. Erenberg, *Steppin' Out* (Chicago, 1984), pp. 79-85, 155, 165-66. Writing in Switzerland in 1916, Andrey Bely refers to the new species taking over the world as "civilized wildmen, white Negroes, tango-dancers." Cited in Konstantin Mochulsky, *Andrei Bely,* trans. Nora Szalavitz (Ann Arbor, 1977), pp. 183-84.

52. Sławomir Mrożek, *The Hunchback,* trans. Jacek Laskowski, unpublished, Act II.

53. Kazimierz Dejmek, *Tygodnik Solidarność,* No. 5, May 1, 1981, n.p.

54. To these works there could also be added Alan Sillitoe's poem "Barbarians" (1973), about Scythians camping in a destroyed city.

55. Howard Brenton, *The Romans in Britain* (London, 1982), pp. 43-44.

56. Ibid, p. 63.

57. Ibid, p. 97.

58. Barrie Keeffe, *Barbarians* (London, 1978), p. 103.

59. J.M. Coetzee, *Waiting for the Barbarians* (Harmondsworth, 1980), p. 133. I am grateful to Susan Brockman for calling my attention to this extraordinary novel.

60. Ibid, p. 143. Mark Horkheimer and Theodor Adorno find that "terror and civilization are inseparable," and that barbarism is "the other face of culture," in *The Dialectic of Enlightenment* (New York, 1972), pp. 111-12.

61. Ibid, p. 147.

THE MYTH OF RITUAL IN THE MARKETPLACE OF SIGNS

BY HERBERT BLAU

The place of ritual in the origin of the drama is shrouded in myth. But the myth I am referring to is not the myth from which it was once thought ritual derived. That myth was formulated by Sir James Frazer in *The Golden Bough,* surely one of the most seminal works in the history of modernism. As Lionel Trilling remarked in his essay "On the Modern Element in Modern Literature," just about the time that the story of Resurrection in its most institutional form was losing its hold on the world, the literary mind was captivated by Frazer's account of death and rebirth,[1] and those falling and rising gods who seemed to assure a cyclical continuity while the center was coming apart. The applications of this myth to drama were made by the Cambridge School of Criticism—Harrison, Murray, Cornford, Cook—also known as the Classical Anthropologists. In the writings of the Cambridge School, the ritual theory of myth coincided with the ritual

305

theory of drama. As Jane Ellen Harrison put it, and almost all theater histories preserve it, the drama had its roots in some aboriginal ritual, an originary rite, the *dromenon* or nuclear event ("the thing done") or the *legomenon* or primal Word ("the thing spoken").[2] What the thing was or the Word that was in the beginning remains a mystery.

There were variations on the nature of the initiating rite—tomb or funerary ceremonies, vegetation cycles, the year-god or sacrificial king and, in recent years, shamanism—but the theory was that the shaping principle of a ritual source eventuated in the classical form of drama and the civic institution of theater. That was pretty much how things looked when I started working in that dubious civic institution, my view of the origins of the drama conditioned soon after by Francis Fergusson's *The Idea of a Theater* which accepted, through the fractures of modernity, the established ritual theory. It was not so much a theory, however, as an allegory constructed by Frazer from diverse ritual manifestations which subsequent anthropologists looked upon as conflicting evidence of a dismembered whole. As James Boon observes in *Other Tribes, Other Scribes,* "the only thing that is whole in *The Golden Bough,* eventually thirteen volumes long, is the allegory itself."[3]

Things have changed considerably since Fergusson's book appeared, with its assumption of a ritual source for the tragic rhythm of action. Even before we began to suspect, with Artaud and Derrida, "that there has never been an origin,"[4] it became apparent that few classical scholars or anthropologists really believe that all myth—including Homeric Epic and the sacred literature of the Near East—has its beginnings in ritual. Classical scholars are skeptical now, too, about the common view that ritual illuminates our conceptions of Greek culture. They are even more skeptical about the ritual origins of drama, whether out of the goat song or tauriform rites or the cult of Dionysus, whose forms we can approach at best as the remembered shards of broken signs. Still, even those alert to the inadequacy of received opinion, like Roland Barthes, can be misleading for a moment, from some old reflex of conditioned history which offers no more verifiable alternative.

In an essay on the Greek theater, written in 1965, Barthes starts with the customary review of the evolution of the theater from the dithyrambic choruses and dances produced in the Dorian region by the Dionysian cult. These were presumably developed by Thespis and Phrynichus into something like tragic drama consecrated by the state and, in 538 B.C., festivalized by Pisastratus to adorn his tyranny. "The sequel is well known," says Barthes: "the theater was established on ground sacred to Dionysus, who remained the genre's patron," though he couldn't or wouldn't impede its rapid decline and the abandonment of its choral structure. The opening paragraphs of the essay are not the disorienting breach of a subject one expects from Barthes. They are, rather, just about what one can still find in most of the histories of the drama. But after repeating the conventional narrative, he adds what we might have guessed: "As 'history,' such an account remains somewhat mythic."[5]

There are still powerfully regressive theories, like that of René Girard, with a strong desire—the more the world reveals itself as a marketplace of signs—to ascribe redemptive value to the illusions and mystifications of ritual.[6] As he goes about reappraising the mythic element in the history, there is a kind of evangelical desperation in the enterprise of Girard. It has the fervor of Artaud's victim signalling through the flames. At that "fragile, fluctuating center where forms never reach,"[7] it's hardly a question of theater being *derived from* ritual, theater *is* ritual—and a far vertiginous cry from the Cambridge theory of the drama's origins. First doubted by Sir Arthur Pickard-Cambridge, that theory was then devastated by Gerald F. Else in the *Origins and Early Form of Greek Tragedy* (1967). According to Else, the ritual theory of tragedy "is not now held, at least in its strictest form, by any leading scholar"[8]—which is why Else was so upset with Fergusson's *The Idea of a Theater* which proceeds from that theory as a kind of gospel, as did Northrop Frye when he displaced the New Criticism with Myth Criticism. A year before Else's book appeared, Richard Schechner—in one of his earliest excursions between theater and anthropology— was also disturbed by Fergusson's insistence on a ritual underpinning to the action of tragedy as a pattern indelible through the history of drama. Despite all the archaeological research in Greece since the turn of the century, the assumptions of the Cambridge group, as Schechner remarks, have never been proved and "no single ritual has been uncovered which contains all the elements of either drama or the Primal Ritual."[9]

As for Frye, he does say in *Spiritus Mundi*—hedging his conviction about myth—that while Frazer gave abundant evidence of the symbolism of a divine-human victim as a latency in the unconscious, it perhaps never emerged in a complete form.[10] Frye never quite yielded up, however, what he said in the earlier *Anatomy of Criticism,* that *The Golden Bough* does provide a key to the origins of drama by reconstructing "an archetypal ritual from which the structural and generic principles of drama may be logically, not chronologically, derived." Keyed in to the archetype, he adds: "It does not matter two pins to the literary critic whether such a ritual had any historical existence or not."[11]

Nor does it matter to this day to certain artists and theater practitioners, who at some rudimentary, nostalgic, or visionary level were confirmed in ritual desire by the alchemical theater of Artaud. Or even before that (if they were sufficiently literary or had read Eric Bentley on the neglected plays[12]) by the occultism of William Butler Yeats. It was he who said, when told that the sun *doesn't* rise, that it should. It would have been hard for Yeats—who could imagine the discursiveness of Greek drama refined exquisitely to its ritual core—to accept the demythicizing view of Else, who speaks of the "quasi-vacuum or low density of mythological tradition in Attica" which permitted its dramatists to subvert the body of myth from within (38). Else refuses to accept the unsubstantiated notion that "Sophocles' audience approached his tragedies in a spirit of 'ritual expectancy' . . . "(4). There is a reality principle in his view that it was not ritual forms but Thespis (separating from the chorus) and Aeschylus (introducing the second actor) who were responsible for the nature and structure of Greek tragedy. For Yeats, however, the ritual expectancy was essential to his idea of theater, even if it had to be imported, as in his own plays, from another culture. Like García Lorca, Cocteau, and T.S. Eliot, Yeats was one of the poetic dramatists of the century who sought in ritual forms an alternative to the domination of theater by realism and naturalism, the materialistic jaundice of the modern, which denies the affirmation of a transcendent principle—a denial of the divine in the name of Man.

For Artaud, as Derrida points out, the Theater of Cruelty is born not only to separate birth from death but to erase that defiled and usurping name. "The theater was never made," said Artaud (quoted by Derrida 233), "to describe man and what he does. . . . " Nevertheless, the history of realism has its own mysteries and occult tendencies or, in the masking of ideology, processes of *occultation*. From Ibsen and Strindberg through O'Neill the skepticism of the modern preserved the residues and shadow-structures of ritual forms, even as the corrosion and distrust of a historicist sensibility eroded their powers. Despite the erosions, and the jaundiced view of ritual origins among classical scholars, the interest in ritual persists from the legacy of early modernism into the postmodern: Brecht and Barthes, Artaud and Derrida pay attention to ritual, however, for quite different reasons, as vision, critique, structures of irony, or instrumentality. Or they see in the idea of the *festival* not only an image of cultural memory but—as Derrida sees it in Artaud—a virtual alternative to the Western metaphysical tradition with its "phallogocentric" structure of domination and power and its vitiating principle of *mimesis*. It is that principle which Girard, aware of the critique of representation, tries to defend for salvational purposes, along with the ineliminable but generative violence of ritual desire.

But let us back up for an older view of salvation to Eliot and Yeats, both of whom valorized the Word and posited—with more or less apocalyptic violence in the vision—a recovery of cultural unity, as classical modernism did. The recovery was not to occur, however, as in the annals of the postmodern or the metaphysics of Artaud, in the perpetual present moment of an infinitely deferred future, *resisting repetition,* but in the epiphanic moment of a rematerializing past. In rethinking the ritual concerns of Eliot and Yeats, we'll be turning up issues which were not at all exhausted by their experiments in the theater. Dormant for some years, those issues were reactivated over the last generation in the revival of Artaud, who has become a talismanic figure in the newer critical theory, which in turn—obsessed with the thought of performance—is beginning to reshape our thinking about the theater.

Eliot's early "Dialogue on Dramatic Poetry" was written in the same year (1928) he announced himself an Anglican in religion, a Royalist in politics, and a Classicist in literature. His interest in ritual had to do not only with an aversion to realism and its falsifying psychology, the vice of humanism, but an appreciation of artifice, the post-Symbolist desire for a pure aesthetic. There was also the desire to ground the drama in its proper speech, not prose—the language of devaluation—but verse, which Ibsen, master of prose drama, felt compelled to abandon as the spirit-world receded into bourgeois appearances. (In the age of Deconstruction, those appearances became the subject of a logorrheic critique which reversed the priority of speech and *writing*. In this reversal, speech is exposed as a ventriloquism of the Logos, while writing is seen as unceasing difference in the play of appearances, refusing the closure of the authoritarian Word. It was a high theoretical conversion of the performative mode of the sixties, with its antiverbal appearances, into a self-reflexive discourse on legitimacy and power.) But as Eliot searched for the grounds of authority in his experiments with the drama, he eventually took his cue from Ibsen and realism, returned to prose, and tried to suggest in surreptitious rhythms the older mythic and ritual forms behind the bourgeois appearances, to reveal the Word within a word unable to speak a word, swaddled in darkness, a sort of tongue-tied pantomime of the play within the play.

In the Dialogue, however, it was ritualized appearance which attracted him. What he valued, for instance, in the artifice of ballet (its amazing popularity now may strike us as a new bourgeois appearance) was precisely *closure*, "permanent form," whose strength "is in a tradition, a training, an askesis. . . . ''[13] Which is to say, as Grotowski later did for the theater, a spiritual discipline, ''a training which is like a moral training'' (Eliot 47). The other participants in the Dialogue having approved of ballet because ''it is a liturgy of very wide adaptability,'' one of Eliot's voices, E, takes the opening for which he has been waiting: ''I say that the consummation of the drama, the perfect and ideal drama, is to be found in the ceremony of the Mass. I say . . . that the drama springs from religious liturgy. . . . And the only dramatic satisfaction that I find now is in a High Mass well performed'' (47). When E adds that the Church ritual through the year affords a complete drama of creation, B takes issue: ''the question is not, whether the Mass is dramatic, but what is the relation of the drama to the Mass?. . . Are we to say that our cravings for drama are fulfilled by the Mass?'' (48).

We are more likely to say today, as Raymond Williams does, that our cravings for drama are being fulfilled by the mass media, so that what we now have, in an overdose of theatricality and supersaturation of image, ''is drama as habitual experience: more in a week, in many cases, than most human beings would previously have seen in a lifetime.''[14] Or, as Jean Baudrillard would put it, so much more that it becomes an obscenity, a religion of appearance, with the simulacra as sacred, the cybernetic inertia of hyperrealism.[15] This impasse of mass culture may seem as distant from the genteel debate over the dramatic properties of the Mass as the Pope himself was when he celebrated the Mass in Papua and used pidgin English while the tribesmen, throwing up clouds of yellow and orange smoke to ward off evil spirits in the offertory process, shouted, ''Mi laikum you Pop!'' We may also remember, however, that as far back as the banyan trees on the cannibal isle in *Sweeney Agonistes,*

312

there was always in Eliot—not only in the irony but in the most civil inflection—an early warning signal. He knew long in advance that in the aesthetic of fascination which now takes us everywhere, with a baggage-load of signs, Walkmen glued to our ears, that "a kind of non-intentional parody hovers over everything" (Baudrillard 150).

There is something queer in the modern sign which, reaching everywhere through the media into everything once sacred, exposing it to derisive eyes, still "dreams of the signs of the past and would well appreciate finding again, in its reference to the real, an *obligation*. . . " (85-86). Well, maybe not too much of an obligation, a reasonable facsimile, perhaps, or simulation of necessity, so long as it feels like a new *experience*. That's what B distrusts in E. He feels that there is something obscene and excessive about this fascination with the Mass. He speaks of it as an orgiastic self-indulgence, an illicit affectivity, and—what looks like second nature in a world of simulacra—a confusion of genres as well, based on unbelief. He says of E what Eliot suspected of himself, that his "dramatic desires were satisfied by the Mass, precisely because he was not interested in the Mass, but in the drama of it. Now what I maintain is, that you have no business to care about the Mass unless you are a believer" (48).

Now what I maintain is what I've already implied, that while ritual interest has shifted from the Christian Mass to the sacred forms of other cultures, the issues of the Dialogue still remain suspended in an age of disbelief. What we are dealing with inevitably is the substance of ritual desire in an era of suspicion whose secularity seems to blush and increase exponentially with every born-again religious impulse. At the same time, our cravings for the drama seem to have weakened in proportion to its mass-mediated availability. It is certainly true that the drama as it comes out of the canonical texts has had a bad press in the last generation of experimental theater. And a case can still be made that the most interesting performance today, to some extent in the theater but mostly elsewhere in the other arts, is still doing without it. Thus, we look to ritual again not only for ideas of community, but for missing energies, psychic liberation, desublimated sexuality, carnival spirits, structures of participation, the redemptive side of repetition, or an awakening festival that relieves us of it, and—so far as there is still an aesthetic in all this—an alternative theatricality. All of it is a legacy of the sixties and its unfulfilled desires, but either more sophisticated, theorized, or ironically mediated, as it is in the quoted figurations of the new Expressionist painting, or, ripping off high and low culture alike, the most cunningly referential of the MTVs.

But one still wonders, with more or less classical rigor, whether one has any business with ritual unless one *is* a believer and not merely a connoisseur of permanent or exotic forms which—almost in proportion to our new ethnological curiosity—are losing their sacred character. As for the ritual performers coming out of the rain forests, ramadas, and precincts of the sacred, manifesting themselves to adoring and despoiling eyes, are they not losing something of their alluring theatricality as well? How do we keep the ritual appearances from becoming only too familiar as they are appropriated, infallibly, into the system of representation which sustains its power by doubling over and representing itself?

There is an understandable interest in borrowing from the theatrical forms of other cultures. But there is always the chastening moment when we realize that whatever it may have been for those others it is inevitably only appearance to us. As we pick up ritual gestures and techniques from Java, Bali, and India, we enter another order of illusion in which it's hard to determine what it is that we have acquired. For what is transferable in performance across cultures has to be able to survive the breakdown of cultural autonomy. Here there is a political issue which we are sometimes only too ready to forget in the ardency of ritual desire. If the transfer is possible at all, it occurs over the ruins of the territorial and despotic, and that applies to both ends of the exchange. If the borrowing doesn't screen out, say, the human cost of the hieratic gesture preserved in that other world, it forgets the taboo or interdiction on which the gesture is based. The remembrance of that content may itself be repressed. The ways of symbolic exchange are such that, in the assumption of an external form, not only false reverence or deceived emulation, but the most sophisticated irony may be the means of repression. What has been forgotten in the gesture has entered a system of denial in the same old economy of desire. It permits us to go on believing as we did through a changing appearance which is nothing more than the appearance of exchange.

In any case, what is being transferred is never what we believe is being transferred. The performative gesture derived from another culture remains in the world of representation from which no culture appears to be exempt, although other cultures appear to have made other adjustments to appearances. These may appear more or less enviable until, indeed, we look into the human cost. What may change, as in the movement of "objective" myth into the contents of the unconscious, is the degree of *subjectivity* in the representation which, once it enters the unconscious, like Oedipus, may be infinitely ramified and extended, but never lost. In this way, ritual borrowings may be metabolized into the secular, which may not be entirely gratifying to ritual desire, attached as it is to longings for absent communication or an irradiated reality touched again by the sacred. Whatever happens to Oedipus in the unconscious, Oedipus himself has no complex. Nor is there any guarantee that the ruptures we live out in the history that he has come to represent will be, as at Colonus, reassumed at last in the eternity of myth. If Freud is attentive to ritual and invokes myth, thereby perpetuating it, he grants it no specificity. There is no Narcissus in the pool of Freud's essay on narcissism.

Performance, however, is specific. That is universal. It is also very local. And it occurs everywhere in the world now, so far as we can see—and all the more *because we're looking*—without miracles. We know we can construct through structures of repetition forms with the apparent resonance of ritual. But that, too, is mere appearance. Ritual structures in our time leak through the activity of perception. If that's true in the Church, it's doubly so in the theater. If the eye altering alters all, it particularly alters those things which appear to cycle through the sacred, from which we're twice removed in the age of modernism by its critical vigilance and suspicion. If desire could restore ritual, it would be subverted by desire, which arouses specular consciousness with—as we see in the plays of Genet—its repetitive fantasies of desire.

As for the repetition which is central to ritual, all those reflexive variations of the Eternal Return, what we have to do is distinguish—and it can at best be a temporal distinction—between ritual and habit. There is the repetition which repeats itself insensibly, the form perhaps of realism's revenge. "Habit is a great deadener," says the tramp in *Waiting for Godot*,[16] that plaintive play of repetitions in which nothing is repeated or nothing *happens,* twice. On no religious grounds whatever, it seems to recuperate a ceremoniousness which merely recurs. Of course, what merely recurs may never have been ceremonious. I was going to say like taking out the garbage. But if we really think of it, nothing, however banal or inconsequential it seems, recurs with any consciousness of its recurrence that is without a ritual element. Habit is after all not merely divided from the living processes of the world. Often it appears, like ritual, to be their mirror image, inverted and unreflecting in the sense of thoughtless. That is, for all the ceremony, what ritual must also be, even if it moves through consciously reiterated phases. Habit, like ritual, also mediates between mind and nature. In the self-reflexiveness of its repetitions, it seems like a projection of the natural within ourselves. Looked at one way, it seems perfectly natural. What we repeat is, however, not at all involuntary but partakes as well of an accretion of choices. Or it reflects those choices—in that resembling the mind's inclination to a settling distinction, through all its restless desire. Language itself is habitual, as is the tendency to dramatize, which is what Aristotle suggested in speaking of imitation as being as natural as rhythm.

What is disturbing about mimesis in our drama is that it has always been insufficient to itself. Through the long oedipal history of the form, it has always been troubled with going through the same old motions of desire, with something desired always missing in the recurrency of desire, which took its habitual toll. This is the recurring subject of our drama, which Beckett perceived as it seemed to be coming to an end. For all its bourgeois values and sedentary theater, the West remains restive with habit. That restiveness has been responsible in our culture, sometimes at terrible and self-destroying risk, for whatever is most volatile and alive. Now that the risks, in a nuclear age, are more alarming, there is still a fine ontological line between ritual repetition and deadening habit. The theater renews itself there, on the threshold of transgression. But as we try to negotiate *that* line, as in a rehearsal (Fr.: *répétition*), thinking of repetition as generative, reawakening desire, the question remains in the ruptured sensibility of a secular age: *What is it that we want to repeat?* We'll return to that question in Artaud, for whom repetition was unforgivable sin.

It is a question that used to be approached through the relationship of poetry and *belief,* which receded in theater and critical discourse with the rising affirmation of *play.* During the period of games and improvisation, when the pleasures of repetitive activity seemed undeniable—to the point of boredom or *jouissance*—we were also taking seriously the possibility of doing without the drama. The return to ritual came with the communitarian dream of the sixties. In the participatory ethos, nobody worried much about the complicated question of credibility of belief nor, like B in Eliot's Dialogue, the ultimate matter of ritual ends. B says in the argument with E that "if we can do without the drama, then let us not pretend that religion is drama"—or, to transpose his argument, that ritual is theater except in a very weakened form. "If we are religious," he says, "then we shall only be aware of the Mass as art, in so far as it is badly done. . . "(48). There may be an aesthetic priggishness in the critical rigor, but not too far afield from certain anomalies of our more godless thought with its rather ungrounded affinity to ritual.

Yeats's affinity was hardly that by the end of his career, when against all the realistic evidence he was holding on to the ritual idea with the rather astonishing ferocity that characterized his old age. Not at all a Christian, he had other ritual ends. He might have appreciated the Mass for unabashedly aesthetic reasons, since he never wavered in his desire, through the weakening of religion, to sanctify art instead. What he admired in ritual was the hieratic forms, and their affinity with dreams and trance. He agitated for a national theater and longed for "the emotion of multitude,"[17] but what seduced him was essentially solitary. What he describes in ritual is an evocative hauntedness, like incense around a High Altar, but no less precise for that, running through the nerves like fire. As for those forms drawing on ritual, he observes how the dancer in the drawing room achieves, with no studied lighting and human means alone, an imaginative intricacy, introversion as distance, the recession of mind into a more powerful and subtle life, the intimacy of a "separating strangeness" (224). What attracted him to the noble plays of Japan that Mrs. Fenollosa entrusted to the translation of Ezra Pound (at the time Yeats's secretary) was their decorous ritual character: verse, music, incantation, "figures, images, symbols . . . too subtle for habitation"—a rich languor of association where the interest is, if achieved by human means, "not in the human form but in the rhythm to which it moves . . ." (231), as in the Sufi whirling and petrified motion of the grand operas of Robert Wilson.

There is in Yeats an early modernist aversion to the tacky worldliness of realistic character, with its tepid humanism and psychological disguise. There is also an impatience with the objective metabolism of the world as we commonly know it, its material gravity, weighed down by history. And there is in the passage that follows a theoretical anticipation of the long-drawn static abeyances and the soporific suggestiveness in the imagery of Wilson's theater: "If the real world is not altogether rejected, it is but touched here and there, and into the places we have left empty we summon rhythm, balance, pattern, images that remind us of vast passions, the vagueness of past times, all the chimeras that haunt the edge of trance; and if we are painters, we shall express personal emotion through ideal form, symbolism handled by the generations, a mask from whose eyes the disembodied looks, a style that remembers many masters that it may escape contemporary suggestion. . . '' (243). With his titles invoking Einstein, Freud, and Stalin, Wilson makes the contemporary suggestion even as he escapes history, evoking but a totem or token. And one may wonder in due historical time whether the real world has in these orchestrations of rhythm, pattern, and chimera been touched sufficiently here and there or, like Yeats in some of his earlier plays, too vaguely.

While Yeats persisted through a long career sustaining ritual desire, he had to abandon the illusion of what, from his reverence of myth and ritual, he had called the emotion of multitude. The truth is that the multitude had abandoned him. While still persuaded at the end of his life that a ritual theater was possible, he couldn't escape contemporary suggestion in the close quarters of Ireland. Nor the material grasp of history. Nor the enraging reality principle of an unheroic old age where the desublimated sexuality was, for all its poetic fervor, physically running down. "I am old, I belong to mythology," says the angry figure of Yeats in *The Death of Cuchulain*, his last play, who feels he's out of fashion but insists now that he wants only "an audience of fifty or a hundred, and if there are more, I beg them not to shuffle their feet or talk when the actors are speaking. I am sure," he adds mordantly, "that as I am producing a play for people I like, it is not probable, in this vile age, that they will be more in number than those who listened to the first performance of

Milton's *Comus*. On the present occasion they must know the old epics and Mr. Yeats's plays about them. . . . "

There's a funny anomalous moment in Sean O'Casey's diaries when the carpenter Fluther Good—who, with the multitude, looted the shops in *The Plough and the Stars*—shows up at one of these performances and reads a newspaper. Fluther is indifferent to the terrible beauty being born, whether at the Post Office in the Easter Rebellion or in Lady Gregory's drawing room. Meanwhile, the Old Man rages: "Emer must dance, there must be severed heads"—and these heads must be iconic, made of painted wood, impassioned by the dancer herself. But where to find now—"upon the same neck love and loathing, life and death"—a dancer of appropriate power? "I spit three times," he says, focusing all his scorn for this vile age and the sweaty historicism of its theater on the painted dancers of Degas. "I spit upon their short bodices, their stiff stays, their toes whereon they spin like peg-tops, above all upon that chambermaid face. They might have looked timeless, Rameses the Great, but not the chambermaid, that old maid history. I spit! I spit! I spit!"[18] Whereupon the stage is darkened and the curtain falls, and the play begins in myth to end in history where—though he also ritualized the theater and probably didn't much like Degas's dancers either— Brecht thought it always belonged.

In his conception of the A-effect, Brecht drew upon ritual forms, but his "separating strangeness" was of another estranging kind. It was not trance or dream that he was after, and if there were ritual incantations, they were likely to be ironic, subject to ideological control. The equivocal attitude conveyed in Brecht's essay on Chinese acting is that while the actor prepares a performance *like* ritual, he makes no ritual claims and, by various technical means, voids the symptoms of regressive, ergotropic behavior that we associate with the more trancelike, shamanistic, or ecstatic aspects of ritual performance. Such behavior is in fact associated by Brecht with our realistic and naturalistic traditions and their ideal of a thoroughly subjective acting out of the Stanislavski Method, with its mystical moments of psychological truth, in which the actor presumably forgets himself in the emotion that carries him away. By contrast, Mei Lan-fang is making *comparisons* and *distinctions,* symbolically shaping reality by a kind of *analytic* in his ideographic technique.

It is a similar analytic that Derrida quite rightly perceives in the theater conceived by Artaud. Far from the "family shamanism" (Eliade's term) which characterized most ritual theater experiments in the sixties, Artaud calls for a rigorous intellectuality and "mathematical meticulousness" in the midst of trance. It is an occult "theater of dreams, but of *cruel* dreams, that is to say, absolutely necessary and determined dreams, dreams calculated and given direction, as opposed to what Artaud believed to be the empirical disorder of spontaneous dreams." Out of the experimental empiricism of the Surrealists, Artaud came to believe that "The ways and figures of dreams can be mastered." It is not the randomness of the unconscious that he favors, but its articulating and linguistic processes, as in recent psychoanalytical theory—though he would have rejected a psychoanalytical theater in the ordinary sense, as he had rejected the psychological theater. "It is the *law* of dreams that must be produced or reproduced," observes Derrida. Despite the lure of the originary Mystery, Artaud refused either a secret interiority or a secret commentary. As he remarks in a passage quoted by Derrida, "The *subconscious* will not play any true role on stage." It is possible to conclude, then, that the Theater of Cruelty is not intended as a theater of the unconscious. What Artaud imagines in the notion of cruelty is an intensification of *consciousness* and, in all its naked and emblooded realization, an "exposed lucidity" (Derrida 242).

Brecht, too, believes that the subconscious will not play any true role on stage. And in a remarkably perceptive passage of the essay on Chinese acting he points out—as Artaud does in the cultural analysis of *The Theater and Its Double*—that "it is becoming increasingly difficult for our actors to bring off the mystery of complete conversion," the sort of conversion we associate with ritual, because the unconscious of our theater has become so unsuspectingly occupied, colonized, politicized, that "their subconscious's memory is getting weaker and weaker, and it is almost impossible to extract the truth from the uncensored intuitions of any member of our class society even when [as in the case of Marlon Brando] the man is a genius."[19]

So far as there is something ritualized in the theatrical strategies of Brecht and Artaud, their stress on consciousness and an exposed lucidity corresponds to the cognitive view of ritual advanced by d'Acquili and Laughlin in *The Spectrum of Ritual,* though the difference between theater and ritual pivots on what they call the "matter of choice":

> . . . given an organism in which the neural mechanisms for abstract thought have evolved, which require causal and antinomous thinking as a highly adaptive trait, that organism must necessarily use these mechanisms in an attempt to explain his existential situation. Such explanation involves the obligatory structuring of myths, complete with the organization of the world into antinomies and with the positing of initial causal termini of strips of observed reality that man calls gods, spirits, demons, and the like. These mechanisms are not a matter of choice but are

necessarily generated by the structure of the brain in response to the cognitive imperative. Once the problem is presented in myth form, man, in common with all animals, attempts to solve it (i.e., to master the environment) in a motor action. In the presence of a problem presented in myth, and with the inherited ritual mechanisms still intact, ritual becomes the motor vehicle by which the problem is solved.

D'Acquili and Laughlin observe that this process doesn't always work, but the ritual remains and is likely to remain "one of the few mechanisms at man's disposal that can possibly solve the ultimate problems and paradoxes of human existence."[20] It's not entirely clear what the word *solve* really means, though when we look further into Artaud we may see that what they say of ritual may be said equally of theater. Which raises another question, about priority and origins. Or gives us another view.

Whatever there was in the beginning, it sometimes appears in Artaud as if the priorities are reversed and that, if anything, *ritual was born of theater.* As for Brecht, he observes in the "Short Organum" that while theater may be said to have been derived from ritual, "that is only to say that it becomes theater once the two have separated; what it brought over from the mysteries was not its former ritual function, but purely and simply the pleasure which accompanied this." That pleasure is not, however, simple, so that we can retrace through it the ritual from which it derived. It is rather a pleasure which attains its climaxes "as cohabitation does through love. . . . " If what we have in ritual is a fixity of signs that can be duplicated and repeated, what we have in theater is an open scrutiny of signs keeping its distance from ritual in the irreversible rupture of history. For Brecht, the pleasures of theater are laminated by history, "more intricate" than ritual, "richer in communication, more contradictory and more productive of results" (181).

The break with myth and ritual occurred (however it occurred) for precise cultural reasons, but it is not a break that occurs only once. The history of the drama—that actively skeptical and interrogative form—is the figurative record of a renewable struggle against the sclerosis of signs in a system which, as obdurately as ritual, insists on repeating itself. Whatever else the drama is, it is for Brecht a struggle for control of signifying practice and, through every image of repression, the power of representation. That includes the right of the excluded (a premise of ritual being exclusion), the unrepresented, to be represented. It is a useless right, however, without the enabling power of activated reason which, instead of abandoning representation to the anti-mimetic delusion, directs it critically to other ends. Brecht refuses, as we see in his critique of tragic drama, to surrender *choice*—including the choice of representations, the construction of the *gestus*—to any sort of arcane necessity, particularly the arcane necessities of class structure. Or to any social determinations that seem god-given or natural, in terms of which we reproduce, as regularly as ritual, the conditions which keep those socially determined illusions alive.

In the essay on Chinese acting, Brecht addresses the issue central to the ritual concerns of contemporary performance: the transferability of ritual techniques. What is often overlooked in that essay is the distinction he makes between the rational appropriation of a technique and the uncritical acceptance of what often goes along with it by way of cultural oppression. "Among all the possible signs," he writes, "certain particular ones are picked out, with careful and visible consideration" (93). Among the signs he doesn't like in the signifying detachment of the Chinese actor is that the A-effect in his performance is achieved "by association with magic" (96). While he could admire the singular performance of Mei Lan-fang, he was put off by the hierarchical structure which preserved, in secrecy for the privileged, the "primitive technology" or "rudimentary science" out of which the performance was made. Brecht had a quick appropriative instinct for "a transportable piece of technique" (95-96) but an equally quick aversion to what it might represent. He knew with his friend Walter Benjamin that behind any cultural treasure there is inevitable human cost, which is the best-kept secret in art, the anonymity of the labor behind the admired object which does not disclose its barbarous truth. Techniques are also cultural productions. They may require in their historical emergence, as in the case of Chinese acting, a repressive social system for the aesthetic pleasure they give. Carried over through the exchange mechanisms of bourgeois culture, the use value of such techniques is in some measure always already soiled, and one would expect that perception to manifest itself in performance, to avoid an obtuse nostalgia, with more or less irony.

When he wrote dramatic criticism, Roland Barthes was alert to such irony. He was also aware of the structural impediments of achieving in our culture—through the manifest "density of our narcissism"—what he perceived, say, in his conception of the system named Japan in his *Empire of Signs,* "one altogether detached from our own." He is not, he says, gazing lovingly at an Oriental essence, the Orient being for him a matter of indifference, but rather suggesting through the practice of an unheard-of system, after a trip to the "real" Japan, "the possibility of a difference, of a mutation, of a revolution in the propriety of symbolic systems.''[21] What Barthes admired in the Bunraku is the unsoiled appearance of its signifying detachment, ''cold like 'a white onion freshly washed.' ''[22] He sees in the Bunraku performance a lesson in writing (the play of signs in the construction of meaning), but an earlier lesson came, actually, from Brecht, on whom he wrote three essays in the fifties—after the Berliner Ensemble came to Paris—defining a Brechtian criticism. His early book on *Mythologies* is a demonstration of this criticism, but mostly not on the theater. It is a remarkable exercise on all kinds of popular forms and commodities—from wrestling through detergents to striptease—of a critical activity directed to the deritualization of thought.

What Barthes means by myth in that book is what we would otherwise call *ideology,* which Marx describes as ''phantoms of the brain.'' What he is interested in exposing is the lexicon of accepted ideas in which ''ideological abuse'' is hidden.[23] He looks askance at what goes without saying, those ideas which are so self-evident they resemble facts of nature, confusing history and nature. Having the force of necessity in human affairs, they are attested to in the rituals of everyday life. One of those accepted ideas in Western theater is what he thinks of as specifically bourgeois, the way in which the actor's body is made into its own lie by the system of representation in which it performs, claiming for itself a visceral truth which only ''borrows from physiology the alibi of an organic unity, the unity of 'life,' '' when its behavior is little more than the behavior of a marionette (*Image-Music-Text* 171). What he sees in Western acting of the non-Brechtian kind is a perversion of use value in a ritual of self-deceit. Beneath an appearance which seems living and natural, the actor serves his body up, divided, as the food of the spectator's fantasy. In this culinary theater, ''Voice, look, figure are in turn eroticized, like so many pieces of the body, like so many fetishes" (171-72).

As with the myths he exposed in his earlier book, the essay on the Bunraku follows Brecht in exposing the mechanisms of concealment in our theater, "the very artifice of the process of revelation (machinery, painting, makeup, sources of light)" (173). This surreptitious ensemble of appearances constitutes a space of deceit, "spied on and relished by a hidden spectator; a theological space, that of moral failing: on the one side, under a light of which he pretends to be unaware, the actor, that is to say, gesture and speech; on the other, in the darkness, the public, that is to say, consciousness and conscience." (Had he pursued the issue further, Barthes might have gone on to say that even with lights up, thrust stages, and the illusion of participation, the fetishism and moral division persist.) By contrast, in the Bunraku "the sources of the theater are exposed in their void. What is expelled from the stage is hysteria, that is theater itself, and what is put in its place is the action necessary for the production of the spectacle—work is substituted for interiority" (173-74). And use value is restored.

There is nothing particularly ritualistic in what he admires in the Bunraku performance which, as he sees it, also eliminates for the actor the alibi of the sacred. Do we forget as we watch the performance the presence of the manipulators? Barthes considers that a vain question. By neither dissimulating nor emphatically disclosing how it does what it does, the Bunraku abolishes "the metaphysical bond that the West cannot stop itself from setting up between soul and body, cause and effect, motor and machine, agent and actor." Nor is there any pretense of spirituality in all this. If the manipulator is not hidden, he can't be turned into a God.

Furthermore, no strings attached. Without an originary thread to an invisible source, there is no metaphor, and thus no spurious linkage to an absent Fate. Having broken the circuit of puppet aping creature aping God, the Bunraku also undoes the major pretense of our psychological theater, behind the rituals of the Private Moment, that the *inner* controls the *outer* (174). If Barthes shares with Brecht an aversion to hysteria, he shares with Artaud—with whom we associate hysteria, whom we think of perhaps as the supreme hysteric of the modern era, its exemplar—a distrust of theater itself.

I'd like to look at that distrust now in Artaud, in connection with the problem of origins and ritual repetition. Unlike Barthes, Artaud has no aversion to the sacred. It is precisely the sacred whose primal energy he wants to restore. But it appears that, in doing so, he would abolish in the interests of the sacred the very basis of ritual, the principle of *repetition,* which is governed "by everything that Artaud wished to destroy, and it has several names: God, Being, Dialectics" (Derrida 245). For Artaud, the rising and falling gods of Frazer are signs of an infinitely repeating death which is thought as eternity and eternally thought, an "eternity whose death," as Derrida states it, "goes on indefinitely, whose death, as difference and repetition, within life, has never ceased to menace life" (245-46). It is the power and scandal of theater that nowhere else is this menace of repetition so orchestrated and well organized. "Nowhere else is one so close to the stage as the origin of repetition, so close to the primitive repetition which would have to be erased, and only by detaching itself from itself as if from its double" (247). What Artaud treasures in theater is precisely its *disappearance,* the resistance in its true nature to the pressure of the very repetition through which it appears. It would thus be, in Derridean terms, "the art of difference and expenditure without economy, without reserve, without return, without history. Pure presence as pure difference. Its act must be forgotten, actively forgotten" (247).

There is a remarkable passage in "No More Masterpieces" where the complexity of Artaud's tutelary image of theater merges with his attitude toward ritual repetition in a cathartic function at the virtual limit of thought: "The theater teaches precisely the uselessness of the action which, once done, is not to be done, and the superior use of the state unused by the action and which, *restored,* produces a purification" (Artaud 82). The word *restored* is of course peculiar to an idea of theater which wants to abolish repetition. And Derrida tries to deal with it at the end of his essay by pointing out that Artaud, whose theater was never achieved, set himself the task of the unachievable, resigning himself "to theater as repetition" but unable to "renounce theater as nonrepetition"—thus, a theater of repetition which, at some unimaginable boundary of its tautological form, does *not* repeat itself (249-50).

As for the act to be forgotten so that the unused state may be restored, that is also implicit in the Brechtian *gestus* where we are meant to see not only the uselessness of the action which, once done, is not to be done, but also the action *not* done which should be. Once again, in Brecht, there is nothing sacred about it. The sign includes an absence which, so long as it continues, marks the victim in history.

The mark of history for René Girard is the inevitability of the victim. The forgotten act which triggers his *Violence and the Sacred* is misleadingly revealed in myth by symbolic substitution, as it is preserved in ritual to the extent that a society lacks a firm judicial system. Even that system, however, is part of a universal coverup which is essential to protect the social order from its own worst fear, that it is incurably violent and wants to destroy itself. For Girard, moreover, "there is . . . hardly any form of violence that cannot be described in terms of sacrifice—as Greek tragedy clearly reveals" (1). What is obscured, however, by the processes of history is how society deflects upon a relatively indifferent victim, a sacrificeable victim, the violence which it fears it will turn upon itself. As violence has an unerring instinct for displacing itself upon the surrogate victim, so "the sacrificial process requires a certain degree of *misunderstanding*" (7). That misunderstanding is incorporated in its emergent rites. "The endless diversity of myths and rituals derives from the fact that they all seek to recollect and reproduce something they never succeed in comprehending" (316). The generative violence must remain hidden, but its aim "is to achieve a radically new type of violence, truly decisive and self-contained, a form of violence that will put an end once and for all to violence itself" (27).

For Girard, the difference between primitive societies and our own—neither less violent nor less hypocritical than the other—is a matter of degrees of containment or, we might say, of strategic misunderstanding. Meanwhile, however secreted, violence and the sacred remain inseparable. In primitive societies, "the covert appropriation by sacrifice of certain properties of violence—particularly the ability of violence to move from one object to another—is hidden from sight by the awesome machinery of ritual" (19). In the superstructure of advanced societies, there are further deflections and substitutions or sublimations. Whatever the social order, so long as there is an order, the generative violence is remembered but remains invisible—like the truth of the victim being signaled through the flames. According to

Derrida, that surrogate victim in Artaud is remembering what seems to be an older and generic violence, the murder that is always "at the origin of cruelty, of the necessity named cruelty. And, first of all, a parricide." It is that which is inscribed in the memory space of theater by "the hand lifted against the abusive wielder of the logos, against the father" (239)—the inaugural violence which opened in one lethal and doubling blow the history of representation and the burden of tragedy. For Artaud, it is the murder of the father that is the primitive repetition that has to be erased so that it can repeat itself again "at the greatest proximity to its origin but *only a single time*—this murder [which] is endless and is repeated indefinitely. It begins," adds Derrida, "by penetrating its own commentary and is accompanied by its own representation" (249).

That is where Girard picks it up in his account of mimetic desire, which he sees as an ineliminable function of the human enterprise. If the great myths are dark, it is because they are concealing as they reveal something criminal and evil at their core. The aspect of ritual which obsesses Girard—as it does the drama, however it got there—is the sacrificial act or its displacements. Artaud does not specify such an act, but they concur in the perception of the primordial violence as both "a *sacred obligation*" and "a sort of *criminal activity*" (Girard 1). What I have been calling ritual desire desires this obligation and is, with more or less romanticism, tempted by such activity, as the outbreak of ritual experiment was preceded in the theater by fascination with the drama of Genet. But the drama remains another matter, abrading upon the sacred, as Genet demonically knew, in the derisively poignant return of those Allegorical Forms.

While there are residues of ritual or ritual elements in the drama, drama is by its nature a more open, risible, and fractious thing. It is doubly so in the theater, if not by virtue of its mysterious Double, then to the degree of its compulsive *doubling*. The representational mechanisms of the form are further confounded by the dispersive activity of perception. The theater neither sustains myth by repetition nor discloses deity like ritual. To the extent that the theater is dramatic, it is both critique and tribunal. (It is perhaps dramatic to that extent.) As far back as the *Oresteia,* it is not ritual practices that are being upheld but the oldest claims of ritual which are being mediated. I say *mediated* specifically. What is set in motion in that etiological drama—which establishes not only the judicial system, but the mechanisms of Western drama as they might have been imagined by myth—has passed through the long semiosis of history. Heraclitus said that justice is strife. Now it can be said that it is only mediation. The liabilities of mediation are compounded by the actual omnipresence of the *media* in our time. That not only demoralizes judgment and justice but, in the proliferation of image and appearance, seems to make a redundancy of theater.

Still, there is in the reflexive memory of theater a congenital tension with the appearances of ritual order, however alluring or consoling they may seem. Whatever it was in the beginning (and the worst we can say of it now), drama is the subversive impulse which moves the theater into an open practice which abstracts itself from ritual ends. From Euripides to Ibsen and Genet, it has turned the myths over and over until, as Marx did with Hegel, they seem to be standing on their head. What we have in the canonical drama, and in revisionist productions of the drama—as well as in the refusal or ripoff of the drama in Performance Art—is the reconstitution of myth by history, and a dissociation from the rigid or static practice and magical purposes of the societies in which ritual prevailed.

There was over the last generation a new incitement to ritual from what appeared to be the signals coming from Artaud. While he seemed to make a fetish of certain hieratic forms, nowhere does he subscribe to the necessarily repressive fixity of ritual. He calls, rather, for "states of an acuteness so intense and so absolute that we sense, beyond the tremors of all music and form, the underlying menace of a chaos as decisive as it is dangerous" (51). And when he raises the question of origins, his notion of an "archetypal, primitive theater" leads "metaphysically" (50) to the materialization of an essential *drama* which implies nothing like the communal unity we associate with ritual. Sexual rupture and carnage are the ontological grounds of an "essential separation" (30-31). What he is reimagining then is "the essential principles of all drama, already *disposed and divided,* not so much to lose their character as principles, but enough to comprise, in a substantial and active fashion (i.e., resonantly), an infinite perspective of conflicts" (50). It is certainly nothing like the tribal and psychedelic manifestations of an earthly paradise, the bull-roaring rituals which petered out in the sixties and seventies, we thought, until elements of it showed up—multi-mediated but solipsistic—in the mutilations and disenchantments of punk, the parody and taxidermy of video and body art, and the sensory overload of the new Expressionism.

What Artaud envisaged is born in a sort of retrospective hypothesis or temporal warp "out of a kind of organized anarchy after philosophical battles which are the passionate aspect of . . . primitive unifications" (51). This can only come about, however, the imagined sublimity of it, *"but with drama,* after a meticulous and unremitting pulverization of every insufficiently fine, insufficiently matured form," since the spirit doesn't leap "until it has passed through all the filters and foundations of existing matter," a labor to be redoubled "at the incandescent edges of the future." We are reminded then that this alchemy is material, historical, subliminal in the sublime. If Artaud wants in "solid and opaque form" the irreducibility of light itself, that is neither the rigidity of ritual nor the mere assumption in some premature rite of passage of now widely available and transportable techniques from the world's repertoire of depleted or dubious signifiers.

What arises from ritual desire in practice is a sort of pathetic *trompe l'oeil* of "collective dramaturgy upon the empty stage of the social" (Baudrillard 48). Our problem with ritual remains, then, political. Nostalgia keeps eluding that issue. Whatever meaning there may be in a High Mass in Bolivia or a Hassidic Seder in Brooklyn, there is no way of having anything like the order of ritual in a society predicated on the open competition of overproduced signs mostly divested of value. For a ritual to have efficacious authority, it must also assume something as irrevocable in the order of signifiers as in the designation of status, caste, practices of exchange. The clarity of the sign depends on the power of the law or interdiction which preserves it from abrasion or slippage. If the characteristic gesture of postmodern performance is parody, that's because—with ritual elements in the *bricolage*—we make a pretense of reveling in the slippage. We play with signs. But it's like a game of Monopoly in the supply-side economy. The currency is false. The ceremony we remember, as Baudrillard says, tolerates no counterfeit, "unless as black magic and sacrilege, and it is thus that any confusion of signs is punished: as grave infraction of the order of things" (84). It is also characteristic of postmodern performance, and the new theoretical discourse which surrounds it, to love in ourselves the image of infraction. What we are playing out, as the signs collapse around us, is a melodrama of transgression.

But who is being transgressed, or deluded? We look to other cultures as if they were somehow exempt from what Barthes once called "the tyranny of uncertain signs." For an uncertain time and a privileged few, perhaps they were. As with the seeming alternatives to the manic aggressiveness of our own culture, we are forced to confront an unsettling truth: those nonaggressive cultures were never what they seemed to be in the *huya iniya* or the flow of the *chi* or the ceremony of *ikebena*. As Brecht observed about Chinese acting, there is the dirty secret of repression in every hallowed gesture. "If we are starting to dream again, today especially," writes Baudrillard, "of a world of sure signs, of a strong 'symbolic order,' make no mistake about it: this order has existed and it was that of a ferocious hierarchy, since transparency and cruelty for signs go together" (84). It was an implication that Artaud could never quite accommodate in his cruel passion for an alphabet of perfect signs, "the dry, naked, linear gesture all our acts could have if they sought the absolute" (66). His own quest for the absolute was better perceived in "those strange games of flying hands" of the Balinese dancers, "like insects in the green air of the evening," which communicate "an inexhaustible mental ratiocination, like a mind ceaselessly taking its bearings in the maze of its unconscious" (63). Without the hierarchical ordering of signs, what seems to remain in the maze is the nearly unbearable ferocity of that mind, discovering beyond exhaustion the certitude which escapes it.

Make no mistake about it either, ritual is fascinating. But the struggle now in performance is naively served by the fantasies of ritual desire. We live in a world of broken reciprocity. In our most radical desires, we dream like Artaud of a body without organs. But our reflexes seem formed by the estrangement of an essential fracture. Whatever ritual has done to heal wounds or seal the divisions of incursive time, it is this fracture which seems ritualized in desire, the anxiety of an absence which we glut with representations. The psychopathology of everyday life is polysatured with them, as natural as breathing, an overmastering convention, the *image* of performance as fundamental need. In this context, ritual is myth, another representation. Even when ritual appears to be purely ritual it still depends on representation, a system of exchange in which divinity can be attested to by the power of its signs. What we are dealing with today, however, is not the faintest shadow of a ritual renewal, a virtual impossibility, but rather the incorporation of ritual desire into the mechanisms of a signifying system where signs are no longer, as Eliot said, taken for wonders, nor an approximation of the real. Where signs are still taken for wonders, we see the power of divinity on the video screen, where we also see the shadows of our most legible desires.

Divinity or desire, what we take for reality is a dominion of signs which extends now through our information systems— by satellite transmission through the green air of the evening—to Bali and Bangkok and Kerala, and all those other parts of the world from which we seek the reassuring plenitude of ritual forms. Our addiction to ritual and ritualized performance has intensified just when those symbolic forms are coming out of temple and bush and suffering the attrition of an exposure they were perhaps never meant to have. Or is it that, in all things of the world, exposure was the first intention? Thus it appears to be with the theater, never more so than today when, however it resembles ritual, it dissolves with it into the real which—without sanction or obligation—must live by resembling itself.

Notes

1. Lionel Trilling, "On the Modern Element in Modern Literature," *Literary Modernism,* ed. and intro. Irving Howe (Greenwich, Conn.: Fawcett, 1967) 69.

2. For a useful review of the status of ritual in contemporary thought—from which I have borrowed some introductory references—see Richard F. Hardin, " 'Ritual' in Recent Criticism:The Elusive Sense of Community," *PMLA,* 98 (1983): 846-59.

3. James Boon, *Other Tribes, Other Scribes: Symbolic Anthropology in the Comparative Study of Cultures, Histories, Religions, and Texts* (New York: Cambridge UP, 1982) 10.

4. Antonin Artaud, quoted by Jacques Derrida, "The Theater of Cruelty and the Closure of Representation," *Writing and Difference,* trans. and intro. Alan Bass (Chicago: U of Chicago P, 1978) 232.

5. Roland Barthes, *The Responsibility of Forms: Critical Essays on Music, Art, and Representation,* trans. Richard Howard (New York: Hill and Wang, 1985) 64.

6. René Girard, *Violence and the Sacred,* trans. Patrick Gregory (Baltimore: Johns Hopkins UP, 1977).

7. Antonin Artaud, *The Theater and Its Double,* trans. Mary Caroline Richards (New York: Grove, 1958) 13.

8. Gerald F. Else, *The Origin and Early Form of Greek Tragedy* (Cambridge: Harvard UP, 1967) 3.

9. Richard Schechner, "Approaches to Theater/Criticism," *Tulane Drama Review,* 10.4 (1966): 22.

10. Northrop Frye, "Expanding Eyes," *Spiritus Mundi: Essays on Literature, Myth, and Society* (Bloomington: Indiana UP, 1976) 111-12.

11. Northrop Frye, *Anatomy of Criticism* (1957; Princeton: Princeton UP, 1973) 109.

12. Eric Bentley, "Yeats's Plays," *In Search of Theater* (New York: Vintage. 1953) 296-306. The essay was written in 1948, just about a decade before *The Theater and Its Double* came on the scene.

13. T.S. Eliot, *Selected Essays,* 3rd ed. (London: Faber, 1953) 47.

14. Raymond Williams, "Drama in a Dramatized Society," *Writing in Society* (London: Verso, n.d.) 12.

15. Jean Baudrillard, *Simulacra,* trans. Paul Foss, Paul Patton, and Philip Beitchman (New York: Semiotext[e], 1983).

16. Samuel Beckett, *Waiting for Godot* (New York: Grove, 1954) 58.

17. William Butler Yeats, *Essays and Introductions* (New York: Macmillan, 1961) 215.

18. William Butler Yeats, *The Collected Plays of W.B. Yeats* (New York: Macmillan, 1953) 438-39.

19. Bertolt Brecht, "Alienation Effects in Chinese Acting," *Brecht on Theater: The Development of an Aesthetic,* ed. and trans. John Willett (New York: Hill and Wang, 1964), 94.

20. Eugene G. d'Acquili and Charles D. Laughlin, "The Neurobiology of Myth and Ritual," *The Spectrum of Ritual: A Biogenetic Structural Analysis,* eds. Eugene G. d'Acquili, Charles D. Laughlin, and John McManus (New York: Columbia UP, 1979) 179.

21. Roland Barthes, *Empire of Signs,* trans. Richard Howard (New York: Hill and Wang, 1982) 3-4.

22. Roland Barthes, *Image-Music-Text,* trans. Stephen Heath (New York: Hill and Wang, 1977) 170.

23. Roland Barthes, *Mythologies,* trans. Annette Lavers (London: Jonathan Cape, 1972) 11.

BIBLIOGRAPHICAL NOTES

Always say everything twice.
—Eric Bentley

1. **Bentley's Principal Works.** The full Bentley bibliography numbers over 400 items and is growing. To include it would burden this book unnecessarily; however, I plan to publish it elsewhere. Many of the principal essays and plays are available in the volumes below.

A. CRITICISM

A Century of Hero-Worship. Philadelphia: Lippincott, 1944; as *The Cult of the Superman,* London: Hale, 1947.

The Playwright as Thinker: A Study of Drama in Modern Times. New York: Reynal and Hitchcock, 1946; as *The Modern Theatre,* London: Hale, 1948.

Bernard Shaw: A Reconsideration. New York: New Directions, 1947; revised 1957; revised London: Methuen, 1967.

In Search of Theater. New York: Knopf, 1953; London: Dobson, 1954.

The Dramatic Event: An American Chronicle. New York: Horizon Press, 1954; London: Dobson, 1954.

What is Theatre? A Query in Chronicle Form. New York: Horizon Press, 1956; London: Dobson, 1957.

The Life of the Drama. New York: Atheneum, 1964; London: Methuen, 1965.

The Theatre of Commitment, and Other Essays on Drama in Our Society. New York: Atheneum, 1967; London: Methuen, 1968.

Theatre of War: Comments on 32 Occasions. New York: Viking Press, 1972; London: Methuen, 1972.
The Brecht Commentaries. New York: Grove Press, 1981; London: Methuen, 1981.
The Brecht Memoir. New York: PAJ Publications, 1986.
The Pirandello Commentaries. Evanston: Northwestern University Press, 1986.
Thinking About the Playwright. Announced for publication with Northwestern University Press.

B. PLAYS

Orpheus in the Underworld (opera libretto). New York: Program Publishing Company, 1956.
A Time to Die & A Time to Live. New York: Grove Press, 1970.
The Red White and Black (music by Brad Burg). New York: in *Liberation,* May 1971.
Expletive Deleted. New York: in *Win,* 6 June 1974.
Rallying Cries: Three Plays (Are You Now or Have You Ever Been; The Recantation of Galileo Galilei; From the Memoirs of Pontius Pilate). Washington, D.C.: New Republic Books, 1977; also as *Are You Now or Have You Ever Been, and Other Plays.* New York: Grove Press, 1981.
The Kleist Variations (Concord; The Fall of the Amazons; Wannsee). Baton Rouge: Oracle Press, 1982.
Monstrous Martyrdoms (Lord Alfred's Lover; H for Hamlet; German Requiem). Buffalo, New York: Prometheus Books, 1985.

C. ANTHOLOGIES

The Importance of Scrutiny. New York: G.W. Stewart, 1948.
From the Modern Repertoire (3 volumes). Bloomington: Indiana University Press, 1949-1956.
The Play: A Critical Anthology. Englewood Cliffs, New Jersey: Prentice-Hall, 1951.
Shaw on Music. Garden City, New York: Doubleday, 1955.
The Modern Theatre (6 volumes). Garden City, New York: Doubleday, 1955-1960.

Let's Get a Divorce! and Other Plays. New York: Hill & Wang, 1958.
The Classic Theatre (4 volumes). Garden City, New York: Doubleday, 1958-1961.
The Storm over "The Deputy." New York: Grove Press, 1964.
The Genius of the Italian Theatre. New York: New American Library, 1964.
The Brecht-Eisler Song Book. New York: Oak Publications, 1966.
The Theory of the Modern Stage. London: Penguin Books, 1968.
The Great Playwrights (2 volumes). Garden City, New York: Doubleday, 1970.
Thirty Years of Treason. New York: Viking Press, 1971.
The Dramatic Repertoire (3 volumes). New York: Applause, 1985.

D. TRANSLATIONS

Naked Masks: Five Plays, by Luigi Pirandello. New York: Dutton, 1952.
Seven Plays, by Bertolt Brecht (and other volumes in the Grove Press edition of Brecht). New York: Grove, 1961.
The Wire Harp, by Wolf Biermann. New York: Harcourt Brace & World, 1968.
Filumena Marturano, by Eduardo De Filippo (in *The Genius of the Italian Theatre*).

E. DISCOGRAPHY

"Bentley on Brecht" (performer). Riverside, 1963; Folkways, 1965.
"Brecht before the Un-American Activities Committee" (commentator and editor). Folkways, 1963.
"A Man's a Man" (adapter and lyricist). Spoken Arts, 1963.
"Songs of Hanns Eisler" (performer). Folkways, 1965.
"The Elephant Calf" and "Dear Old Democracy" (adapter, lyricist, and narrator). Folkways, 1967.
"Bentley on Biermann" (performer and translator). Folkways, 1968.
"Eric Bentley Sings The Queen of 42nd Street" (performer). Folkways, 1969.

2. **What Editions To Look For.** Classics such as *The Playwright as Thinker* have been in continuous print since published. *In Search of Theater* and *Life of the Drama* are with Atheneum. *What is Theatre?* (which for many years has incorporated *The Dramatic Event*), and *Bernard Shaw* have been reissued recently by Limelight Editions (New York). Keeping drama before the public is an uphill struggle in America, and several of the anthologies have been allowed to go out of print, such as *Seven Plays,* by Brecht. Bentley reissues them as he can. Most of Bentley's own plays are published individually, but are more readily available in the editions cited.

3. **How To Find Out More.** A large number of his essays, and most of his shorter criticism (book reviews, etc.) are not represented above. For such articles as "Education and the Literary Heritage," or "The Meaning of Robert Penn Warren's Novels," the reader should consult the annual indexes of the following periodicals: *The Kenyon Review* (1945-1955), *The New Republic* (1952-1960), *The Nation* (1943-1944, 1965-1968), *Tulane Drama Review* (1955-1970), *The New York Times: Book Review* (1945-1950) and *Arts and Leisure* (1967-1973), *Theater* (1980-1986), and the full file of *Theatre Arts*. New York's *Village Voice,* the various Shaw bulletins, and the pages of the Gay press. Those interested in performing Bentley's drama can contact his English agent, Joy Westendarp, The International Copyright Bureau, London; or his American agent, Samuel French, New York.

M.B.

CONTRIBUTORS

JACQUES BARZUN, for many years University Professor and Provost of Columbia University, is widely known as a scholar, teacher, and author. Among his many books are *Darwin, Marx, Wagner;* and *A Stroll with William James.*

BERNARD BECKERMAN, author of *Shakespeare at the Globe, 1599-1609* and *Dynamics of Drama: Theory and Method of Analysis,* was Brander Matthews Professor of Dramatic Literature at Columbia University.

ALBERT BERMEL, a playwright and Professor of Theatre at Lehman College and the Graduate Center of the City University of New York, has taught film history and aesthetics, but never acting. He is the author of *Contradictory Characters, Farce,* and *Artaud's Theatre of Cruelty.*

MICHAEL BERTIN, the editor of this volume, is writing a critical study of Eric Bentley for Twayne's United States Authors Series.

HERBERT BLAU served as a director of the Actor's Workshop of San Francisco and of the Vivian Beaumont Theatre of Lincoln Center, and is now Distinguished Professor of English at the University of Wisconsin–Milwaukee. His latest book is *Blooded Thought: Occasions of Theatre.*

ROBERT BRUSTEIN is director of the American Repertory Theatre, theatre critic for *The New Republic,* Professor of English at Harvard University and, most recently, author of *Making Scenes.*

RUBY COHN, Professor of Comparative Drama at the University of California (Davis), has published widely on modern drama. Her books include *Samuel Beckett: The Comic Gamut* and *Currents in Contemporary Drama.*

MARTIN ESSLIN is Professor of Drama at Stanford University, and the author of *Brecht: A Choice of Evils* and *The Theatre of the Absurd.*

ROLF FJELDE, poet and playwright, has translated Ibsen's *Peer Gynt* and the *Complete Major Prose Plays,* and is the founding president of the Ibsen Society of America. He teaches drama, poetry, and film at Pratt Institute in New York City.

JOHN FUEGI is Professor and Director of the Comparative Literature Program of the University of Maryland, editor of the *Brecht Yearbook,* and author of *The Essential Brecht* and *Brecht the Director: Chaos, According to Plan.*

ARTHUR GANZ, the author of *George Bernard Shaw* and *Realms of the Self: Variations on a Theme in Modern Drama,* is Professor of English at the City College of CUNY.

DANIEL GEROULD, an anthologist and translator, has published studies of *Witkacy* and *Twentieth-Century Polish Avant-Garde Drama.* He is Professor of Theatre and Comparative Literature at the CUNY Graduate Center.

RICHARD GILMAN is Professor of Playwriting and Criticism at the Yale School of Drama, and the author of *The Making of Modern Drama* and *Decadence: The Strange Life of an Epithet.*

MICHAEL GOLDMAN's books include *Shakespeare and the Energies of Drama, The Actor's Freedom: Toward a Theory of Drama,* and *Acting and Action in Shakespearean Tragedy.* He is Professor of English at Princeton University.

IRENE HAUPT specializes in theatrical photography. Her subjects have included the world premiere of Beckett's *Rockaby,* and her work has appeared in *The New York Times* and *Saturday Review*.

STANLEY KAUFFMANN is the film critic of *The New Republic* and has been the theatre critic of *The New York Times, The New Republic,* and *Saturday Review.* For many years on the faculty of the Yale School of Drama, he teaches at the CUNY Graduate Center. His latest book is *Theater Criticisms.*

JAN KOTT, Professor Emeritus of English and Comparative Literature of the State University of New York at Stony Brook, is a Getty Scholar at the Getty Center for the History of Art and the Humanities. His most recent book is *The Theater of Essence.*

C.S. LEWIS is famed for his children's stories and popular books on Christian subjects and for his studies of medieval literature. A good account of his life is provided in Humphrey Carpenter's *The Inklings.*

JAMES MCFARLANE has published several books on Ibsen and on Scandinavian literature, and is general editor and translator of *The Oxford Ibsen.* He recently retired as Professor of European Literature from the University of East Anglia in Norwich.

ANNE PAOLUCCI is Chairman of the English Department of St. John's University, Jamaica, New York; president of the Pirandello Society of America, and author of *Pirandello's Theatre: The Recovery of the Modern Stage for Dramatic Art.*

GORDON ROGOFF is Professor of Theatre at Brooklyn College (CUNY). His collected criticism will be published by Northwestern University Press in 1986, and he is writing a study of Luchino Visconti for Summit Books entitled *Borrowed Glory* . . .

EVERT SPRINCHORN is Professor of Drama at Vassar College, the author of *Strindberg as Dramatist,* and the editor-translator of *Ibsen: Letters and Speeches.*

LILLIAN VALLEE is a free-lance translator whose work includes *Bells in Winter*, *A Prisoner of Martial Law*, and *Grotowski and His Laboratory*. She is translating Witold Gombrowicz's *Diary* for Northwestern University Press.

MICHAEL BERTIN

Michael Bertin was born in New York City in 1947. His parents had met in Casablanca during the war; his mother French and from Algeria, his father an American career Air Force colonel. He grew up under a variety of influences, not least the inspiration of his Parisian relatives—the writers Claude Henri Leconte and Jacques Delile—and his mother Suzanne's grand spirit. In the late seventies he found his father, Oscar Heinlein, his sister and brother, Catharine and Tex, and his American roots. He is happy to say that he attended his parents' wedding in 1980; their love had endured a thirty-year separation.

In 1977, Bertin went to the Yale School of Drama on scholarship, and upon graduation worked for Temple University, teaching undergraduate and graduate classes in theatre history, criticism and dramaturgy, and serving as director of Temple's London branch in 1985. On leave from teaching to write, he recalls with fondness the fine group of students he had, and thanks them for the lively classes they gave him.

As with many people in his profession, Bertin finds that his greatest intellectual debt is to Eric Bentley, and so it is no mere chance that his first books should be on the man. Editing this volume with the support of a publication grant from the NEA, he is also writing a study of Bentley for Twayne. He is a contributor to *The Times Literary Supplement, Theater* and *Shakespeare Quarterly,* and Washington correspondent of *Plays International.*

Michael Bertin lives in Arlington, Virginia with his wife Maggie—a museum professional and writer, his daughter Madeleine—an avid reader and flautist, and his son Richard—a dogged pursuer of causes and clues.

The Play and its critic

DATE DUE			
AUG 26 1993			
OCT 05 1995			
MAY 5 1997			
APR 13 1999			